PRAISE FOR RAIFORD PALMER AND *I JUST WANT THIS DONE*

"Having worked with 100,000+ women all around the world, I have seen firsthand how an entrepreneur's marriage can make or break their business. Divorce can be the worst financial crisis a business owner has ever endured, or it can be the beginning of a new season in life. Raif Palmer teaches women and men how to respectfully part ways from their spouse with as much money, dignity, and self-respect intact as possible. I highly recommend *I Just Want This Done* to any entrepreneur considering a divorce."

—**Danielle Canty**, Co-Founder & President, *BossBabe*

"I have settled numerous divorce cases with Raif over the last fifteen years. I am both a lawyer and a licensed counselor, and I can tell you that Raif's approach to resolving divorce cases is top-notch. This book contains tons of useful tips and advice that is honest, practical, and will save you money, time, and aggravation. If you are thinking of getting divorced, or if you are in the middle of a divorce—get this book. You'll be glad you did."

—**James J. Lenahan, J.D.**, *The Law Offices of James Lenahan*

"*I Just Want this Done* is a book that should be read by any sophisticated person wanting insights regarding how to work with their lawyer, how to understand the rules of the game and how to best make emotionally intelligent decisions in this most difficult time of your life. I cannot recommend Raif's book more strongly!"

—**Gunnar J. Gitlin, J.D., AAML**, Principal, *Gitlin Law Firm*, Author, *Gitlin on Divorce*

"I found Raif's book of special value to me and my podcast audience, *The Luxury of Self Care*, because it provides realistic advice to anyone considering or involved in divorce. As a child of divorce myself, I know the damage that can be harmful to children without the intention. As I approach my own marriage, I found Raif's point of view insightful on many aspects, from years in his professional practice, to his own personal failed marriage vs. his current successful one. We can all learn from our mistakes and years of experience. I found *I Just Want This Done* helps divorcing couples peacefully, respectfully separate without wasting time, money, or energy. I recommend everyone considering divorce read it and take Raif's unique advice to heart, I know I did."

—**Ahnastasia Albert**, Host, *The Luxury of Self Care Podcast*

"Raif wrote a book on divorce that needed to be written. It is insightful, smart and candid. I will be giving a copy to all my divorce clients."

—**Ryan Kalamaya, J.D.**, Shareholder, *Kalamaya | Gosha*, Aspen, CO

I JUST WANT THIS DONE

I JUST WANT THIS DONE

How Smart, Successful People Get Divorced without Losing Their Kids, Money, and Minds

Raiford Dalton Palmer, J.D., AAML

E. James Publishing Company

E. James Publishing Company, Inc.

Elmhurst, IL

E. James Publishing
Company

E. James Publishing Company, Inc.
Elmhurst, IL
www.EJamesPublishing.com
Send feedback to Feedback@EJamesPublishing.net

Publisher's Cataloging-In-Publication Data

Names: Palmer, Raiford Dalton, author.
Title: I just want this done : how smart, successful people get divorced without losing their kids, money, and minds / Raiford Dalton Palmer, J.D., AAML.
Description: Elmhurst, Illinois : E. James Publishing Company, Inc., [2021] | Includes bibliographical references.
Identifiers: ISBN 9781737208907 (softcover paperback) | ISBN 9781737208914 (jacketed case laminate hardcover) | ISBN 9781737208921 (Kindle ebook)
Subjects: LCSH: Divorce--Law and legislation--United States. | Divorce--Economic aspects. | Professional employees--Family relationships. | Businesspeople--Family relationships.
Classification: LCC KF535 .P35 2021 (print) | LCC KF535 (ebook) | DDC 346.730166--dc23

Special discounts for bulk sales are available.
Please contact Sales@EJamesPublishing.net

To my wife and law partner, Juli Gumina, who supports me all the way in life and in business. Your trust in me made this book possible. To my former wife, Stephanie Palmer, for backing me through ups and downs in my career and raising two great sons with me. You are both inspirations for this book and each in your own way helped me write it.

"You can be right, or you can be happy."
— Douglas W. Palmer, borrowed from Gerald Jampolsky

Don't get caught in the swamp!

CONTENTS

Tell Me What You Think

Let other readers know what you thought of *I Just Want This done*. Please write an honest review for this book on your favorite online bookshop.

★ ★ ★ ★ ★

FOREWORD

By Gunnar J. Gitlin, JD, AAML

S everal years ago, my daughter's university in Chicago was in dire need of lawyers to judge their mock trial invitational tournament. I put out the "Bat Signal," asking Chicago-area members of the American Academy of Matrimonial Lawyers to volunteer for the two-day competition. Raif volunteered and I had the opportunity to judge with him. I learned that he had been a college mock trial coach. He was one of the best judges for the weekend, providing excellent guidance to these potentially aspiring lawyers. Raif brings with him a deep knowledge of trial practice, as well as an emotional intelligence that's obvious from reading his book, or from simply having a conversation with him.

I'm a divorce lawyer, and I've written my own book about divorce law. (Mine's geared toward fellow attorneys.) And while I was writing the book, I was also going through my *own* divorce. So I know what's out there in terms of resources for people navigating a divorce. There is one thing lacking from all the websites and Q&A's you've probably already stumbled upon in your Google searches: a practical guide for those going through a divorce that speaks to how to work with your lawyer to effectively navigate this most difficult time in your life.

Reading this book is not necessary for the simplest of divorces. It's possible for divorce to be easy. But I have seen that sometimes what should be the simplest of divorces goes awry for reasons you might not anticipate if you're going through a divorce for the first time.

Sun Tsu in the *Art of War* tells us: "If you know the other and know yourself, you need not fear the result of a hundred battles." From where you're sitting, we lawyers are "The Other." (Some translations even translate "other" as "enemy".) If Sun Tsu were to get divorced in the 2020s, I think he'd start by learning the rules of the game that lawyers play by. Raif's book begins by demystifying the legal profession:

explaining how lawyers are trained, from law school forward. Under-standing the mindset of your prospective divorce lawyers will help you choose the right lawyer and cost-effectively navigate your own divorce. Raif is a big-city lawyer, working in Chicago. But his entire book applies almost equally well to the rules of the legal game outside a large metropolitan area.

You may initially think that divorce lawyers are in the business of maximizing the number of divorces in the world. But, perhaps surpris-ingly, *I Just Want this Done* first focuses on whether reconciliation is possible. Divorce lawyers find that if you're scheduling an appoint-ment with us, you've probably come to the decision that a divorce is necessary, and has been for quite some time. The client's instincts are often correct, and it's usually too late. Yet as Raif points out, we divorce lawyers perform our duty best when we urge the client to first explore individual and marital counseling to clarify that divorce is 100% the best decision. In the case of a longer-term marriage, it's a big question–a question of how someone wants to spend the *rest of their life.*

My cousin from Chicago once quipped, "I'd move to California, but I'd have to bring myself with me," his own take on the Murakami quote "No matter how far you travel, you can never get away from yourself." In the same way, once you're divorced, you'll still have a relationship with yourself. After all, Sun Tsu says you need to know the other *and* yourself to win the battle. If a divorce proves necessary, then counseling or therapy may help you see your past more clearly and understand how to more effectively move forward.

The Fourth Chapter in Raif's book provides invaluable insight regarding how to choose the right divorce lawyer. From there, he addresses the partnership necessary for a good lawyer-client relation-ship. I will tell clients that lawyers and clients succeed or fail as a team: when the teamwork is seamless, in every encounter the client's expec-tation will likely be met.

Raif then explores 20 "divorce myths." Reviewing these can provide valuable insights for traps to try to avoid. Every divorce lawyer hears from time to time, for example, *""I Need to Teach My Ex a Lesson. It's about the Principle.""* This is a myth because when one is getting a divorce, it is time to focus on one's own future, not to focus on "teaching a lesson" to the person who is divorcing. By understanding mindsets that one should strive to avoid, one can more effectively make decisions and try to engage in a reasoned cost-benefit analysis. And this, indeed, is the through-line of the book.

Chapter 7 of Raif's book presents the "nuts and bolts" options regarding choices that can be made rather than simply engaging in "traditional adversarial representation." There is a concept in cognitive bias that "if all you have is a hammer, everything looks like a nail." Fortunately, Raif has in-the-trench experience as a litigator with experience in when and how to use alternative dispute resolution for cost-effective resolutions within divorce cases.

This book provides much more than some of the initial highlights. I will leave that up to the reader to encounter in this engaging book that reads nothing like any book regarding divorce that has been written before.

I Just Want this Done is a book that should be read by any sophisticated person wanting insights regarding how to work with their lawyer, how to understand the rules of the game and how to best make emotionally intelligent decisions in this most difficult time of your life. I cannot recommend Raif's book more strongly!

PREFACE

I was the first lawyer in my family. I was a golf caddie in high school. I ran punch presses in a factory. I set up and operated a hot dog stand on a pontoon boat in college. I finished college in three years and worked full time in a law firm to see what the law business was like. I've done a little bit of everything as a private practice lawyer. After graduating and passing the bar, I started out as a lawyer doing civil litigation, defending people involved in auto accident cases. I handled eviction cases and a little criminal defense. Later I did some personal injury trial work, this time on the plaintiff's side, representing people injured in accidents. I tried three jury trials all the way to verdict. I set up corporations and LLCs, and I did real estate deals.

My first divorce client was originally a personal injury client of mine. One day, she called, and asked me to do her divorce. I told her I didn't do divorce work. She said, "You can do it for me; it can't be that hard!" I referred her to the guy I always used. (I found him in my Rolodex, back when people still used a Rolodex.) She called a week later: "That guy's an asshole!" I was stunned since I had never heard any complaints about him.

She insisted again that I handle her case. I decided to do it. (At the time, I needed the money.) I told her I would learn on the job, but on my dime. I bought a couple of books about Illinois divorce, and I was off to the races. That case went well, and she sent a couple of friends, they sent friends, and pretty soon I was in the divorce business.

But I also did business litigation up to about 2009. I had a lot of experience working for business and individual clients. They are a unique group—they demand results and do not have unlimited budgets. Working with this type of client, you quickly learn the importance of a cost-benefit analysis. When a client has a $5,000 problem, spending $5,000 in legal fees isn't going to make them happy. And they will call you to complain if they aren't happy. Imagine my surprise when I got to divorce court . . . and learned that things were very different than I experienced in other civil courts.

First, not many divorce lawyers are good trial lawyers. They don't have a lot of real trial experience. Most divorce cases settle. Sometimes they settle within a few months, sometimes well in advance of trial, and sometimes on the day of trial (not recommended). So there aren't many opportunities to present a case at trial and gain experience in the first place.

Second, there are no juries—a judge decides divorce cases. (Except in Texas, where they still have jury trials in some cases.) Generally speaking, judges are relaxed with the rules of evidence in divorce court (at least where I practice). In fact, they can be relaxed with procedural rules overall. There is some understandable logic in this. Following every rule of evidence could mean hours in court simply trying to get financial statements admitted into evidence, for example. So, to streamline things, courts tend to allow some "bending" of the rules. The downside of this is that it can make for some lazy lawyering and allow a lot of bad habits to form. A lack of trial experience generally results in a lack of focus during discovery (the process in which parties exchange information and documents in a lawsuit) and a meandering effort to resolve cases that results in cases taking much longer than they should and "accidental" trials. Because of this, some lawyers don't know exactly what proof they need, so they cast a needlessly huge net in discovery and demand every document in the universe. More on that later.

Third, and maybe most important: many lawyers handling divorce work are not skilled at assessing your real chances in a case and don't do frequent cost-benefit analyses. You end up chasing low-value things in your case and digging into expensive litigation when ultimately, it is not worth the trouble. My former insurance company and commercial clients would not have tolerated it. They know how it works. They won't spend money on lawyers unless it makes financial sense. Unlike these clients, the typical divorce client (even our high-income, highly educated clients) don't know what to look for. They have no frame of reference.

Some divorce lawyers won't tell you this. It's not necessarily out of malice or greed but training and force of habit. For example, not long ago, the best lawyers in town had the best law libraries. Literal libraries full of law books. The books were expensive, and this was a major barrier to entry for new law firms. Long-established firms with good law libraries literally had better access to legal knowledge than their newer competition and could use this to their advantage. The internet has democratized legal knowledge. Now a lawyer right out of school has access to most of the same information that only the largest law firms had back when I was starting out in this profession.

Law school focuses on teaching people to be good law students and leaves graduates unprepared for the actual private practice of law. Graduates learn the law but not how to handle cases for actual paying clients. Law school education only began to move into alternative dispute resolution in the 1990s—yet still with a much greater emphasis on trial practice and appellate court (litigation) courses. The majority of law school graduates are trained primarily in litigation and trial practice - to fight and be a gladiator for their clients.

Further, typical law firm revenue is generated on an hourly time and expense basis. This means there is no direct incentive for most lawyers to be efficient in case handling. Also, attorney ethics rules require that lawyers provide "zealous" representation of clients. This can quickly morph into "overzealous." Again, not intentionally, but this can happen in the ordinary course of work. There is a subtle undertone in the representation. If the client thinks they want a war, their lawyer may not dissuade them from that. It is easy under the guise of "zealous representation" to add unnecessary complexity to a case. The mindset "We're not going to leave any stone unturned" is frequently misguided—in many divorce cases an attorney can safely leave a lot of "stones" unturned and still get a good result.

The business of law has changed, but most people don't know it. Movies, TV, social media, and Google searches don't accurately portray how the legal system works. Some lawyers don't have "the memo" yet either. Law is a hidebound profession. The huge changes in technology that have radically altered every industry have only recently hit the law business.

Thus, a lot of what some lawyers tell clients is from an outdated perspective, one that does not value efficiency and a cost-benefit-sensitive approach.

You want to get the best value. You should pay for what matters and for the attorney or law firm that will get the work done for you as efficiently as possible.

WHY THIS BOOK?

In a word, education. Over the years, I have learned that while every divorce is different, with different facts and different people involved (and, indeed, the law changes constantly in this area as well), situations in cases would recur, and patterns began to form in my mind. After hearing a client tell me their story, I would respond with advice and sometimes tell them, "I wish I had a book with all this stuff in it for you, and I could just tell you to read Chapter so-and-so to help you understand this."

I want to help make sense of a difficult time in your life. I want to try to save you time, money, and emotional grief in divorce (especially for you and your kids). I want to show you a better way to get divorced.

Therefore, this book. This book is about telling you what matters and what doesn't so you can get divorced without losing your kids, your money, or your mind.

CAN I HIRE YOU TO HELP ME?

Yes! The team at STG Divorce Law offers several services to individuals in the state of Illinois and out. We represent clients in Illinois and also coach and counsel anyone contemplating or going through divorce anywhere worldwide. To find out more, contact us at www. STGLawFirm.com.

CHAPTER 1

A DIRE SITUATION

C hris Stevens was on top of the world. His company was success-ful, and his wife and kids were good. Chris's wife, Jennifer, was a teacher at the local high school. They had two teenage kids, Callie and Tyler. Callie, on the high school JV volleyball team, had a busy social life, and Tyler, with a 3.3 GPA, liked his fraternity at the University of Illinois.

People always told Chris that he had the "perfect" family. Thanks to Chris's success, he and Jennifer were able to build a beautiful, large brick home in a nice suburb with a three-car garage and a pool. They were able to fill the garage with nice cars for themselves and the kids and even had a vacation condo and boat on Marco Island.

Chris was a shareholder of a logistics company located in the Chi-cago suburbs. He shared ownership with his friend and colleague Steve. Chris's analytical, quick mind helped the company stand out. They acquired clients quickly thanks to Steve's sales ability and Chris's inno-vative ideas. The company grew quickly, as did their incomes.

Married since college, Chris figured his relationship with Jennifer was typical, much like that of his parents, who were still happily mar-ried. When they met, Chris was a quiet, thoughtful, and hardworking engineering student. Jennifer was always the life of the party: fun, interesting, and extroverted. Chris was drawn to her—she was everything he wanted to be. The relationship was romantic at the start and affectionate. They got busy with the kids, houses, and their jobs.

In the last few years, Jennifer had started to complain: "We never go on dates." "We don't go on vacations." "I'm not having fun." Chris did not know what to do—this was the way things had been for a long time, and it wasn't a problem before. They had a great life, and Chris always told Jennifer he loved her. He hoped it was a phase and that Jennifer's new interest in fitness was a good distraction.

Chris worked out at his local CrossFit box that morning and went to work. At the end of the day, Chris came home. Soon after, Jennifer returned from her regular yoga class and came into the kitchen. She put her phone down and went upstairs to change. Chris opened the refrigerator to get a snack. Jennifer yelled down from the master bedroom: "Can you bring my phone up?" and Chris grabbed the phone and began walking upstairs.

While he was walking up, the phone buzzed, and Chris saw an instant message pop up:

How are you, baby? ❤ ❤

His heart stopped. He didn't recognize the sender. His heart raced, and he kept staring at the four words on the screen. He tried to unlock the phone but couldn't. He had always known her password before . . .

Chris resumed climbing the stairs, feeling a tightening in his throat. He walked into the bedroom and held out the phone to Jennifer.

"Do you have a boyfriend?" he said.

Jennifer looked startled, then composed herself and calmly took the phone. After a long pause, she said, "No . . . This? This is just Ray . . . joking around with me."

Chris knew that Ray Colbert worked at the high school. His chest felt tight, he was breathing quickly, and he wanted to scream.

Finally, he said, "Joking . . . OK, um, that's weird," not knowing what else to say or do. He thought quickly. He said, "We need to go to counseling."

"About what? We're fine," said Jennifer, dismissing him with a wave of her hand. Chris's rising panic had his heart pounding.

After the conversation, Jennifer acted as if nothing had happened. But Chris knew he was in trouble. He couldn't stop thinking about it. He couldn't eat and stared blankly while Jennifer and Callie talked about school. His sense of dread grew. His gut ached. Chris couldn't sleep, right next to Jennifer in bed. She slept soundly.

The next day, Jennifer texted before Chris got home from work that she was out late with her yoga friends. Chris remembered he had helped Jen find her phone once with an app on his phone. He clicked the log-in and saw a GPS blip at a house in the next town—an address he didn't recognize—not the restaurant Jen had said she was visiting.

Chris drove to the house. He saw Jennifer's car in the driveway, with a red, older Porsche parked in front of it. His heart raced. He recognized the car—it belonged to Ray Colbert. Chris suddenly felt powerless and pathetic, like all the air had been let out of him.

Chris texted Jennifer: You f—ing cheater!

Jennifer texted back: Don't come home tonight. She added, I'm done. You need to move out. I'm telling the kids we're getting divorced.

Chris felt like he had been punched in the gut. The bottom fell out. He didn't know what to do. He decided to stay at a hotel in the area that night.

Sitting in the hotel room, mindlessly scrolling social media, Chris thought to do a quick Google search: "divorce lawyers near me." He looked at several websites, mostly showing scowling lawyers in suits with their arms folded. He'd never shopped for a lawyer before outside of buying a house.

WHAT DO I DO NOW?

There are two ways to handle a divorce for people like Chris. One route usually devolves into an expensive war—expensive not only in terms of money but also in terms of emotional damage and collateral damage to career and personal relationships, especially within the family.

The other way is a calm, reasoned approach that obtains a better overall result with lower expenditure of energy, time, and money; preserves relationships; and has less collateral damage.

The purpose of this book is to help you take the second way. Because the first way is rarely the best option. Nobody "wins" a divorce. There is only losing better with less heartache—minimizing damage to your kids, yourself, and your property while reaching a reasonable, acceptable conclusion. This book will show you how to keep the relative peace, and save money and time in the bargain. This book should be subtitled *Secrets Divorce Lawyers Won't Tell*. If everyone knew and lived by the principles in this book, we'd have a lot less work to do as divorce lawyers. I'm kidding, but there is some truth in this.

Nevertheless, if you're about to go through a divorce, you need to know your options. Divorce doesn't have to be World War III. Our law firm has advised thousands of clients on how to navigate divorce successfully. I'm not just a divorce lawyer; I've been divorced, too. I've been where you are. I have kids; owned a business; and had a couple of homes, cars, and retirement accounts. My world was thrown into turmoil. For a time in my life, I felt like I had no control and was afraid of what might happen.

THIS IS MY STORY, TOO

It was a beautiful sunny day in late June, ironically one day before my twenty-fourth wedding anniversary with the woman I thought would be my wife forever. I picked up a laundry basket with a pillow, bedsheets, and a blanket. My wife prepared the basket for me, a final act showing the kind of person she is. I looked at our Labrador, Samantha, and pug, Oscar. I petted both and told them I would miss them much. I looked around the family room. Family pictures. Familiar surroundings. Home. I took a deep breath and turned for the back door.

Driving to my parents' house only a few minutes away, I cried. I cried for the loss of my marriage and family, for the pain suffered by my wife and our sons. I cried because I felt like I'd let my family down. I cried because I would miss my wife, our sons, our dogs, the house we'd fixed up together, our neighborhood, and our past life.

My folks had bought the house a couple of weeks before and weren't ready to move in, so I could stay there alone for a while. I didn't have an apartment yet and was scrambling to find one. My doctor hoped my high blood pressure would return to normal—I went to see him when I started feeling a pounding in my head after I'd told my wife I wanted a divorce.

I walked into my parents' empty house, hauling in boxes of stuff from my SUV. I put the two bags of groceries on the folding table in the dining room. I hadn't bought groceries for one since I was a junior in college, twenty-five years before.

My heart ached. I wasn't sure if I was doing the right thing. For a long time afterward, I teared up at random times—triggered by anything. A song on the radio. Seeing a young family walking down the street together. Flowers in front of a house. Little kids playing in a front yard.

The hardest thing I've done in my entire life was telling the kids we were getting divorced. We said all the "right" things they tell you to say.

"It will be all right."

"We love you; that will never change."

"We just aren't going to be in the same house, but we are still your mom and dad."

It doesn't matter what you say. It's the worst thing you'll ever tell your kids. It took all my willpower not to break down. My older son, then eighteen, ran out of the house in tears. His younger brother, about to start high school, asked us, "Will things be OK? We're going to be OK, right?" I wanted to die.

The second hardest thing I've ever done in my life was move out of our family home. The first time I tried, I broke down, cancelled my order for a new bed, and went back home. My wife gave me an anniversary card. Guess I have great timing.

Nothing happened right—the boys' birthdays took place right around the time I told her I wanted a divorce. Then prom. Then graduation—for both of them. It was awful.

Several days later, I realized that we would never be back to "normal," and we wouldn't work, and I got up the will to leave again. During the short time I was home, I had hoped it could work—I wanted it to work. But my heart knew the pieces would never go back together again.

I wrote my wife a card that I never sent.

> Thank you for the good times. Thank you for the boys. Thank you for your hard work. Thank you for supporting me and my career. Thank you for being strong when the law firm broke up.

No matter what happens, it takes two people to get married and two to get divorced. And it hurts like hell when it's over. Divorce is the intersection of love, sex, kids, and money. It's everything we all hold dear rolled into one. And like my laundry basket, it gets loaded onto a moving truck. Because it was over. At least, the way things had been. There was no going back.

This was not supposed to happen to me. I was the eldest child, the first grandchild, and expectations were high. I had a great childhood and loving parents. (Luckily, I still do.) I did well in school, went to a great college, and did well in law school. I married a beautiful, hardworking woman who became a successful teacher and later a school administrator. We bought and fixed up three homes together. We built a vacation home in Michigan. We had nice cars. We took the kids on nice vacations. We were winners. My wife supported me when my former law firm broke up during the recession. All of our parents were still married. And yet, we fell out of love. We didn't go on dates. We went on only a few vacations together in twenty-four years without the kids—and one of those was our honeymoon. We didn't have many friends. We worked and took care of our kids. Somewhere, we lost track of us.

We had tried marriage counseling. When that didn't work, we each hired a personal counselor to help us understand and deal with everything. Previously, I had been the divorce lawyer who was above it—immune to it. My wife and I were too smart, too nice, and too good to get divorced. For years, I sat in consultations with divorcing people, listening to their stories, glad this would never happen to me. Now it was happening to me, and it felt like there was nothing I could do to fix it.

After living at my parents' home for a few weeks while a crew painted the interior of the house (my new bed was in the living room), I moved to a tiny, rented house nearby. I bought (and built) IKEA furniture—I was their best customer for a while. I spent night after night alone in my house putting furniture together to make a bedroom for my sons and a place they would want to come to. I framed T-shirts from places the boys loved and hung them on the wall in their bedroom. I saved toys from when they were little boys and brought them to my house. I drove my oldest son to college to help him move in. I no longer saw my younger son every day—I texted him "goodnight" every night. Life stacked one hard thing on top of the next.

After some time passed, we realized that we were going to get divorced. Luckily, we still trusted each other about the finances and the kids. We worked out most of the details of the divorce on the dining room table in a few hours with our laptops flipped open. She hired a lawyer I recommended, and I had one of my partners help me. We worked it out within several weeks at minimal expense. I moved out in June. We were divorced by August.

Is that turnaround time typical? No. Can it be for you? Possibly. You can get a lot closer to a few months instead of three or more years—if you heed the advice in this book. In these pages, I'm going to tell you all the things I've told my clients over the years—the stuff you don't find online. The advice I would give my best friend if they were getting divorced. This is valuable information learned the hard way over twenty-five-plus years of practicing law in multiple areas, especially divorce law. This advice works not just in my home state but anywhere in the USA. And it is timeless. This advice will stand up whether you read this book right after it's published or twenty years later. This is not tactical information about alimony, child support, and how property is divided in divorce. You can get that anywhere. (But be careful—there is a lot of outdated and plain wrong information about divorce online.) This book is less about A + B = C and more about how to get to C with the least damage done to your wallet, your emotions, and your family.

In this book, you'll learn:

- What matters and what doesn't in divorce
- How to know if reconciliation is possible or not
- How typical legal advice risks everything
- How to choose the right divorce lawyer
- How to be a smart client
- The twenty-two myths most people believe about divorce
- Your four case resolution options
- What the "meta case" is and how to win it
- The four true costs of divorce and how to minimize them
- How to protect your business and career during divorce
- The dos and don'ts of child custody
- How (and why) to hire a divorce coach
- How to handle new significant others
- How not to be painted as a jerk

Chris got divorced without losing everything. So did I. And you can, too.

Which brings us back to Chris's story. He followed the same advice you'll receive from this book. He sought out an experienced, dedicated divorce law firm with a high number of positive reviews online—our law firm. Together, we quickly gathered and organized Chris's financial records. We kept the lines of communication open with Chris's wife to avoid misunderstandings. Most importantly, we helped Chris put his ego aside and use his head when thinking about his divorce case and following our advice. Chris realized that being perhaps a little more generous and easygoing now would benefit him in the end. We encouraged Chris and his wife to avoid a court process and instead negotiate a solution in their case. We were able to resolve the case in nine months. Both parties ended up satisfied with the outcome. Most importantly, we preserved Chris's family, realizing that life is a long haul and that they will need to deal with each other in the future for the kids.

Chris did everything right as best he could. Still, divorce was one of the most painful experiences of his life. If divorce is at all avoidable, avoid it. If the marriage is salvageable, save it. If it's possible.

Is it possible? It just might be, which is why we're headed there first.

CHAPTER 2

IS IT TOO LATE?

(HOW TO KNOW IF RECONCILIATION IS POSSIBLE)

I could not believe Michael and Susan were getting divorced. A handsome doctor. A beautiful wife. Both intelligent, friendly, well-adjusted people you would be glad to have as friends. They raised four great kids who all "launched" and were well adjusted. They had money. They were comfortable.

All this went through my head as I sat with Michael and Susan during our third settlement meeting. As in the previous two meetings, they were pleasant with each other. Easy communication. They even laughed together at times. Both seemed sad to move ahead with divorce.

During a break, I spoke with Susan's lawyer privately.

"I think there's more here. They should stay married," the other lawyer said. We'd done several cases together before and got along well. "What do you think, Raif?"

"Yeah, they seem great together. I'm wondering if they can work out their problems and stay married," I said. "Michael seems happy. He wants to stay married. He's only upset by the fact that she wants out."

"Because she feels trapped. Her husband has been her identity," Susan's lawyer said. "Divorce is her way of saying she wants to feel independent."

Good points. Susan was well educated and had a career before they had children but had been a stay-at-home mom for nearly twenty years. Michael handled all financial matters. Her life had revolved around the children, their activities, and their interests, as well as her husband's professional and social life, which involved a lot of get-togethers with other doctors and hospital executives. From what we could tell, Susan had simply lost herself in the marriage. Now that the kids were grown and gone, she didn't know what to do with herself.

Her lawyer and I had some ideas.

• • • •

Staying happily married is better than getting divorced. This is the reality we divorce lawyers face. Couples like Michael and Susan whose relationship is not fundamentally broken can still reconcile. Good for them, but not good for those of us who make our living on divorce cases. Most lawyers would have encouraged Michael and Susan to proceed. It's how we get paid.

And that's exactly why doing the right thing is the best thing. Helping clients solve their divorce problems efficiently isn't always financially rewarding, but it's personally satisfying. Divorce attorneys get a bad rap, deservedly so sometimes, but divorce attorneys are also some of the most sensitive problem solvers who have a front row seat to a family in crisis. Exploring reconciliation rather than divorce may result in less income for the lawyer, but it is so important. Suggesting reconciliation rather than divorce is so important that it's a rule of the American Academy of Matrimonial Lawyers, the only national vetting organization for divorce lawyers. Rule 1.2 of the Bounds of Advocacy states:

> An attorney should advise the client of the emotional and economic impact of divorce and explore the feasibility of reconciliation.

The Bounds of Advocacy go on to say:

> The divorce process can exact a heavy economic and emotional toll. The decision to divorce should never be made casually. An attorney should discuss reconciliation and whether the client has considered marriage counseling or therapy. If the client exhibits uncertainty or ambivalence, the lawyer should assist in obtaining help.

Why reconcile, especially if you've already started the process? Because divorce is costly. Much more than just in money. In your heart, you know this. (We discuss the many "costs" of divorce in detail in Chapter 9.) Reconciliation takes work—a lot of it. But you avoid the serious destruction divorce can cause. You avoid the many costs of divorce. Your family will be better for it. Your kids will appreciate it. You owe it to yourself to see if reconciliation is an option for your family.

I was married for twenty-four years, and it was a good marriage in many ways. I would have preferred to stay married to my first wife if we could have worked things out. I got remarried a few years after my divorce. I'm pro-marriage. I would love to see happy couples (and their kids) stick together if possible.

I would love nothing more than for you not to need to hire me. Potential clients often call and discuss the possibility of divorce—the pros and cons, how property will be divided, how alimony is computed, and what will happen with the kids. Clearly, many people contemplate divorce, sometimes months or years in advance. I tell them to at least consider reconciliation.

Make your marriage work by all means. "Why would you want me to reconcile?" you ask. "You'll make money if I get a divorce." That's true. But we have plenty of work to do even if you reconcile. The world needs good marriages to thrive. Our law firm is busy without your case.

WHY IS THIS HAPPENING NOW?

The reason divorces seem to happen most frequently when the kids are in high school and college is by that time, you have more time for yourselves. Usually by then, both spouses have stable careers, or perhaps one of them has been at home for a while with the kids. The marriage is maybe fifteen to twenty-five years old at this point. The spouses finally have mental space and time. They think about what makes them happy—many times this has been deferred in the rush toward a career, a home, maybe a second home, cars, and the college 529. Likely the parents have focused (sometimes entirely) on the children. No dates together, no vacations without the kids. And one or both spouses are unhappy. This is what many people call a "midlife crisis."

Do I want to be with this person for the next chapter of life? The couple hasn't shared adventures and experiences. It's the empty-nest challenge. If the kids and careers have been effectively in the way of the marriage, some people feel that they need a major reset, which can lead people to divorce. *This person isn't interesting to me anymore.*

SAVING A MARRIAGE
FROM VAMPIRES

Many books and articles about relationships discuss "vampires"—things that suck the life out of a marriage. These are things that take the energy away from one or both people such that they don't have energy to devote to the relationship. Examples of this are addictions, whether they are to alcohol or drugs, sports, video games, gambling, or something else. They can include "sports widows": one person has an all-consuming hobby or passion that drains energy from the relationship. One of the people in the couple is devoting so much energy to the "vampire" that they have no energy to put into the other person and the relationship; the other person suffers, and resentment grows. Generally, these situations might be fixable, but the vampire has to be addressed first. Until that is resolved, there is no room for the marriage. This, admittedly, can be extraordinarily difficult or impossible.

This is no substitute for professional advice on this or any other emotion- or communication-related topic in this book. By all means consult a licensed psychiatrist, psychologist, or counselor about these issues.

REIGNITING PASSION WHEN YOU'RE "BORED" AND HAVE "GROWN APART"

Another situation is perhaps more common but no less destructive to a relationship. Many people have fairly normal, stable marriages. But some couples have potentially differing needs that may not have been apparent at the outset of the relationship or were just plastered over by the needs of the moment (grad school, career, rehabbing the house, the traveling soccer team). When time and space permit, these differences grow to be real problems in the marriage. Sexual need imbalance, differences about money, varying ideas about where to live, differing ideas about retirement, and more fall into this category.

I'm not a psychologist, but I've become a long-term student of human relationships in both my personal and professional lives. I've learned some important things along the way.

I've learned one big thing: *times change, people don't.* I don't buy the line "they changed." Change is hard for people. Most people never change. We have a hard enough time changing habits—the diet industry alone is a $70+ billion market. It's even harder if not impossible to change personality traits. What I think happens is that after fifteen or twenty years, people finally have the time to understand what they want in life. They also decide that the things they don't like about the other person are a problem that needs correction or that they need to leave.

My counselor asked me during my divorce, "Is what's bothering you in the marriage based on habits, or are they bedrock personality traits that won't change?" People can change habits, but even that is hard. Personality traits are nearly impossible to change. Examples are do they like vacations? Do they prefer saving money over spending? Does the person have a quick temper? And so on. If traits can't be changed, the next question is whether you (or your spouse) can live with them the way they are.

DEALING WITH AFFAIRS: MORE THAN JUST SEX

There are many kinds of affairs, and they operate as relationship vampires as well. There are many books on these topics. I just want to cover the initial concepts here.

The Two Types of Affairs

There are two kinds of emotional and sexual affairs. One is a one-time fling. The person in the affair is lacking emotional or sexual satisfaction in their relationship and craves what they are missing. Usually, the marriage is repairable. The other type of cheater is someone who shouldn't be married at all. They are serial cheaters and won't ever change. The thrill of the chase is always more interesting than a committed relationship.

Affairs take many forms, but they all have one key element: they are destructive to the marriage because of the diversion of energy away from the relationship—they are a vampire writ large. Google "types of affairs" and you will find dozens of articles on the topic. Some claim there are twelve kinds of affairs; some claim only two, as do I. That said, the two types of affairs take a few different forms.

Examples of Affairs

- The one-night-stand affair: the person in the affair wants to feel sexually free outside the marriage. They drink too much, go too far, and have a one-time relationship with a person outside the marriage.
- The revenge affair: the person is trying to "punish" their spouse by having an outside relationship.
- The emotional affair: the relationship is platonic, not sexual, with the person spending a lot of time communicating (online or in real life) with another person or people.
- The serial-cheater affair: this person (example below) has one affair after another, maybe more than one at a time.
- The "exit-strategy" affair: the person is secretly hoping to get caught and escape the relationship.

These categories are typical reasons people involved in affairs have for the affair. They don't make it any easier.

The breach of trust occurring in an affair can be difficult if not impossible to recover from. Again, umpteen books exist on this topic. But from a divorce standpoint, I think some useful things can be gleaned.

My favorite story about the second kind of affair is a divorce I handled early in my career: "the seventeen-day marriage."

A young wife came into my office for a consultation a few days after returning from her honeymoon.

She told me, "My husband cheated on me, and I want a divorce."

I asked, "When did this happen?"

She said, "On our honeymoon."

Shocked, I asked, "Did he ever cheat on you before that?"

And she replied, "Yes, more than once while we were dating. But I thought he would be better once we got engaged. He promised he wouldn't cheat again."

I asked, "How long were you dating?"

"A year."

I immediately thought to myself, *Cheating on the honeymoon? This guy can't be fixed.*

A divorce in that case is inevitable. He's the "serial cheater" if there ever was one.

Which leads me to another thing I am asked a lot, usually by wives dealing with cheaters: If my husband isn't happy with me, why does he stay with me and not leave me for his girlfriend?

The answer is that he still gets a lot out of your relationship, and he loves you and his family. He would like to have his girlfriend *and* his wife and family. Sometimes perhaps this is cynical, like the spouse does not want to suffer the social and financial consequences of the divorce. But it also can be real and practical. The husband may like a lot of things about his wife and family but need a sexual/emotional outlet he does not get at home. Frequently, the wives in these situations end up filing the divorce case, simply because the husband is satisfied with the situation, and, naturally, most of the wives aren't. (As an aside, this happens in the other direction as well, when the wife has the affair.)

The only affair a marriage can recover from is the one in which the person was missing something and stepped out of the marriage to meet that need. With counseling and a desire to work together, the couple might find they can remain married and be happy.

SURPRISING SIGNS IT'S POSSIBLE TO RECONCILE

- You get along well on a daily basis.
- You share the same values (money, religion, politics, child-rearing).
- You enjoy your spouse's company.

HAVE YOU LOOKED INWARD?

Athol Kay's book *The Mindful Attraction Plan* argues that one must improve themselves first to help fix relationship problems. Common issues that cause your spouse to lose interest in you are:

- Loss of job (and lack of effort in a job)
- Overweight, out of shape
- No attention to grooming or personal appearance
- No hobbies or other interests

This makes sense. Understandably, people who don't take care of themselves, have no interest or pursuits in life, and aren't making any effort aren't interesting as friends—much less sexual mates.

Have you had adventures with your spouse? You may be old hat, but new adventures make your spouse excited. Do you exercise, travel, have hobbies? Or are you stuck in neutral in life?

Associate Professor Brian Olgolsky at the University of Illinois identified things that married couples can do to improve their relationships. Here are the top five:

- Keep lines of communication open, making sure that you are accessible and being positive.
- Talk about the relationship and check in with each other.
- Respond to each other. Engage with the other person and pay attention.
- Use humor. The use of humor during stressful times can defuse problem situations and make hard times easier to handle.

- Do fun things together. Exciting and fun experiences increase communication, create shared memories, and increase satisfaction with the marriage.[1]

I cannot overstate the importance of doing new and fun things together. Shared exciting activities *always* improve relationship quality. Research shows that doing exciting things together makes you ascribe the excitement to the other person.[2] In short, the excitement of the event is connected in your mind to your spouse, improving your relationship.

Again, these are *shared* activities. Not solo activities. Here's what happens when spouses have fun on their own.

I once represented a woman in a divorce who was outdoorsy and athletic, and her husband was into watching sports on TV. She wanted to bike and kayak with her husband. But he turned her down multiple times, preferring to stay inside and watch TV. It turned out that the next-door neighbor husband was also interested in kayaking and biking, and the wife struck up a friendship with the man. Every weekend they would go either on long bike rides or kayak trips—at first, totally platonic. Over time, however, she grew to care about the man and see him as a major improvement over her husband. They got involved romantically, and the couple ended up in my office for a divorce.

---

1   Belinda Luscombe, "A Guy Read 50 Years Worth of Relationship Studies. He Came Up With 17 Strategies, Yahoo, www.yahoo.com/now/guy-read-50-years-worth-152458561.html?guccounter=1&guce_referrer=aHR0cHM6Ly93d3cuZ29vZ2xlLmNvbS8&guce_referrer_sig=AQAAAC-Zb-Nfs1GWRKpEg072Sphdz4boH6iYsaZH1AGcLPqqv07qp8R5M12oDpD3ex-O4MfoTRyjaglYl4UI8z46Px77wI9NICdoZqK8TIlxn0JtAuGdUuOEZkXSYaOn-wAg-Jy8xzQclEf6uY4DgdwNvnq52n5fbNiEnT9Prc_Aybnrj3n.

2   A. Aron, C. C. Norman, E. N. Aron, C. McKenna, and R. E. Heyman, "Couples' Shared Participation in Novel and Arousing Activities and Experienced Relationship Quality, *Journal of Personality and Social Psychology*, 78, no. 2 (February 2000): 273–284, https://doi.org/10.1037//0022-3514.78.2.273.

THE AFFAIR WASN'T YOUR FAULT. OR WAS IT?

I've been surprised in consultations with the "victims" of affairs that they claim to be "shocked" by the affair. But when they discuss the nature of the marriage, the affair should not have been a surprise at all. Common issues include "I haven't slept with him in two years." "We've been in separate bedrooms for a long time." "We don't do anything together."

A story from an actual case: During a divorce pretrial conference with a veteran family law judge, the wife's counsel explained the wife was "blindsided" by the divorce in an attempt to gain sympathy from the court. After being pressed by me about the facts of the relationship, the judge was incredulous when the wife's counsel admitted the parties had not had sex in six years.

It takes two people to get married and two to get divorced. The majority of affairs are a *symptom* of the problems in the relationship, not the disease itself. Meaning if you examine the relationship, you can find the seeds of its destruction. Happily married people don't seek out affairs. No one wants the stress, risk, and possible fallout: divorce, public shame, damage to family and children. Many times, the relationship is lacking something one person needs, and they get desperate enough to seek it outside the marriage, or an opportunity presents itself that, under ordinary circumstances, they would have ignored.

MICHAEL'S STORY, CONTINUED

After Susan's lawyer and I wrapped our chat, we confronted the otherwise happy couple.

"Maybe you should consider staying married," I said to both parties.

"This is not about marriage but about life," Susan's lawyer said. "That is, a divorce may not fix what is upsetting you. You have an amazing life and seem to get along so well, and you seem so sad about this divorce."

Susan was shocked, but Michael was nodding with a knowing look on his face.

"Why don't we just try talking to someone?" Michael glanced at the other lawyer and me. "A counselor?"

They talked it over and agreed to meet with the marriage counselor we recommended. They put the divorce on hold.

After several counseling sessions, Susan realized that the freedom she sought she could get inside the marriage by pursuing her interests (church missionary work, writing) and by getting access to the family finances. Previously, Michael had handled all the financial matters. Susan found freedom that she hadn't thought was possible. What she thought she wanted was a divorce—but that was not what was bothering her. What she needed was her own identity, and that was for her to determine. Susan had been only a wife and mother for such a long time that this resulted in a rebirth as an independent adult. Ten years later, Michael and Susan are still married.

CHAPTER 3

HOW TO TURN $5 MILLION INTO $500,000 THE HARD WAY

(THE WORST WAY TO HANDLE YOUR DIVORCE CASE)

Dave was desperate. I could feel his fear and hopelessness as he told me his story.

"I've been in court in Chicago for nearly four years. *Four years*," Dave told me over the phone. "There's no end in sight. This . . . *sucks*."

Dave was spending $12,500+ per month in court-ordered temporary support. Worse yet, he had been forced out of the family business he co-owned with his brother and now had no income, and his lawyer had not been able to reduce the support payment, so he was paying with his nonmarital assets.

The divorce case was filed in 2011. Dave had been paying the temporary support by court order since April 2013. We started representing Dave in spring 2015. The case wouldn't be finished until late 2016.

"I hired somebody else back in 2011. I got nothing. The guy made no progress. For years."

I gathered from Dave that his wife, Ellen, hired a lawyer who intentionally delayed the divorce process. That lawyer filed motion after motion and did everything possible to drag Dave into court.

Dave's case was complex from a financial standpoint. Dave had formerly owned half of the family business but sold it and was holding the proceeds. (And more money was slated to come in payments over time.) One big issue raised by Ellen's lawyers was whether the business was marital property or nonmarital property. Based on the documents I saw and from talking with Dave, it appeared pretty clear that it was nonmarital, meaning his wife would not share in that cash.

After four years of machinations in court, out of desperation, Dave wanted a second opinion. He was referred to a veteran, skilled divorce lawyer in the suburbs. She was smart, experienced, and had the right mindset but was not equipped to handle a major trial against a big-city divorce firm, which was why Dave called me.

Normally, I'd take a pass. The second time (or third time) is usually not the charm for divorce clients. If a client does not click with his first divorce lawyer, that can happen. If they don't click with two lawyers, that usually means something is wrong with the client.

Dave was a nice guy who had a big problem. A major Chicago law firm known for WWIII tactics and big fees represented Ellen. Dave had a big marital estate, which meant dollar signs and potentially big fees for these guys. More zeros on a client's balance sheet should not necessarily mean more zeroes for legal fees. Plus, the lawyer who was helping Dave was nice, had a phenomenal memory, and was sharp on the law and the facts of his complex case.

I quickly realized the best strategy was two pronged: try to settle the case quickly and push for a trial date in the case to stop the bleeding of cash. Every month cost Dave $15,000 in temporary support with the possibility of no reimbursement. And all for a fairly short marriage. (Based on Illinois law, the marriage was measured from the date of marriage to the date the case was filed.) So even a not-so-great settlement or trial result would be better than Dave's present, seemingly endless nightmare in court. If we could work with Ellen's attorney, I thought we'd have a good shot at doing a great job for Dave.

We took the case.

We pushed for the trial date and got one. Right before Christmas, of course.

The trial started with a bang—the night before trial was to begin, Ellen's lawyers pulled the dirty trick of dismissing the wife's case in an attempt to catch us off guard. Instead of starting with Ellen's case and witnesses, I had to start with Dave's case. If you aren't prepared to do that, you're screwed—or, more accurately, your client is screwed. The good news was that I was ready for this and put Dave on the stand to testify right away, which would likely take a few days.

Nearly a year later, my partner, Laura, and I were sitting at counsel's table in a dimly lit courtroom at the Daley Center in Chicago. Dave was on the stand answering questions from the other attorney.

The trial took forever. Two things made it much worse: First, the judge would only hear the trial a day or two every few weeks and then only from about 1:30 p.m. to maybe 4:30 p.m. Second, Ellen's lawyers (who had an office only a couple of blocks from the courthouse) seemed to be late to court more often than not as well. So we would get rolling by about 2:00 p.m. and quit many times by 4:00 p.m. Generally, this meant only about two hours of effective trial time per day. Worse yet, the judge was forgetful, and I doubted she would recall the evidence or our arguments when it was all over.

We couldn't get Ellen and her counsel to come to the table to settle. Meanwhile, the sizable assets the parties had—whether marital or nonmarital (due to the husband selling his interest in a family business)—were dwindling, as the enormous attorneys' fees (and the fact that the wife was spending a lot of money and was not employed) made things worse.

At the time, the case had been in litigation for three years. In Cook County (Chicago and the Chicago area), cases can take a long time to get to trial for a number of reasons. The caseload per judge is high. The judges generally don't exercise strong control over their courtrooms and are not eager to penalize lawyers who blow deadlines and break the rules. The courts allow multiple continuances (rescheduling) of trial and hearing dates, compounding the problem. Many of the judges in the county also have a court call, so the judge who hears the case before trial might not be the judge who runs the trial. This means that any institutional memory the court might have about the case (and who has been behaving or misbehaving during the case) is lost.

Would we be able to help Dave and get him out of this mess?

High-net-worth individuals like Dave incur huge costs with little benefit if they act irrationally. Acting rationally as a client in a divorce case is easier said than done. Because divorce is the intersection of everything we hold dear—kids, money, sex, and love—with it comes the fear that some or all of those things will be endangered or at least changed. With fear comes anger and pain. When a client is in the thick of a nasty, litigated divorce, emotions can easily get in the way of clear thinking.

For example, your soon-to-be ex just went to Florida with her boyfriend on your dime. Or your husband gets to do what he wants on the weekends while you're stuck with the kids. These things make people mad.

Emotional turbulence makes you (or your spouse) susceptible to a lawyer telling you they will "win," "get you yours," et cetera. You're scared and angry, and you know you're going to lose half your assets, and life with your kids will never be the same again. That makes you susceptible to the desire for revenge through litigation. Unfortunately, some attorneys either take advantage of these negative emotions or just don't make an effort to tamp them down. If lawyers are paid by the hour, drama in a case equals more work, and more work equals more fees. Drama is expensive. The more there is, the more lawyers can charge—justifiably. The hardest thing for any lawyer to do is tell their clients no. So most lawyers don't. What is in your best interest might not be in your attorney's best interest. When I recommend a settlement proposal and the client resists, I always say, "Why do you think I would recommend this deal? Our firm makes more money if you *don't* settle." That's how you know you can trust the advice.

When your soon-to-be ex-spouse "gets your goat," your rational mind shuts down, and your reptilian brain kicks in. You want to "win." There is an allure to the big, movie-finale courtroom drama. Maybe you feel like you will "teach a lesson" to your spouse. (More on this and other divorce myths in Chapter 6.) Some divorce lawyers won't dissuade you from the battle. (Not necessarily with evil intent, as we explain later in this chapter.)

So you're primed for a fight. Will cooler heads prevail? The right approach—and the right lawyer—makes all the difference. The lawyer focused on "winning" the divorce case may not rationally evaluate your case with a cost-benefit analysis: taking into account your goals and fears to give you an unbiased, reality-based look at your chances.

WHY LAWYERS FIGHT

Most divorce lawyers want to fight, fight, fight.

Why? Of course, there is the obvious financial incentive. But that is one reason among many. The combative, court-based approach is hard-wired into many divorce attorneys. It's how we are trained. First, law school is an important component. Next, our training as law clerks and junior lawyers has an important effect. Then, our work experience as attorneys shapes us with concerns of liability and ethics complaints. The general lawyerly culture also contributes to the court-first bias.

I realize it looks like I am slamming attorneys here. I am not. I believe in the system, but it's not one size fits all and can use substantial improvement. The court system is not the best way to resolve *most* family law disputes. I like attorneys—I'm married to one! We have a tough job. Lawyers do so much good for people daily in our system of justice. Most divorce attorneys genuinely believe they are fighting the good fight on behalf of their client and upholding their ethical obligation to zealously represent them. Yet some fail to look beyond the balance sheet or impact on children in the name of "client advocacy," "fairness," and "winning" for their client. At the same time, the client feels justified with exacting an emotional and financial toll from their soon-to-be ex-spouse.

The way the system works and the way attorneys are "brought up" in that system can help you effectively navigate your divorce.

THE IMPACT OF LAW SCHOOL

Law school is a zero-defect culture. Think about it. The students who make it to law school generally were A students in high school and college. Then they took a difficult exam to get into law school and scored well on that. At the time of publication of this book, the acceptance rate for the top ten law schools in the United States is around 10 percent. Law schools are loaded with perfectionists and type-A personalities. Plus, in law school, the heart of what students learn is based on broken cases—when things went so wrong that a lawsuit was filed, and then the trial decision was so disliked by one party that they appealed it to a higher court. Most law school classes are taught using case law as examples—appellate case reports. But think about that. Things that go *right* don't end up as contested lawsuits, and they sure don't wind up in an appellate court. Law schools are also geared toward litigation and trial practice. As of the publication of this book, the University of Illinois Law School has six courses relating to evidence and trial practice and several more focused on litigation.[3] It has only two related to mediation and alternative dispute resolution.

This emphasis on litigation and how things can go wrong means that lawyers are trained to look out for the one percent worst case scenario—and to treat every case the same way.

---

3 "Courses," Illinois College of Law, https://law.illinois.edu/academics/courses/.

THE INFLUENCE OF MENTORS AND EMPLOYERS

The mentoring and training new lawyers receive in the early part of their careers is critically important. Since much training of lawyers is on the job, your lawyer's on-the-job training has a tremendous influence on how they practice law. A good mentor and training for a lawyer means a solid understanding of not only trial practice but also what is required for trial: how to prepare for it, and therefore how best to settle without trial. Some of the best lawyers who settle cases happen to be skilled trial lawyers. They know what the client is in for, and they know how things can go sideways at trial. They deal in the art of the possible. Like soldiers returning from war are the first to warn against the next war, a lawyer with a lot of trial experience knows what you face and does not have an unrealistic view of what can be accomplished. Further, if the partners running the law firm have a trial-oriented mindset, they will teach this mind-set to their younger lawyers. If they believe in alternative dispute resolution (ADR)—that is, any method of resolving a case without using the court—they will pass that on to their younger lawyers as well. ADR includes mediation (dispute resolution using a neutral person, usually a lawyer trained in mediation, collaborative practice, and arbitration. These concepts are described in detail in Chapter 7.

THE IMPACT OF RISK AVOIDANCE

The law business itself is a tough world, but even more so in divorce with raw emotions and the intersection of so many aspects of life and the legal world. Lawyers are exposed to personal liability if they make a mistake. You can't sue the owner of General Motors if something is wrong with your car, but you can sue the owner of a law firm personally if one of the lawyers in the firm commits malpractice. A bad trial result can be pinned on a judge while a client unhappy with a settlement result blames the lawyer.

One of my mentors, the great Honorable James F. McCluskey, told me, "Lawyers never get in trouble by doing stuff; they get in trouble by not doing stuff." And he's right. He meant that taking timely action was always better than doing nothing or waiting too long. Lawyers almost always get in trouble legally and ethically for not doing things, rather than for making mistakes of commission.

Lawyers obsess over bad news. We read the list of colleagues who have been suspended or disbarred for ethical lapses. We read stories of malpractice lawsuits, worried we will somehow make a similar mistake. We attend continuing education courses about changes in the law and ethics rules to avoid foul-ups. There are hundreds of ways to screw up in our business that can cost a lawyer lots of money—maybe all their money—their career, or both. Plus we always learn about new ways lawyers made mistakes.

Over time, attorneys become more risk avoidant. No one wants to get sued for malpractice, draw an ethics complaint, or have to reply to a bad review online. In this culture, the "leave no stone unturned" mentality becomes understandable and defensible. When you are supposed to zealously represent your clients and not doing "stuff" gets you in trouble, it is best and easiest to simply "do stuff" and not have those worries. This mindset can justify pressing ahead in court and leaving "no stone unturned" in order to avoid blame for missing something or recommending a settlement with which the client might be later dissatisfied.

IMPACT OF POP CULTURE

Many clients have little to no awareness of alternatives to court. Thank pop culture for that. Dramatic trials are "sexy." They're what people see in the movies and TV, and they have an irresistible "gunslinger" or "gladiator" vibe, so the classes in law school are popular. Trial is more like a competition and has all the elements of an exciting game. (Not so exciting for clients paying the bills later on.) Some clients also are suspicious of making a deal, for fear they are giving up too much and that the only "fair" result would come from a court hearing.

TECHNOLOGY

Law firms are conservative by nature and therefore notoriously technologically challenged. When I worked as a young law clerk for a small firm in Chicago in the early 1990s, I asked the head staff person if I could get a computer because I would be much more productive with one. (At this time, laptops were uncommon among students, and the internet as we know it did not exist.) She said that the owner of the firm told her she could buy any office equipment she wanted "as long as it didn't have a screen on it." Years later, in a meeting where I discussed stopping our firm's practice of snail mailing copies of documents to clients and instead emailing a scan, one of my colleagues was concerned we'd lose revenue since the staff would take much less time performing this function.

This attitude is not unusual in the law business. There is also a legitimate concern about the security and confidentiality of technology related to our ethics rules, making lawyers reluctant to adopt new technology. So conservatism reigns among older lawyers and, you'd be surprised to hear, a lack of imagination among younger lawyers. This coupled with the lack of desire to spend money on technology and systems results in a cautious approach. This often results in firms adopting software and systems years after they become commonplace in the business world.

THE TYRANNY OF THE BILLABLE HOUR

The law firm's culture also contributes to whether the lawyer working on your case promotes settlement or recommends litigation. The way most divorce legal work is billed to clients in the United States contributes to litigation. Billing clients on a time-and-expense basis (charging for hours worked) is the predominant method in divorce law firms (and most any litigation law firm in general in the United States). It is a system well known to law firm owners, and most lawyers "grew up" in firms that billed on a time-and-expense basis. Billable hours equal revenue. For the firm owners, each billing employee (attorneys and perhaps paralegals) needs to bill (and collect payment on) a certain number of hours each month to cover expenses and turn a profit. These are substantial expenses. Employment expenses alone can range from 40 to 60 percent of divorce law firm revenue. Net profit margin is tighter than you might expect. If the law firm has a large staff and big, high-end office space, the pressure to bill and collect is that much greater.

With the hourly-fee model, there is no strong incentive to use technology to increase productivity. It is not that lawyers want or intend to run up high bills—most can stand behind the time charged to clients. It can simply be a product of this system. There is no disincentive to put in a lot of time on a case unless the client cannot pay for the work.

It gets worse. Many family law firms have a billable-hour minimum. These range from 1,800 to 2,200—akin to a 46-hour weekly requirement, assuming four weeks off per year. But working as a lawyer, you don't bill eight hours just because you were at the office for eight hours. Law firm billing software company Clio's 2020 Legal Trends Report shows that on average, across all practice areas, law firms bill only one-third of the hours worked to clients (2.66 hours in an 8-hour day), and of that, about 80 percent of the billable time (or 2.1 hours) lands on a bill. What's more, on average, law firms only collect about 90 percent of the hours billed (or 1.9 hours).

Consider a law firm whose goal for billable hours allows each team member to have a normal workday without being pushed to bill hours. The driving goal is to accomplish the client's goals in the most efficient manner, not simply to run up a bill. In the end, we are looking for client satisfaction, positive reviews, and referrals—emptying a client's bank account for our fees won't accomplish that. As of publication of this book, the firm is moving to use fixed fees even for litigation cases, to free our clients and team from the constraints of billable hours entirely.

All these reasons fuel the drive to litigate, to make the case bigger than it needs to be. When you call with a concern, will the lawyer advise you just to deal with it: explaining that you will spend $5,000 on a $3,500 problem? Or will the lawyer tell you, "Yes, I will file a motion about that right away"? A profit-first lawyer may overlook a careful cost-benefit analysis. They might not discourage court action. Just as every action has an equal and opposite reaction, fighting begets more fighting, so court action will provoke more court action from your spouse. And you and your spouse go down a spiral of increasing acrimony and litigation. This leads to the "black hole" or "swamp" of interim litigation.

The worst situation is when the cases "run away" and go to trial, and the fees owed to the lawyers are greater than the difference in financial outcomes for the parties to the case. They can dwarf the issue the lawyers were hired to resolve. The parties are almost forced to go to trial to "win" and hope that the other party is forced to pay the fees, which rarely happens.

THE POWER OF SUGGESTION AND THE SWAMP

Lawyers have tremendous power over clients. Clients look to the lawyer for guidance and counsel, especially in divorce cases with emotions running high. Similar to the power a psychologist has over a patient, the lawyer has power over a typical divorce client because they have an audience willing to believe what they are told, especially if it is bad stuff about their spouse. They are susceptible to the power of suggestion. So it is easy for lawyers to use language that ratchets up litigation. This is how illusionists control an audience's perceptions and how hypnotists influence clients' beliefs and behaviors.

THE "RED FLAG" STORY

I had a case in which the parties had been married for about ten years and had no children. I represented the husband. The wife had previously been married and had obtained a substantial estate from her prior divorce as well as alimony. This was his first marriage. He owned real estate and a business that predated the marriage. They did not have a prenuptial agreement.

When the client called me for the initial consultation, he confidently said, "This is an easy case." (*Famous last words*, I always think to myself.)

"OK, tell me what is going on."

"My wife and I agreed that the only thing we will split is our home, which we bought jointly. Each of us will keep our own stuff. And no alimony—she makes about what I make. We've kept all our assets and income separate since the beginning of the marriage at her request."

I was skeptical because things rarely are as easy as clients think they will be.

He retained me. His wife hired a lawyer in a big-city firm, largely known for their high-profile cases. They don't have a reputation as a firm that engages in ADR. I was concerned, knowing the law firm I was dealing with. I told my client as much. In any event, he wanted me to propose an early settlement along those lines. Which we did—we sent a settlement agreement containing the terms that the couple discussed before hiring attorneys.

The lawyer hired by the wife markets herself as a collaborative attorney, but the lawyer's words told me this was going to get complicated. They admitted to me that her client was OK with settling the case. But, the attorney said, "I have a lot of concerns about the case." They expressed concern that my client was "in a hurry to settle" and that the settlement proposal could not be considered until their law firm conducted extensive discovery, hired experts to value his non-marital businesses, and valued all of his real estate holdings. *Oh. Only that?* I thought.

I pointed out that the major issue was whether his stuff was marital property and therefore subject to division because it seemed from the overall information that all his property minus the home was nonmarital. The other lawyer said, "We will have to investigate that as well." Plus, against my client's wishes, the lawyer wanted to file the case with the court, which would mean needlessly increased fees since we could exchange documents and get the information we need without the help of the court. (And normal collaborative practice is to stay out of court generally until a case is settled.)

So, in other words, the other lawyer wanted to search the proverbial haystack when she could have asked our client for the needle. If there were concerns about the information provided, the client would have cooperated to provide more proof. We could have at least made an effort to do things by agreement and stay out of court.

The wife initially wanted to settle out of court. But what else would the client do if she was scared and prone to accept the lawyer's suggestion to do an extensive investigation?

My guess is that at the consultation, the wife told her lawyer about the deal that was on the table. At this moment, the client is primed to follow the lawyer's guidance. There were two ways to go about it from the lawyer's perspective. The attorney can say, "We can do that for you, but we recommend some minimal investigation to be sure you're covered." Or they can push them to "verify everything" because "we don't know what we don't know." Which is true! But this book urges a cost-benefit analysis. How much do you already know? How much risk is involved in a narrowly focused investigation? Is the cost worth the potential gain? By scaring the wife, the lawyer now had her sold on a full-blown investigation that may not have been necessary.

Here's the kicker to the story. After my client learned that the other attorney a) filed the case in court and b) wanted to get every document related to his finances for the past ten years and value all his property, whether marital or nonmarital, he terminated our firm and hired a similar large divorce firm fearing he needed a "bulldog" to represent him. He got scared and decided to jump into the swamp with his wife. My prediction was that the couple might spend $150,000+ on their case and end up right where they started with the proposed settlement, only now each person will be $75,000 poorer.

THE "I KNOW HE'S A CHEATER" STORY

I represented the husband in another case. They had a long-term marriage (25-plus years). He had recently retired from a mid-six-figure job and had banked several million dollars in assets. His wife had been a stay-at-home mom, but the kids were now grown. A couple of years earlier, they had separated; my client had moved out, then they reconciled some months later. Then, my client realized it would not work out and moved into a condo he purchased.

His wife suspected that my client had a girlfriend. I didn't think so. Not that I'm naïve; this is common, but in this case, I believed him.

"What effect would a girlfriend have on my case?" he asked me as a hypothetical.

He seemed like a man who wanted to know in his heart he was doing the right thing and to be able to say so to his adult sons.

In any event, legally, affairs have no effect on division of assets or payment of alimony in Illinois. The only caveat is that money spent on a significant other is considered "dissipation of marital assets"—money spent outside the marriage for a nonmarital purpose after the marriage has broken down.

So an affair in this case wouldn't have mattered from a legal standpoint. But my client's wife was angry about it.

We got involved in the case, and shortly before the first professionals' meeting, my client called me, upset.

He said, "My wife is telling our sons that her lawyer says I have a girlfriend. My boys are heartbroken."

I didn't think the other lawyer said that to his client. But again, the power of suggestion is strong. Also, people hear what they want to hear, and they may hide behind their lawyers to add perceived authority to the things they say.

My guess is that the wife, upset about the divorce to begin with, said to the other lawyer, "I bet he has a girlfriend." And instead of emphasizing the fact that it doesn't matter in our state from a legal standpoint, the attorney may have said, "They all do" or something similarly cynical. Of course, at the time, the lawyer had no evidence of any girlfriend. Neither did the wife. Lawyers should avoid tossing around comments like that. Clients are looking for guidance, and they seize upon things their lawyers tell them.After hearing that, the wife told family and friends (including the parties' children) that my client had a girlfriend, and of course, my client became upset. This is the kind of misguided "advice" from attorneys that blows up cases and drags people into the swamp.

In both these examples, the lawyer planted a negative thought in the client's head when they were susceptible to suggestion. At the least, they didn't dissuade the client from their downward mental spiral. The statements made by the attorneys may not have been a direct assertion or may have been intended as sarcasm, but coupled with the client's mindset, the statements were equally damaging. There is a power imbalance between lawyer and client. If the lawyer senses that a client is looking for a cheerleader and a strong fighter, there is a temptation to go along with client desires, even if the evidence may not support the ideas and even if pursuing it won't hold up to a cost-benefit analysis.

It's like an ostensibly healthy 30-year-old with no medical complaints coming in for a checkup, and the doctor issues $10,000 worth of tests because the patient *might* have one condition or another. But is that best for them? Chances are it's not. But if the doctor suggested that other similarly positioned 30-year-olds have disproportionately had cancer or some other malady, she could convince the patient to have the tests quite easily.

Be aware of this and consider your susceptibility to suggestions from your family, friends, and lawyer. They may tell you what you want to hear and lead you down the wrong path. This is not to say this is intentional on the part of lawyers but a decade or two of practice tends to make attorneys cynical. Just as a drug addiction counselor may start to think that "everyone" has an addiction, we divorce lawyers get a skewed view of things. Since attorneys are risk averse and are trained to defend against the one percent chance of failure in a zero-defect culture, we assume the worst and start there with our analysis, even if it might not be right for every case.

THE INTERIM LITIGATION SWAMP

These cases are examples of what I call the "interim litigation swamp." And the typical divorce lawyer gets mired (sometimes happily) in the swamp and brings their client with them. Interim litigation is the court action that happens between the start of a case and the final trial—think issues like temporary child support or permission to have the kids go on a trip out of the country. Such petitions might be necessary in a case in which the working spouse isn't giving the stay-at-home spouse access to funds. (We discuss why not to be that person later in Chapter 16.) Interim litigation can also involve motions related to parenting time and discovery, such as a motion to force financial records turnover. Some interim litigation is essential, and some is a waste of time and money. It all depends on context. Wasted interim litigation is expensive.

The case goes on and on, around in circles seemingly in endless repetition, and it never seems like you are making progress because all you are doing is addressing temporary issues, not the ultimate issues in the case.

Getting mired in the swamp can include email wars between the lawyers. This "trial by email" is a complete waste of effort. The "office tiger" lawyers who love to engage in this (and in the telephone version) spout all kinds of tough talk and bad-mouth your client, but to what end? Of course, the judge does not see the emails or hear the phone conversations. What the lawyer writes in an email is not evidence that will be useful in court.

Arguments between the lawyers via email (or in person) are seldom worthwhile. If the judge won't read it or hear it, what's the point? This is not to say you don't want to hear the other side's point of view—a good lawyer should always be willing to listen to the other attorney to learn facts or law that they might not be aware of. The problem lies where you've already made it clear to the other attorney that you understand their point of view, and your client disagrees with it. Some attorneys seem to think that by yelling loudly enough or bombing you with emails, they will convince you and your client of the error of your ways.

In these situations, my response to the lawyer is "If you know of facts or law that would change my mind, I am more than willing to consider that information." A good attorney should always be willing to talk with the other lawyer and be open to facts and law they might not be aware of. But just repeating the same arguments that my client is wrong or a bad person won't make me see things the other way.

THE WOLF IN SHEEP'S CLOTHING

Another swamp creature is the wolf in sheep's clothing. This type of lawyer says the right buzzwords about alternative dispute resolution, has had the appropriate training in mediation and collaborative law, and has joined the local collaborative law organization. However, they don't walk the walk. They advertise ADR because they know clients are seeking it (in their understandable desire to stay away from the swamp). But in the end, this kind of lawyer takes their swamp-dwelling ways and transfers them to the ADR realm. In collaborative practice, the attorneys regularly working in this space soon find out who these people are and stay away from them.

These attorneys masquerade as "settlement-minded" attorneys who just relabel the same old approach to negotiating divorce cases. This takes several forms. This kind of lawyer advises their clients to avoid signing the collaborative participation agreement, telling them that it is more cost effective to keep them as their attorney if negotiations fail and the case winds up in court. They file the case in court when that is not necessary. (There are some occasions where filing a case is necessary, even in collaborative or other ADR practice, such as to preserve the length of the marriage for alimony purposes in Illinois.) They seek overly extensive discovery when it isn't necessary. They push a "maximum" and unrealistic result for the case for their client, even when the client would be satisfied with an "acceptable" result (see the Venn diagram in Figure 1) at a much lower cost.

With the wolf in sheep's clothing, you might as well have just been in court despite outward appearances, whether you are in "assisted mediation" or arbitration or "cooperative practice." This is essentially collaborative law without a participation agreement, so the lawyers stay on if the settlement negotiation fails, and the case goes to court. I find it a waste of time. You either choose fish or fowl. You end up battling a swamp dweller with all the related grief that comes with it.

Is interim litigation necessary in your case? Ask yourself, "Will this get me *more* divorced?" Meaning, is this advancing your case or just making you feel good temporarily? Always apply a cost-benefit analysis. You can figure that at today's typical rates, any interim petition or motion will cost $2,500 to $5,000. Weigh that against the size of the problem. Is it worth it? If it's not, it's not. Many lawyers don't ask you about your thoughts about the cost-benefit in the first place, and you are in danger of heading into the swamp.

TRIAL DATES: OR, HOW TO GET OUT OF THE SWAMP

If you already are in litigation, trial dates are the best way to resolve a case. In the way that sunlight is the best disinfectant, a trial means the court will decide the case, and this causes everyone, including the lawyers and the parties to a divorce, to get real about their chances. Since the vast majority of divorce cases settle, this forced attention on the case typically causes negotiations and, in turn, settlement of a case, as the parties and lawyers typically want to avoid the expense of a trial and the chances of an adverse outcome that might be worse than a negotiated settlement.

At the trial, the lawyers will offer evidence and make legal arguments on the issues in the case, and the judge ultimately will decide the outcome. Once the trial date arrives, you must be ready. Judges aren't likely to reschedule without a good reason. You need to have your witnesses and documents ready to be presented, and the attorney must have command of the law and the facts of the case. A trial is the opportunity for the attorney to teach the judge about the case and their client's point of view. I should mention that although I believe trial dates are great drivers of settlement—or at least of case resolution—they are not a panacea. We discuss the commonly held misconceptions about trials in Chapter 6.

In my experience, many divorce lawyers are allergic to trial dates. I have some theories as to why this is the case. Personal injury and commercial litigation lawyers aren't afraid of trial dates; on the plaintiff's side, they push for them. Most civil litigation lawyers want momentum, and they want a conclusion to the case. They don't want the case to take forever, and neither do their clients. But in divorce court, it is at times difficult to get lawyers to advance the case to a conclusion.

WHY SOME DIVORCE LAWYERS DON'T LIKE TRIALS

1. **Trials are tons of work.** Typically, a lawyer will be working twelve- to sixteen-hour days when at trial. They are preparing at night and on the weekends and have to know everything about the client's case. Trials disrupt all of their other cases and everything else they are doing as a lawyer. The trial judge is in control of the lawyers' calendars at that point, and the trial dates take priority over any of the lawyer's other clients. When an attorney is at trial, it's all-consuming. They aren't just busy during the trial itself. They are talking with their client before, during, and after; they are talking with witnesses, reviewing evidence, organizing exhibits, and much more. This takes a tremendous amount of work and time, and every hour the lawyers are working on the trial is billable to the client.

2. **Being at trial totally disrupts the rest of the lawyer's practice.** The lawyer cannot do any other work outside the trial. It becomes all consuming. Perhaps attorneys and staff in their firm are also tied up working on the trial, making them unavailable for other work. Meanwhile, their other clients get zero attention as they become totally absorbed by a trial. (This is where a larger firm can shine, with resources

to both help with the trial and provide backup for the other cases the trial lawyer is handling.)

3. **The court will decide the case**, and the lawyers—and parties—lose control over the outcome.

Courts in our jurisdiction won't issue a trial date until you have a "pretrial conference," where you discuss the facts of the case with the court (without the parties present) and without witnesses. The judge reads memoranda the lawyers prepare for this conference; reviews financial affidavits illustrating the assets, liabilities, income, and expenses of the parties; discusses the case for about 30 minutes or so; and gives recommendations for settlement. These can be useful. But "We aren't ready for pretrial" is a common refrain from counsel looking to buy more time, file more interim motions, and generate more smoke around the case. They tell the judge, "We need more discovery." And ironically, as time passes, the data change (you make more money, spend money, asset values change), so you generate the need for even more discovery because now the parties need to update the documents they already produced. So the nature of the problem becomes evident.

There certainly is a time and place for trial, when your client cannot accept the settlement offer from the other party or when the cost-benefit analysis indicates that the potential trial outcomes are better than the deal on the table, even taking costs into account. (More on the four true costs of divorce in Chapter 9.) In divorce cases, it is uncommon that a trial is the best option. It can be the best or, indeed, the only option in cases of child or spousal abuse or neglect or when a parent demands sole custody. But in most cases, especially those involving finances, most often the data can be fully ascertained, the costs realistically weighed against potential outcomes, and clarity reached about a reasonable settlement.

Being a strong advocate for your client does not mean fighting is always the best option. Furthermore, not fighting does not equal weakness. Likely in the divorce context, it means the lawyer has a good assessment of their client's case, their chances of success, and the costs involved and is confident that negotiation, not litigation, is in the client's best interest.

A flexible approach to case resolution is best. There are cases that should be settled and cases that certainly should be tried. The important thing is having a lawyer who can distinguish the two and give you good advice about which way to go. There are lawyers in the divorce field who shun all forms of alternative dispute resolution, such as collaborative law and mediation. They will tell you that the only way to properly fight for your rights is in court. They will say that only the court can "protect" you from your spouse and that any settlement is a compromise that you shouldn't make. But people make compromises all the time that work just fine for them. You work out the problem, and you move on. Others say you have to do collaborative or mediation only. These attorneys will tell you that trial is never the answer—that all disputes can be worked out collaboratively or by mediation if people make the effort.

Both types are partly wrong. The best approach is to have experience in all forms of dispute resolution. This is the "mixed martial arts" of divorce law. Not just one approach, but experience in all approaches so the attorney can apply the best one for the task at hand. This is not to knock attorneys concentrating in one area or another. For example, there are excellent lawyers who are purely collaborative, just as there are outstanding divorce trial lawyers out there. The important thing is getting a realistic assessment of your case so you know what is the best approach for you.

Hands down, the worst strategy is what many traditional divorce lawyers do. They battle for months, or worse, years, in interim litigation with no clear focus on the endgame at great expense to the client. Then shortly before trial, the lawyer whispers to the client something like, "If this goes to trial, here's what could happen . . ." followed by the worst-case scenario. They scramble to make a deal, the client panics, and the settlement is worse for everyone than it could have been if that was the priority from the outset.

"I JUST WANT THIS DONE"

From the client's perspective, reaching a settlement they can live with as quickly as possible is the highest priority. It ought to be the goal for us lawyers, too. Because divorce cases don't age like fine wines. No one brags to their friends that their divorce case took three years. A major indicator of divorce law client satisfaction is "time to close": how long the case lasted from start to finish. At our law firm, we track this statistic for our cases. At some point, every client announces they "just want this done." Lawyers don't always understand that the client doesn't want a divorce case; they just want to *be* divorced. As time passes, divorcing people who live together get emotions rubbed raw. Tensions build in the family. The children are emotionally worn out by the tone in the household. The family is in suspended animation awaiting the divorce. I've never met a client who wished their divorce took longer.

This brings us to the all-important question: What's the best way to Get This Done?

SETTLEMENT PHILOSOPHY

If you can settle, by all means settle; if you and your spouse can't reach an acceptable agreement, have a trial. Oftentimes, the facts aren't in dispute in divorce cases, but the desired outcomes are. The numbers are the numbers.

If you can reach an acceptable agreement, negotiation and settlement is the best way to meet your goals. If you are the "moneyed" spouse (the higher wage earner, the one who stands to pay support, the one who generated more of the marital assets), getting the case done sooner is generally better. Providing the financial data, opening a dialogue about the children, and advancing the case toward an acceptable agreement are in your best interest, considering that time passing increases costs and generally makes cases worse. (See Chapter 9 about the four costs of divorce.) If this means that the moneyed spouse is a little more generous than the law requires to resolve the case, that's fine, provided it is within the range of acceptable outcomes, taking the costs into account. There is real value in just being finished.

Just because you're involved in litigation does not mean you must abandon ADR methods. You can still pursue negotiations and mediation and work out a settlement, and you should keep trying to reach an agreement if possible before trial. The various ways to resolve cases outside trial are discussed in detail in Chapter 7. You also may be able to narrow the disputed issues by settling parts of your case, thereby potentially leading to a global settlement or at least shortening the trial, controlling risk and expense.

If you wish to have any hope of settling a case, you need to provide an offer that is in the "dealing range": that realistic range of outcomes we discuss in Chapter 9, taking into account the costs. And you need to be realistic about the dealing range. Just like cornering an animal, giving your soon-to-be ex no options in settlement is a risky move. If they feel that they have no option other than to accept a bad deal or go to trial, you are likely to push the case to trial. You cannot expect your spouse to negotiate with you if you provide no realistic outcome for them. If your settlement offer is your best case at trial (and their cost-benefit analysis means a trial is worth their trouble), do not be shocked when they insist on going to trial.

THE VENN DIAGRAM OF SETTLEMENT

The best settlement philosophy is depicted in a Venn diagram (see Figure 1). The range of acceptable settlement options lies where your interests and your spouse's interests overlap and, moreover, inside the range of realistic trial outcomes. Finding this middle ground is known as "interest-based negotiation" and is at the core of the foundational principles of mediation and collaborative practice described in Chapter 7. Most lawyers might start negotiating at the outside edge of your circle. These extremes are impossible, "ask for the moon" demands. The conventional wisdom is that this will leave "room" to negotiate. No one wants to be the first one to jump into the water with an offer, for fear they will leave something on the proverbial table. So the thinking is to demand your client's best-case scenario, and the client won't get in trouble. This kind of demand seems great at first, until the other party makes a similar offer at the outer limit "best case" for them that is also impossible at trial. But judges rarely give a majority of assets to one person, deny alimony when the facts support it, or award sole custody to a parent. A range of outcomes somewhere around the middle is more realistic. The parties then spend a lot of money and time fooling around, going back and forth with diminishing demands until they get inside the range of realistic outcomes and finally strike a deal. So much of this time and money for fees can be saved by making a realistic offer at the outset.

Experienced lawyers know how these cases generally turn out based on the facts and the law. A good attorney will work hard to skip the unrealistic stuff and tell you what can reasonably be accomplished and a realistic range of court outcomes.

Divorcing couples frequently spend a tremendous amount of money and time fighting over a relatively small difference in possible outcomes. The savvy client avoids spending more in total costs than the "delta" or difference in outcomes is worth. (More about the four costs of divorce in Chapter 9.)

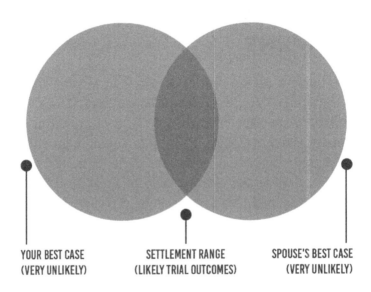

| YOUR BEST CASE | SETTLEMENT RANGE | SPOUSE'S BEST CASE |
| (VERY UNLIKELY) | (LIKELY TRIAL OUTCOMES) | (VERY UNLIKELY) |

Figure 1. Settlement Venn Diagram

52

Consider that settlement range of most likely trial outcomes. In my experience, clients too often spend more trying to move the "needle" 5 to 10 percent one way or the other than the effort is worth in the typical divorce case.

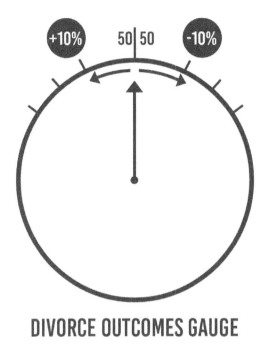

DIVORCE OUTCOMES GAUGE

Figure 2. Divorce Outcomes Gauge

Ultimately, people getting divorced want to know the truth, what their real chances are—not fantasy, pie-in-the-sky magical thinking. In my divorce, I talked to other lawyers in my firm to have them help me assess what outcomes were realistic. The bottom line is that generally speaking, you're going to get some of the money and some of the time with the kids, and so is your spouse. It is much less common for people not to have these outcomes. Examples include cases of child abuse, neglect, or a total failure of parents to communicate with respect to custody and visitation. For financial cases, outliers include cases in which one party has a huge nonmarital estate (lots of inherited money outside the marriage), or one party has a high income, but the family has limited accumulated assets. These kinds of circumstances can "move the needle" in the direction of one spouse more (sometimes much more) than in the average case, and good legal advice is key in those cases to get the best outcome.

THREE STEPS TO RESOLVE A DIVORCE: EVALUATE, NEGOTIATE, LITIGATE

Evaluate, negotiate, and only if necessary, litigate. This is the best process for resolving divorce matters in the proper order of priority.

Evaluate

First, carefully evaluate your case. Discuss goals and concerns with your attorney. Provide financial documentation and other relevant evidence requested by your attorney. At this stage, it is important to communicate well so that your attorney understands the facts of the case, as well as the key issues, and can assess potential outcomes and costs and the strengths and weaknesses of your case. The cost-benefit analysis figures in here. As information becomes available, both from you and from your spouse, the assessment of your case may change over time. It is likely that an ongoing review of potential trial outcomes, costs, and a reasonable settlement range is required.

Negotiate

Second, negotiate.

Divorce courts are an imperfect way to resolve divorce disputes. Judges do the best they can under the circumstances, but they have heavy caseloads. At best, they have limited time to learn about your case. So the judge is not the best person to make major decisions about your life. Within a few short hours, two lawyers will use witness testimony and documents to convey a lifetime (or at least several years) of information to the judge and hope that the decisions made by the judge about children and money are acceptable to their clients. The judge, at best, views your lives through a narrow window, hearing testimony of witnesses and reviewing some financial documents. No judge can be expected to come up with a perfectly tailored, custom solution for you and your ex under those conditions. You and your lawyers are in the best position to work out an arrangement that works for your family.

Ninety-five percent of cases on average ultimately settle. Some settle within a few months of filing, some on the eve of trial. Most divorce trials are avoidable. If the lawyers and the clients put in the work to understand the financial information and the applicable law, and they can be reasonable with regard to parenting, custody, and visitation, then they should be able to settle the case. Also, the judge can be a useful sounding board when in litigation to advise the parties as to a realistic range of trial outcomes in the event that they cannot agree.

Trials in divorce are most often avoidable. Sometimes not—for example, when a win/lose type of issue exists (Dad wants sole custody, and Mom wants sole custody), or Mom wants to take the kids out of state, and Dad wants them to stay. These are yes/no win/loss things that need to be decided by the court. There is no way parties can meet halfway on these kinds of issues. (Sometimes they might be able to, though; more on that later.) If the parties can agree on the data set (the evidence, accounts, balances, etc.), they should be able to reach agreement on the case issues. Child support has been reduced to a formula in Illinois, as has alimony. (States vary on this, but the trend is toward the use of formulas.)

Before you go to war and spend a lot of time and money, have you asked nicely? Try to communicate in order to settle before filing motions and spending money and time in court. This is true for interim issues (like temporary visitation and temporary alimony) and for the case as a whole. If at all possible, work out an agreement before you have to fight. You may be surprised to find out what can be accomplished with a simple phone call. Face-to-face meetings are best to discuss settlement for cases. Next, video conferencing. Then phone calls and, finally, written communications.

I have resolved many disputes big and small simply by calling the other lawyer and talking. You can resolve problems much better by listening to what the other side has to say. You don't have to agree with them, but it is important to listen. You might learn something and gain insight, leading you to a solution for your client. Before calling your lawyer to file a motion, have you asked your spouse to fix the problem? It is the best time to ask, before you both spend time and money dealing with lawyers when the solution might be simple. (And you may be pleasantly surprised to find that they agree.)

Cases in litigation frequently settle at the deposition of one of the parties (the information-gathering phase of divorce). Why? Because everyone is forced to sit together in a room (or on Zoom) and look at the case. Almost like magic, this causes everyone to focus on the case, think about what is important, and reach an agreement.

Unfortunately, too many lawyers hide behind their keyboards. They send lengthy letters and emails, lacking tone and emotion. (Sorry, emoticons aren't enough.) It is too easy to fire off an email or text when it is convenient, compared to reaching out to talk to someone. So misunderstandings occur, or simply a lack of connection, leading to poor results. Conversations are best to iron out differences, ask questions, and move to a common understanding. If the parties simply talk and look over the relevant information together, and their attorneys communicate better, needless litigation can be minimized.

The Art of Settlement

There are many excellent books about negotiation strategy, and I will not attempt to cover that ground here. I do wish to cover best practices and lessons learned in the course of handling hundreds of divorce cases.

1. **Knowing your goals and concerns is crucial.** Being able to identify whether the terms of the proposed deal mesh with

your goals (or don't) is key to negotiating the deal you want. If you know your goals, you will be able to know what to ask for and what to avoid. You can't begin to consider the terms of a deal if you don't know what you want.

2. **Gather and validate the financial data, share it, and make sure you have the same from your spouse.** A big obstacle to settlement is when the parties are not on the same page with information. The faster you provide your financial information and get information from your soon-to-be ex, the faster both of you will trust the information, enabling you both to understand the financial situation. This will allow you to consider proposed divisions of assets and liabilities and evaluate alimony and child support for settlement. One tip: when we assemble a balance sheet for our clients, it is fully annotated with reference to the source of the data (example: "Chase Bank Checking #0433 June 15, 2021 statement"). This helps everyone have confidence in the information in the balance sheet and know how fresh the information is. Double-check information provided by your spouse. This might require cross-checking other records, interviewing or taking depositions of witnesses, or consulting with an appropriate expert. My favorite maxim here is the Ronald Reagan line: "Trust but verify."

3. **Understand the data.** Discuss the information with your attorney (and a financial planner or CPA if you need help). If you feel unsure about finances, this is the time to get help from a qualified financial planner or accountant. There are many available and also many who are trained in collaborative practice happy to help you understand your finances. There are several great books available on basic finance, explaining everything from 401(k)s to pensions and taxes as well. Understanding your finances will help you make decisions about your goals in settlement.

4. **Know your chances of success and likely range of trial outcomes.** You need to know what your chances are at a trial

and what the range of likely outcomes is in order to properly evaluate an offer made by your soon-to-be ex or to formulate your own offer. Later chapters in this book will help you understand these considerations, but a full discussion with a qualified divorce lawyer is key—their experience with the specific state law and your locality (and your judge) will be essential to give you a realistic assessment of the potential outcomes of your case.

5. **Know the costs.** Work with your attorney to assess the true costs of your divorce (or at least do some math yourself) to know what it will take to go through trial (and possibly an appeal) versus whatever offer you are considering. Consider the costs in time, money, and emotional energy—not just for you but for your children, family, and friends. There is much more information about the true costs of divorce in Chapter 9.

6. **Understand where your spouse is coming from.** Understand their point of view. Having perspective is valuable. For example, if you are the "moneyed" spouse, your soon-to-be ex is likely terrified about their future. They see the divorce as being pushed off a financial cliff. We've seen this concern even in high-asset divorce cases in which the less-moneyed spouse will likely receive millions of dollars. If you are the primary breadwinner, you may feel like you are giving money away that your hard work created and that your spouse does not deserve. These feelings are understandable and affect negotiations. Looking at the case from your spouse's point of view will help you better understand how they may react to a given settlement offer or why their offer is structured a certain way.

7. **Be clear with settlement terms.** While a detailed email can be sufficient to set forth settlement terms, once the basic terms are ironed out, it is most effective to make proposals in the form of a complete marital settlement agreement (MSA) and custody and visitation agreement. Summary settlement

proposals are useful initially but are too brief and lacking in information to be of much value as discussions advance. In all cases, the devil is in the details. It is best to have fully detailed settlement documents to make your proposals clear. Similarly, when responding to a settlement proposal in the form of an MSA or custody/visitation agreement, it is most efficient to make edits in-line (for example, in a Word document with changes tracked) so the other attorney and spouse can see precisely what you added and removed.

8. **Think clearly about the practical effect of a deal.** Custody is a good example on this point. A custody or visitation offer or proposed parenting plan becomes much easier to understand when you sketch out the schedule on a calendar rather than just reading words on a page.

For example, the following language is from an actual parenting judgment:

ARTICLE VI

PARENTING TIME

*1. **Regular Weekday Parenting Schedule**. SUSAN shall have parenting time with D.S. & M.S. every Monday and Tuesday and VINCENT shall have parenting time with D.S. & M.S. every Wednesday and Thursday. The parent that has the children with him or her shall be responsible for taking the children to school on the mornings that parent has the children and also for picking the children up or making arrangements to get them home after school or to their extracurricular activities and other appointments on their respective parenting days.*

59

*2. **Weekend Parenting Schedule**. The parents shall each have the children with them on alternating weekends beginning from after school on Friday and continuing through Monday morning when the parent shall transport the children to school on Monday morning.*

This type of written document may be difficult to visualize. So sketching out the parenting plan as in Figure 3 makes sense. Now that the plan is represented visually, you can see that there are long blocks of time with each parent, when a reading of the written plan appeared to be a simple equal split of time (Monday and Tuesday for Susan and Wednesday and Thursday for Vincent, followed by an alternating weekend, but the parenting times run to the next morning.) The net result may be blocks of time that were longer than either parent wanted, and this only becomes clear when you can look at the problem visually.

PARENTING CALENDAR

SUNDAY	MONDAY	TUESDAY	WEDNESDAY	THURSDAY	FRIDAY	SATURDAY
VINCENT	SUSAN	SUSAN	VINCENT	VINCENT	SUSAN	SUSAN
SUSAN	SUSAN	SUSAN	VINCENT	VINCENT	VINCENT	VINCENT
VINCENT	SUSAN	SUSAN	VINCENT	VINCENT	SUSAN	SUSAN
SUSAN	SUSAN	SUSAN	VINCENT	VINCENT	VINCENT	VINCENT
VINCENT	SUSAN	SUSAN	VINCENT	VINCENT	SUSAN	SUSAN

Figure 3. Sample Parenting Calendar

9. **No BS offers or demands.** There are few annoyances in the divorce business that are worse than receiving a totally unrealistic offer. That is, there is no way the outcome set forth in the offer will be achievable in court. This may be for a few reasons: first, your soon-to-be ex (or worse, their attorney) has no clue what a realistic outcome of the case might be and likely has not taken costs into account. Second, they or their lawyer may use this as their go-to strategy: ask for "the Moon," then have "lots of room to negotiate." (At least, that's the thinking.) The concept is ridiculous because any divorce lawyer with a modicum of experience will know the offer is silly and just ignore it.

I'll tell a story to illustrate this point. In a past life, I owned a different law firm with a great guy, Michael Angelina (his real name). We did "door law" in the early 2000s before I started doing divorce work. That means, if the case came in the door, we handled it! We did real estate, personal injury, probate, small criminal defense stuff, business law, you name it. I handled a number of small personal injury cases back then—auto accidents with mild to moderate damage and injuries. At that time, the auto insurance carriers had become tough with negotiations. They would offer much smaller amounts to settle claims than they had only a few years before. (I knew this because I started out as an auto accident defense lawyer out of law school.) A case with, say, $5,000 in medical bills in the "old days" was considered a $15,000 case in total value. And insurance companies would offer that kind of money to settle, many times before you had to file a lawsuit. Eventually, the insurance companies realized that a better strategy was to reduce the offers to maybe 1.5 to 2 times the medical bills. If your client wanted more, you'd have to put in all the work required for a lawsuit, which from a cost-benefit standpoint was not worth the trouble. One day, I was frustrated about negotiating with the insurance companies because I thought our clients were being nickeled and dimed. At lunch one day, I told Mike, "From now on, we're going to be known as the Million Dollar Demand law firm. For every one of these cases, we will start off with a one-million-dollar demand on the insurance company. Maybe they offer just the medical bills to start, say twenty-five hundred. We then make a counteroffer at ten thousand dollars, and when they complain and ask what the basis is for the ten-thousand-dollar counter, we say 'Hey, we just came down nine hundred ninety-nine thousand dollars, and you're complaining?'"

The point is, if the offer is silly, and the other attorney knows it, they will just ignore it, and everyone wasted time and money. Further, you might also damage your chances in the meta case if the judge gets wind of your never-gonna-happen demands. (Much more on the meta case in Chapter 8.)

10. **Have a realistic bottom line.** As I've said, your goal should take the realistic range of trial outcomes into account and contemplate the four costs of divorce as well.

11. **Be careful about lines in the sand.** One of my mentors, the Honorable James F. McCluskey, told me to be careful about "drawing lines in the sand" early on in my career. At first glance, it looks like this is a viable strategy: to say, "We won't take a penny less!" The problem with this is what do you do when your spouse asks for $5,000 more? Or $10,000 more? Are you going to say, "See you in court"? Depending on the case, assuming $100,000 equals one percentage point of the total marital estate, what if you offered an equal split of the estate, and your soon-to-be ex wants 51 percent? Are you going to walk away then?? This kind of amateur brinkmanship rarely works. It results in the person engaging in it looking foolish. Also, this type of hard-nosed bargaining might work in the business world, but you can't get another

vendor or customer in divorce court. You're stuck negotiating with the person—or the judge will decide for you. If your soon-to-be ex draws a line in the sand with a demand, just respond by doing what you are comfortable with—what is acceptable to you.

12. **When it's OK to draw a line in the sand.** A corollary to avoiding lines in the sand: only say "this is my bottom line" or "best and final offer" when it is your bottom line. Lawyers—and you as a party to a divorce case—need to maintain your credibility. Goof around with unrealistic offers and fake bottom lines, and again watch your meta case go down the drain as now the other lawyer and your soon-to-be ex stop taking you seriously.

13. **If you do draw a line in the sand, you had better back it up.** If you say it is your bottom line, and they won't accept your offer, be fully prepared to go to trial and stick to your guns. But also, keep an ear to the ground. Your soon-to-be ex may make an offer that is close enough to be acceptable to you down the road.

14. **Splitting the difference?** There is no rule forcing you to "split the difference." This is the classic situation when each party has stated a position, and the one party offers to settle for a point halfway between the two. It's best to never split the difference, assuming you're at your bottom line, it's realistic, and sticking to your position makes sense. Splitting the difference might be just fine, provided you assess your realistic range of outcomes, assess the costs, and determine that splitting the difference falls into an acceptable range of outcomes.

15. **Settle some issues even if you can't settle all of them.** I don't subscribe to the popular trial lawyer "all or nothing" deal: if you don't agree to all my client's terms, we won't agree to anything. That's silly and not how trials in the rest of the courthouse work. Lawyers in personal injury cases sometimes concede liability but try the issue of damages.

Or they agree to a high-low verdict range to cap the amount of damages, protecting both parties from extreme results. Many issues can be settled and taken off the table, giving clients some peace of mind for those issues and making the lawyer's job easier, saving everyone time and money in the bargain. This has the benefit of making the judge happy as well, with a shorter, more efficient trial. Why not focus only on the issues on which there is disagreement?

16. **Avoid backsliding.** Backsliding is another move to avoid in negotiations. You make offer X; they make offer Y. You don't like it, so you offer X minus 10 percent. Similar to fake lines in the sand, moving backward is disingenuous, and you lose credibility. You may reject their offer and stick with yours, but moving backward as some kind of "punishment" is a poor strategy. Again, you are stuck with this person in the negotiations. You can't move on to make a deal with someone else.

17. **Don't push one slider up while you pull the other one back.** This is similar to backsliding. In this strategy, the party appears to improve the deal in your favor, but there is a catch: they move backward on another aspect of the deal. I visualize settlements as a series of sliding switches on a control panel. You push up the assets slider to point X and move the alimony slider to point Y. They then move their assets slider to point X, right where you wanted it, but push the alimony slider to new (too high) point Z, and you lose interest in the proposal. This is not to say that creative solutions can't be found. They can be. And sometimes mixing up the terms of the deal by moving the "sliders" around can be a creative way to reach an acceptable settlement. There are numerous variables in divorce cases that can be adjusted to reach an acceptable deal, if the parties are willing to communicate. As an example, I had a case in which we proposed a settlement offer with cash assets and a fixed sum and term of maintenance. The spouse agreed to the maintenance terms but asked

for more asset cash. My client's initial reaction was to give the additional cash and simply reduce the alimony to match the increase. I dissuaded him from that plan. It was bound to only upset his spouse and derail the settlement talks, which had proceeded smoothly up to that point. His spouse and their attorney weren't stupid, and they'd see right through the offer for what it was and think he was dealing in bad faith. The better choice was to simply choose to increase the asset offer however high my client was comfortable with and tell the spouse that was his bottom line at that point.

18. **Be creative.** Maybe you can find a middle ground in unexpected ways. Perhaps keeping the marital home is more important to your soon-to-be ex than some money. Maybe your spouse is dating someone and may want to marry them (which in Illinois terminates alimony), so perhaps you offer a fixed-length term of alimony, which limits your liability, but agree to remove the marriage termination event so your spouse can remarry without losing the alimony. In that example, you've limited your liability to a fixed term of years, and your soon-to-be ex is free to remarry rather than play the games people play to avoid "remarriage" and an alimony termination. (One person rents a tiny apartment but is always over at the other person's house; they keep separate bank accounts but do everything together; et cetera.) This specific example is perhaps unique to my state, but it demonstrates how some creative thinking might arrive at a settlement proposal that falls in the middle of the settlement Venn diagram for the couple.

19. **Keep scale in mind.** Keep the deal in perspective. People anchor on numbers and can lose sight of the fact that what they are requesting is not far from what the other person wants, and the actual differences are insignificant in the overall scheme of things. For example, $50,000 might seem like a lot of money, and it is in abstract terms, but not when

weighed against the size of the marital estate and the four costs of divorce.

Litigate

If you have to fight, then fight smart.

1. **Be clear about your goals** and concerns, and if any change, inform your lawyer of the changes.
2. **Gather the evidence your attorney will need for your case.** This includes financial information (assets, liabilities, income, and expenses), as well as information about your children. Make sure your attorney has this information and explain anything that might not be easily understood.
3. **Have the attorney educate you about the applicable law for your case.** This should include a discussion of the legal issues involved and how the evidence works with respect to those issues to point to a given outcome.
4. **Get an assessment from your lawyer about the range of potential outcomes at trial** and what the most likely outcome will be. Find out the estimated costs to get through trial. (These figures may change over time.) Discuss acceptable settlement outcomes taking the costs into account.
5. **Start the discovery process promptly and cooperate with your lawyer** to provide documents requested by your soon-to-be ex's attorney so delays don't extend the length of the case. The sooner information is exchanged between the lawyers, the sooner you can work on settlement.
6. **Have your attorney prepare a divorce property statement** to show you all the marital assets and liabilities. Check the information to verify that it is accurate.
7. **Work with your attorney to determine support scenarios, if applicable.** Get a clear idea of your income and your spouse's income and a legal analysis from your attorney

so you can determine likely alimony and child support amounts, if any.

8. **Work with your attorney or a parenting specialist to prepare a custody and visitation plan**, including your desired parenting outcomes (custody, basic visitation schedule, transportation, etc.).

Doing more of the work up front in your case forces you to evaluate the facts and issues thoroughly earlier, making you better able to succeed at trial and also getting you in a position for settlement sooner.

THE VALUE OF KEEPING THE STATUS QUO

People getting divorced should maintain the status quo at the outset of a case (and preferably throughout). What does that mean? It means keeping things the same if at all possible. People don't like change. In a divorce, a lot of things are changing already in a major way. Adding new bank accounts, real estate, and other expenses to that mix is dangerous. Examples: cutting off money sources for the other spouse (canceling credit cards). Taking keys away from a child for a car without good reason. Buying a car without permission from your spouse. (You are still married and are in the same financial boat legally, right?) These kinds of actions only serve to anger your spouse and cause them to want to retaliate or worse, not deal with you except via their lawyer. They might bring a motion to restore credit card access. They might seek court relief to get you to pay temporary alimony and child support. If you block access to the kids, your spouse is likely to run into court with a petition to demand parenting time. These things only serve to stir up trouble and move the case in a negative direction.

THE 90/10 RULE

Anger and emotion do not translate well to the courtroom. The hard thing about divorce (among many hard things) is that 90 percent of what bothers you can't be addressed by a court. Examples of the 90 percent: snide remarks your spouse makes to you, comments made to your kids about how you are a jerk, your former family friends stop talking to you, your soon-to-be ex smears you on social media. These things are real and cause you plenty of grief, but the court is unable to do anything about them., the court does not have time for it. The cause of your divorce and the little things you do to drive each other crazy aren't something the court wants to deal with. The reason you are getting divorced does not matter. In fact, Illinois is a no-fault divorce state. Divorcing people are not even allowed to plead a reason for getting divorced other than "irreconcilable differences." In most states, you no longer need to prove fault to get a divorce. (In Illinois, the previous reasons included "chronic drunkenness," infertility, abuse, and adultery.)

WHY IS MY CASE DRAGGING?

You feel like there is no progress in your case. Nothing is happening. You haven't heard from your lawyer in a while. There are times when you will feel like things are dragging, and you will want to see action and progress.

Why is this happening (or, more accurately, not happening)?

1. **It is a strategy.** Sometimes taking no action is, indeed, a strategy, which will be explained in more detail.
2. **Waiting on third parties.** Waiting for information from the other lawyer, waiting for subpoena responses, et cetera. common. The lawyer is waiting for stuff from the other side (like discovery) or waiting for information from a third party.

3. **The court is slow.** Some county courts are overloaded, and things just take a long time. For example, in Cook County (Chicago area), Illinois, you can wait months for a hearing on a simple motion.

4. **Overwork.** The lawyer is buried. A symptom of this: the lawyer is slow to return calls or emails or simply fails to reply. A more critical symptom of this: the lawyer misses court dates.

5. **Short-term surge.** The lawyer has a trial or other pressing deadlines in other cases, and your case does not presently require immediate attention.

6. **No funds.** You haven't paid your lawyer. The paying client tends to get calls returned much more quickly, and the case gets attention. Ethically, if you represent a client, money or no, you are supposed to work on the case. But do you think the paying client might just get a *little* more attention than the person who is behind on their bill? It's human nature. We'll discuss this in How to Be a Smart Client, Chapter 5. A criminal defense lawyer I like once told me, "You have to put money into the jukebox, or the music won't play."

7. **Laziness, medical problems, drug/alcohol addiction, et cetera.** As a lawyer, I hope this is never the case, both for the client and the lawyers involved. But it happens sometimes. Lawyers are disciplined by the bar from time to time for neglecting client matters.

LEGAL ISSUES THAT CAN PUSH YOU INTO THE LITIGATION SWAMP

Dissipation of Assets

People can spend a lot of time and money chasing money they believe was wasted by the other spouse. This is called "dissipation of marital assets" in Illinois. One spouse claims that the other spent money outside the marriage after it broke down and demands that the money be refunded to the marriage. Classic example: wife spends $4,000 on a trip to Cancun with her boyfriend after husband moved out of the house. But many times, people try to lump in ordinary spending with these claims. Frequently, this devolves into a finger-pointing battle about who spent what and why it was wrong. Courts hate these claims. They are hard to prove, subjective, and most often simply not worth the money and time spent chasing them.

Many times, in divorce cases, people will get completely sidetracked in discovery, believing that they deserve an accounting of every dollar spent by each party during the entire marriage, and they get on a wild goose chase related to who spent what, when, and for whom., these claims usually are people being upset about a significant other, and they soon find out that they don't get anything back for an affair. They can't do anything about that. Or there may have been a disparity in spending habits in the marriage, and one spouse disapproves of spending by the other spouse. So a dissipation claim becomes the outlet for these feelings. The only way they think they can punish the other person is by going on an expedition, digging out information related to the third party, trying to find dissipation. These claims rarely pan out. The dollars spent on the financial discovery effort and delay of the case are seldom worth it. It completely derails and delays what would otherwise be normal settlement negotiations.

We've heard lawyers defend these extensive searches, telling about the time they uncovered some large sum of money and got it back for the client. Statistically speaking, it is a long shot at best. The vast majority of dissipation "safaris," the wild goose chases, don't get reported. The lawyer won't tell you about the case in which $50,000 in retirement account spending was never explained well, and they let it go because it wasn't worth pursuing.

It's akin to gamblers in Vegas. They never tell you about all the times they lost at the slots.

A lot of this comes from the "wronged" spouse out of anger about the case and the future. That person feels like they need to scrap and fight for every dollar, and maybe, on top of that, they are upset about an affair. So this motivates a dissipation claim that, in the overwhelming majority of cases, will have no impact on the case outcome, despite being costly.

Courts are not interested in engaging in a full accounting of the spending of the parties during the marriage. Buying a car during the divorce is not dissipation. Buying clothing and food during the divorce is not dissipation. The court has little patience for these claims, and most of the spending one person finds objectionable is typically not dissipation under the legal definition. Will the court get excited about jewelry and vacations purchased for a significant other? Yes. Will the court care about dinner for two at a fancy steakhouse? Not likely.

The bottom line with regard to dissipation: do your best to avoid making these claims (or keep them in your back pocket to help nudge negotiations later). If you are on the receiving end of a dissipation claim, the best thing to do is put as much daylight on it as possible. The biggest mistake people make in that situation is either delaying providing information or worse, hiding the ball. This only makes the other lawyer and party look like victims as they hunt for the information (that rightfully should have been provided), and the meta case for that person is harmed. Plus, it needlessly drags out the discovery phase of the case, raising costs for everyone.

If you did dissipate assets (and don't assume you did until a qualified attorney reviews the evidence and advises you), front the information and get it out of the way. Hiding from it benefits no one, especially not you. The smart people here say, "Yep, I bought her a ring. It was five thousand dollars. Here is the receipt." This builds trust, keeps the case moving, and keeps costs down. The meta case moves in that person's favor.

Proving Fault (In Some States)

This is a common way to get sucked into the swamp. You are angry about the divorce, that your spouse cheated, whatever it may be - and that is understandable. No-fault divorce is recognized in all fifty states in the United States. But you want to embarrass him and put that stuff into the divorce pleadings. Common bases of fault for divorce are chronic alcoholism, physical abuse, and adultery. In several states, these are no longer legal grounds for divorce. (As in Illinois, where the only valid basis for divorce is irreconcilable differences.) Prior to the amendment to Illinois divorce law barring fault allegations, they were routinely set forth in divorce court filings as a way to make the other person look bad and to attempt to gain some kind of moral high ground in a divorce. It rarely had the intended effect, usually just angering the other spouse and making it more likely that the case would be sucked into litigation as the accused person now wanted to "clear their name." Moreover, fault had no effect on the division of assets, support, or custody, so there was no other point aside from eye poking.

Kid Issues (Custody) with Older Teen Kids

This is a classic failure to consider a cost-benefit analysis. Custody and visitation battles over older teen children are a major waste of time. These kids are going to do what they want anyway. A kid over thirteen years of age has friends, a mobile phone, activities, and school—they aren't like six-year-olds whom Mom and Dad can hand back and forth. Chances are they will see the other parent as much as the "outside" parent—that is, not much. Example: the parties' child is sixteen. She has her own car and a part-time job. She has a boyfriend and is a volleyball player. She couldn't care less about a visitation schedule or who has "custody," yet parents fight over it, spending tens of thousands of dollars in the process. Then, several months after the divorce case is done, the daughter turns eighteen, and the custody court order that was so hard fought is worthless.

HOW TO SETTLE A DIVORCE BY TAKING THE HIGH ROAD

When you think the other party lacks a realistic assessment of the case and perhaps has not taken into account the costs, the best option is to send not only a settlement offer but also an explanatory letter to sell the offer. Ethics rules require counsel to communicate all settlement offers to their clients, so they have to send this to their client even if they don't like it. (It does not hurt to have your client mention to the spouse, "Did your lawyer send you a copy of the settlement letter from my lawyer?")

A fully fleshed-out marital settlement agreement and parenting judgment is best so all details are worked out. Normally, as divorce lawyers, we avoid writing these letters. The other lawyer may view this kind of letter as pontificating or preaching from us, and they will ignore it, poohpooh it, and downplay it for their client. Experienced divorce lawyers know the chances of success in a case and the costs and should explain these to their clients. But many don't—at least not with sufficient clarity and emphasis to fully inform the client of the true risks involved and the chances of success. Or, worse yet, they have made every effort to do so, and your soon-to-be ex has not listened.

So the extended direct settlement letter does the following: presents a reasonable range of outcomes (best for you, best for their client), lays out the likely costs of continuing down the current path, and compares this to the settlement being proposed. This illustrates how the offer is within the reasonable range of outcomes and is an acceptable deal for their client. It provides a cost-benefit analysis for the other party, just as the attorney would for their own client. This can effectively cut through the noise and resonate with a recalcitrant opposing attorney or spouse. Maintaining credibility with this letter is critical. That is, the claims in the letter must pass the smell test. The range of likely outcomes for the case and the range of costs illustrated must be in line with reality. If that isn't the case, the other lawyer and your soon-to-be ex can easily dismiss the entire letter as fiction. You'll instantly lose credibility, and the entire effort is wasted.

DAVE'S STORY, CONTINUED

I knew that the trial would take many more months and that an appeal was possible if either party didn't like the outcome. Also, the case would cost far more money than it already had. The temporary support was burning through Dave's nonmarital cash while Dave wasn't earning much money since he had been forced to sell his part of the company, and the judge blocked us from trying to reduce the temporary support payment. So I resorted to a Hail Mary. I sent the cost-benefit settlement letter to the other lawyer, along with a fully fleshed-out settlement agreement.

S|T|G
SULLIVAN TAYLOR & GUMINA, P.C.
Naperville · Chicago · Hanover Park

1250 E. Diehl Road, Suite 400 Naperville, Illinois 60563
PH 630.665.7676 | FAX 630.384.1149 | *stglawfirm.com*

Attorneys at Law:
MAUREEN SULLIVAN TAYLOR‡
JULI A. GUMINA†
RAIFORD D. PALMER†‡
EMILY R. CARRARA
SEAN M. McCUMBER*∞
JOSEPH F. EMMERTH IV

ANIQUE K. DROUIN‡
LAURA I. BALDWIN
MICHAEL R. HUDZIK
ANTHONY E. VECHIOLA
MELISSA J. WEBBER

Senior Counsel:
ELLIOT HEIDELBERGER†

October ▮

Chicago, IL 60601

FOR SETTLEMENT PURPOSES ONLY

Re: The Marriage of ▮

Dear Mr. ▮ and Ms. ▮,

Enclosed is a proposed Marital Settlement Agreement. The proposal is a global resolution to the many issues being tried in this matter, and is made in consideration of the range of possible outcomes at trial.

At this point, the parties stand to continue at trial for perhaps another three to six months. Closing arguments will likely be written, meaning substantial time and expense required to prepare them. It is likely the Court will take a lengthy amount of time to consider the arguments and evidence before entering a judgment. If the Court asks the parties to submit proposed judgments, it is also highly probably that the terms of the Judgment will be contested as both parties and their counsel seek to interpret the Court's ruling to their client's best advantage. Also likely is either party appealing an adverse trial court decision, adding another year to the tally. All told, this case could potentially take another year to two years to be resolved.

The Court recently awarded ▮ in excess of $400,000 in interim fees, bringing ▮'s total outlay for fees to date to about $550,000.00. ▮'s attorney fee spend is something near $300,000.00 to date. The parties stand to incur at least another $200,000.00 in fees conservatively, plus $50,000 for an appeal. That totals **$1,000,000.00 in fees.**

The major problem is this: the parties are largely at trial due to the debate about whether a portion of ▮ is marital property (and to a lesser extent due to a disagreement about support). However, ▮ received $2,500,000 of the $3,500,000 he is owed in the ▮ settlement. **And it is almost gone.** ▮ received $1,500,000 from his father's estate – clearly non marital property – and

† *Fellow: American Academy of Matrimonial Lawyers*
‡ *Fellow: International Academy of Collaborative Professionals*
* *Fellow: American Academy of Adoption Attorneys*
∞ *Fellow: American Academy of Assisted Reproduction Technology Attorneys*

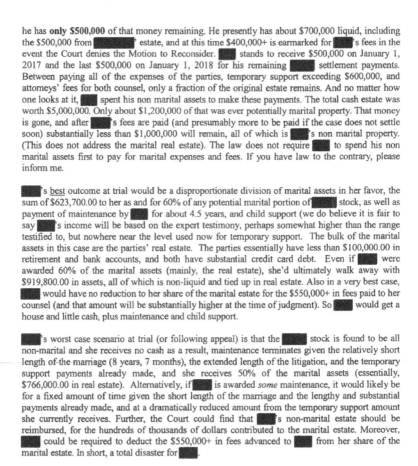

S|T|G
SULLIVAN TAYLOR & GUMINA, P.C.

he has **only $500,000** of that money remaining. He presently has about $700,000 liquid, including the $500,000 from ███████ ' estate, and at this time $400,000+ is earmarked for ██ 's fees in the event the Court denies the Motion to Reconsider. ███ stands to receive $500,000 on January 1, 2017 and the last $500,000 on January 1, 2018 for his remaining ███ settlement payments. Between paying all of the expenses of the parties, temporary support exceeding $600,000, and attorneys' fees for both counsel, only a fraction of the original estate remains. And no matter how one looks at it, ███ spent his non marital assets to make these payments. The total cash estate was worth $5,000,000. Only about $1,200,000 of that was ever potentially marital property. That money is gone, and after ███ 's fees are paid (and presumably more to be paid if the case does not settle soon) substantially less than $1,000,000 will remain, all of which is ███ 's non marital property. (This does not address the marital real estate). The law does not require ███ to spend his non marital assets first to pay for marital expenses and fees. If you have law to the contrary, please inform me.

███ 's <u>best</u> outcome at trial would be a disproportionate division of marital assets in her favor, the sum of $623,700.00 to her as and for 60% of any potential marital portion of ██████ stock, as well as payment of maintenance by ███ for about 4.5 years, and child support (we do believe it is fair to say ███ 's income will be based on the expert testimony, perhaps somewhat higher than the range testified to, but nowhere near the level used now for temporary support. The bulk of the marital assets in this case are the parties' real estate. The parties essentially have less than $100,000.00 in retirement and bank accounts, and both have substantial credit card debt. Even if ███ were awarded 60% of the marital assets (mainly, the real estate), she'd ultimately walk away with $919,800.00 in assets, all of which is non-liquid and tied up in real estate. Also in a very best case, ███ would have no reduction to her share of the marital estate for the $550,000+ in fees paid to her counsel (and that amount will be substantially higher at the time of judgment). So ███ would get a house and little cash, plus maintenance and child support.

███ 's worst case scenario at trial (or following appeal) is that the ████ stock is found to be all non-marital and she receives no cash as a result, maintenance terminates given the relatively short length of the marriage (8 years, 7 months), the extended length of the litigation, and the temporary support payments already made, and she receives 50% of the marital assets (essentially, $766,000.00 in real estate). Alternatively, if ███ is awarded *some* maintenance, it would likely be for a fixed amount of time given the short length of the marriage and the lengthy and substantial payments already made, and at a dramatically reduced amount from the temporary support amount she currently receives. Further, the Court could find that ███ 's non-marital estate should be reimbursed, for the hundreds of thousands of dollars contributed to the marital estate. Moreover, ███ could be required to deduct the $550,000+ in fees advanced to ███ from her share of the marital estate. In short, a total disaster for ███ .

S|T|G
SULLIVAN TAYLOR & GUMINA, P.C.

Based on the foregoing, awarding ▇ the ▇▇▇▇ home in its entirety and awarding ▇ the ▇▇▇ properties is more than a 60/40 division in ▇'s favor. She is then able to remain in the family home without having to take a loan on the property. Additionally, ▇'s maintenance in gross proposal gives her a substantial amount of liquid cash up front, which she would only receive in her "best case scenario," and additional payments over a two year period to assist in her everyday living expenses while she works to become self-sufficient.

Please review the proposed MSA with Ms. ▇▇▇. I am sincerely interested in talking about what ▇ believes are her best and worst case scenarios and the applicable law. I am willing to consider any thoughts you may have in the interest of resolving this case.

Very truly yours,

SULLIVAN TAYLOR & GUMINA, P.C.

RAIFORD D. PALMER

RDP/lkg
Cc: ▇▇▇▇

After some back and forth, it worked. We finally settled the case once the wife "looked over the cliff" and saw how far down the bottom was. She realized that at the end of the case, even with a "win," she'd have no money to put in her pocket. Our client was delighted and escaped with a substantial chunk of assets intact. Plus, his wife had money to work with as well. Had we proceeded, we'd have ground up the modest amount of money remaining in legal fees.

I JUST WANT THIS DONE

CHAPTER 4

HOW TO CHOOSE THE RIGHT DIVORCE LAWYER

Alec was stuck in the swamp and couldn't get out. In his forties and successful, he married a beautiful, young woman, Danielle, and shortly after, they had a daughter. Unfortunately, things didn't go well for the marriage. Alec wanted Danielle to be a stay-at-home mom, but she soon regretted the role. Cue Danielle's "quarter-life" crisis at twenty-five. She resented being "trapped" by their daughter and wanted the fun party lifestyle she had led before the marriage. Alec couldn't understand why Danielle wasn't happy. They had everything they could want: a nice home, cars, and help around the house. Danielle amped up her resistance and resented Alec, accusing him of being "controlling." Danielle started posting nearly nude photos on an anonymous social media account constantly, drawing comments from random men. Alec, understandably, was upset that Danielle was partying and not paying attention to their daughter and also became suspicious that she was running around with other men.

There was more. On the nights Danielle went out, she wouldn't tell Alec where she was going or who she was with. She would return home late, drunk, high, or both. When Alec found out she had left their daughter with a neighbor in the middle of the day so she could go out drinking, he'd had enough. They had only been married for five years, and, sadly, the marriage was over.

As a successful type-A executive, Alec first got recommendations from colleagues for a divorce lawyer. He was referred to a "big name" divorce lawyer in the city. He figured that if he threw a lot of money at this attorney, known for being a "bulldog," he would get the best results. What he got was, in fact, a bulldog and a dogfight to match. Alec was their ideal client—high income, high assets, and upset. His lawyer took him down the road of multiple rapid-fire petitions, lots of court action, and pushing for sole custody.

Alec said on the phone, "I can't believe it. I've only been in this case nine months, and I've spent seventy-five thousand dollars! I'm just following my lawyer's advice, and I'm getting nowhere."

"What have you done so far?" I asked.

Alec described a series of petitions filed to restrict his wife's time with their child, as part of an overall effort to get sole custody of his daughter and shut out his wife. To this end, following his lawyer's advice, he'd hired expert psychologist witnesses to perform custody evaluations at a cost of $15,000 to $30,000 each.

All that lawyer's advice meant tons of money and a major battle—at Alec's expense. All fees are paid out of marital funds, meaning Alec was paying his wife's lawyers, too.

Now, to be fair, if you want sole custody and the facts support that claim, by all means, this is the way you need to do things unless your spouse will agree to your terms. However, in my assessment, the facts as related by Alec did not support the custody claim and would ultimately fail in court.

"Alec, this is tremendously expensive litigation anywhere but especially in this county. This will take you three years and two hundred and fifty thousand dollars before it's all over."

He was shocked but knew it was true because of his current cash spending rate.

"Courts don't want to keep moms away from a child unless you have serious evidence of abuse and neglect," I said. "Someone partying and being irresponsible is unfortunately not enough. Judges see people who are physically abusing their kids, addicted to hard drugs, and so just saying your wife is irresponsible—even with evidence to back it up—is not going to cut it."

"But my lawyer says I have a chance to get custody."

"Sure, you have 'a chance,' but did he estimate the degree of the chance?"

"Well . . . no."

"Then I'll estimate it. You have a ten percent chance of gaining sole custody. That's it. As a lawyer, I can't promise much. But I can guarantee you'll spend a ton of money in litigation for at least two to three years. And your daughter's first memories will be of her rich dad dragging her broke mom to court."

Alec was silent for a moment.

I continued. "Getting this case over with ASAP is the best move you can make. I suggest you talk with Danielle about backing out of court and trying mediation or collaborative practice. It won't hurt to try. If it doesn't work, you can always go back to court."

Alec decided to take my advice, and he hired me.

In our next conversation, I explained how different our approach would be. Previously, there had been a total lack of cost-benefit analysis and a lack of consideration of where his wife was coming from. We needed to understand Danielle if we were going to reach a settlement.

"Can you tell me about Danielle?" I asked Alec as I asked every client. "What are her goals? What are her fears?"

Alec did not know. He had not spoken to her in some time; they only communicated by text about their child. I further explained why we needed to know.

"We want to understand your wife's mindset and motivation in the most unbiased way possible. Assume she's a good person first and work from there. Warfare only begets warfare."

Then and there, Alec decided he would do whatever it took to make peace—and keep it. Even if that meant he did not get sole custody. Had

Alec taken the collaborative approach at the outset rather than the other lawyer's one-size-fits-all win-at-all-costs strategy, his divorce might have already been resolved.

More than a few of my clients are like Alec. My law firm is the second firm they contact after hiring an attorney who turned a broken marriage into World War III. Let their expensive lesson be a warning to you: choose the right lawyer from the beginning. Here is what to look for:

1. **Experience.** How long has the lawyer been practicing law? How long has the lawyer practiced family law and divorce? I'd suggest looking for a lead attorney with at least five years' experience, and preferably over ten years. That is approximately how long it takes to accumulate ten thousand hours of experience—and mastery. There is so much to learn in divorce law that a person with more experience will generally outmatch a newer attorney (if unsupervised by a more experienced one). They also will have firsthand knowledge of the local attorneys and the judges practicing in the area— very valuable intel for you that plays into your outcomes and cost analysis.

2. **Expertise.** A lawyer concentrating in divorce is a better choice than a lawyer who is a jack-of-all-trades. Divorce law is constantly changing and demanding, and to stay on top of it, one needs to be dedicated to that area of practice. For example, in Illinois, the state legislature overhauled the divorce law dramatically in 2015, followed by major amendments each year after that. Our child support law totally changed to a dual-income "income shares" model in 2017. If your lawyer is doing wills and trusts, some real estate, and some personal injury, they aren't able to keep up with developments in the law, and they are also at times preoccupied with other case types. Also, their systems and staff aren't able to focus and get good at one area of practice. Ever

notice how a Swiss Army knife has a lousy pair of scissors? Yes. That's what I'm talking about.

3. **Clean disciplinary background.** You can check the licensure for lawyers in your state to see whether they have been disciplined for misconduct. First, you want to verify that they have a valid license that is not revoked or suspended. Then, check their background. Attorney disciplinary cases are public records. In Illinois, the documents are available for viewing right on the Attorney Registration and Disciplinary Commission's website. The ARDC in Illinois is under the purview of the Illinois Supreme Court. They issue law licenses and manage continuing legal education requirements, as well as attorney discipline based on ethics violations. The American Bar Association maintains Model Rules of Professional Conduct. Each state has its own ethics code, which usually includes rules about confidentiality, client money, and customer service. Ethics violation penalties include "censure"—essentially a public reprimand; "suspension"—the lawyer's license to practice law is suspended for a period of time; and the most severe, "disbarment"—the lawyer loses their license to practice law. Most lawyers have a clean disciplinary record. If the lawyer has a disciplinary record, steer clear. Why take a chance hiring someone with a record of past ethical lapses?

4. **Positive online reviews.** Google is the best place to look for these, but Avvo.com also has decent attorney reviews. Facebook can also have useful reviews. Four five-star reviews don't tell you much, but a hundred reviews in the 4.5+ range give you a good idea you are dealing with a great lawyer. Look at the written comments for more information. You'll notice that the comments rarely say, "Great trial lawyer!" or "Really took a great deposition!" The reviews focus on how people felt they were treated, as they should. Was the client happy with the lawyer's level of communication? Did the

lawyer understand the client's problem? Were they responsive to requests and accessible to the client?

5. **Personal referral.** If this is from a person you trust, these can be gold. Ask for a referral from other professionals you know. Lawyers are a good place to start. Your business or personal attorney likely knows the better divorce lawyers in your area. Your accountant or counselor is likely to know at least one divorce lawyer they recommend. Wealth planners can be a good source of referrals. But be sure to cross-reference and research using the other tools we discuss here. Also consider the source and age of the information and the nature of the issue at hand. The lawyer who was great fifteen years ago might be off their game today.

6. **Divorce certification** (in some states). This is a state-based training-and-testing program through which a lawyer can get certified for a particular specialty, and many states have programs for family law. For example, in Florida, one of the certification requirements is to have handled at least twenty-five contested marital and family law cases in the five years immediately preceding application, with at least seven trials. Note that this is an optional lawyer criterion. Some states like Illinois do not have a certification process. (In fact, per Illinois ethics rules, attorneys cannot say that they "specialize" in any practice area. They are allowed to say that they "concentrate" in that area, though—go figure.) If a lawyer has a certification in divorce or family law, you can have additional confidence that the lawyer specializes in that field, has done additional study on the subject, and took a challenging test on the subject to be certified in that specialty. Additionally, they must be recertified periodically.

7. **American Academy of Matrimonial Lawyers fellowship** (in any state). The AAML has been dedicated to improving the practice of matrimonial law for decades. Founded in the 1960s, the AAML is the preeminent family law organization in the United States. To be admitted, a lawyer must submit

an extensive application detailing their experience and the lawyers and judges they have worked with and describe the last several cases they resolved by trial or settlement. They must have seven to ten years' experience in family law. The AAML gathers information about them from the lawyers and judges who worked with them in the past. The applicant must also pass a rigorous essay-writing and examination process similar to state-specific certification to screen for experience and judgment.

8. **SuperLawyers or Leading Lawyers designation.** These are designations given to lawyers in a peer-selected process in which actual research is put into choosing the lawyers who receive the designation. You aren't guaranteed to get either one from year to year, and you can't "buy" them. I say that because many other attorney review companies are marketing gimmicks. Don't be impressed by seeing ten "great lawyer" badges on a website. I receive letters all the time from these plaque factories stating "I have been chosen"— for only $495, I can get a plaque and a badge for my website. Maybe I should form the "American Divorce Attorneys of America" to make some bucks selling plaques and website badges myself!

9. **Willingness to approach a case with multiple strategies.** Is the lawyer known for "WWIII"-style litigation every time, or do they consider settlement? Is the lawyer a trained mediator? Collaborative practice lawyer? This training and background makes a big difference. Take into consideration your case and the personalities involved. What will be needed? Recognizing the options can help you get it over sooner. Also seeing what strategy your spouse is using helps you know the best approach. Look for the attorney who seems well suited to the needs of your case.

10. **Teaching credentials.** Does the lawyer write articles, author books, teach at a college or university, or lecture other attorneys on topics related to divorce? These are positive signs

of professionalism and recognition of skill by the attorney's peers.

11. **Diversity.** Our firm's lawyers come from a wide variety of backgrounds and viewpoints, and each has concentrations in family law and divorce, but they also concentrate in areas within divorce law. For example, we have lawyers with a concentration in business related to divorce, people who are focused on child-related issues, and folks with a litigation background, as well as people who can mediate or practice using collaborative law methods. We also have lawyers with extensive experience in adoption, guardianship, cohabitation agreements, assisted reproduction, and LGBTQIA issues. All this means that whatever comes up, we are prepared to help a client with it and don't have to send them elsewhere.

12. **Productive consultation.** In the consultation, does the lawyer listen? Or does the lawyer do all the talking? Does the attorney tell you your goals in the consult, before they've had the chance to ask what you want? If any statements are made that seem too good to be true, they probably are. You are looking for a general assessment of whether the lawyer is a good fit for your case. No experienced divorce lawyer is going to give you promises of how assets will be divided or how custody will be awarded until they have seen the evidence and been able to investigate the facts.

13. **Fixed fees.** There are several advantages to working with fixed fees rather than traditional hourly rates.

    a)   *Certainty*. The client knows the costs of the case up front and knows the cost of any actions they may want to take up front, just like with an a la carte menu.

    b)   *Client-lawyer alignment.* We are financially incentivized to get the case over sooner rather than later. We make more money if the case is resolved quickly, aligning us with the interest of our client, who also wants it done sooner. We are not incentivized to increase litigation, make things more complex, or take more time to get the case resolved.

c)   *Client-attorney communication.* Contact between attorney and client is dramatically enhanced. With the client not concerned that they will be billed for every phone call, they are encouraged to talk with their attorneys and the law firm, helping us better serve the client, keeping the client happier, and leading to a resolution sooner. Also, the law firm makes more money when the case is resolved sooner, therefore motivating attorneys to communicate with clients and get all the relevant information about a case early.

This is not to say that hourly rates are bad. You pay for time spent on your case and expenses incurred with an hourly pricing model, and the vast majority of firms still work on an hourly basis. But there are some real advantages to fixed fees.

WHAT TO AVOID

1. **Free consultation.** The consultation is the meeting, video conference, or phone call during which you discuss your case with the law firm and give the firm the basic facts about your case, your goals, and your concerns. At the conclusion of the consultation, you and the attorney should be able to decide whether you and your case would be a good fit for the law firm. Ideally, the lawyer should take about an hour with you to discuss all this. It takes time to do it properly, and time is money. So why do lawyers offer free consultations? Competition. Many firms offer free consultations, so these lawyers are worried that they will miss a potential client if they don't offer them as well. Our law firm offers one-hour paid consultations. That's real value—real advice that potential clients can use right away whether they hire us

or not. Our time is valuable. We charge a reduced rate for the consultation. We don't offer no-charge consults because we don't need to. We have enough potential clients coming to the law firm that we can afford to charge for the consultation. We want the potential client to understand that their time and our time are valuable. We aren't going to apologize for it, just like the Porsche salesman doesn't apologize for the price when someone tells them that the 911 Carrera in the show-room is overpriced. Charging for the consultation is also a litmus test. If they refuse to pay for our time at the outset, they either are not serious—"tire kickers"—or do not value a professional's time and will not be a good fit. Understand also that often what is advertised as a "free consultation" turns out to be a fifteen-minute discussion with a staff person or a few minutes with a lawyer. Which leads to . . .

2. **Salesperson or nonlawyer consultation.** You should be able to meet the lawyer who will work on your case, or at least the firm should be upfront about the fact that the person who will handle your case might not be the person who meets with you initially. Law firms all handle intake of new clients differently. In a larger firm like ours, it is common to have a staff person answer initial calls, emails, and text messages and gather basic information, then schedule a con-sultation with an attorney, usually the lawyer who will be responsible for handling your case. In a smaller firm or with a sole practitioner, the attorney might handle all incoming new client calls. In some cases, lawyers will speak briefly with potential clients to screen them before scheduling a full consultation. (We have our new client staff handle this step.)

3. **One-size-fits-all strategy.** The lawyer knows the solution before you're finished telling them the problem. They inter-rupt you with questions and don't give you time to explain the problem and your concerns. They jump into solving your problems before listening to what you have to say. They have a solution way too soon. The problem here is a lack of

listening. Although the lawyer has seen many divorce cases, perhaps hundreds, you haven't—this is all new to you. An attorney who is not cognizant of that and not willing to listen to you will miss important information you have to tell them. Just because you have a divorce case that is similar to others does not mean your goals and concerns are the same as those of other people or that the best way to handle your case will be the same as in other cases. Every case is unique.

4. **Lowball retainers.** This is a typical way for the average lawyer to grab a client. New clients are understandably sensitive to retainer or first fixed-fee payment numbers. In an hourly billing case, it is customary to get a retainer, which is a deposit against future work to be performed. Some retainers are refundable; some are not. If refundable, in the event the attorney-client relationship is terminated, you will pay for all work performed up to that point but be entitled to a refund of the remainder of your deposit. In a fixed-fee case, the law firm will ask for a nonrefundable first payment for the first part of the work. However, the retainer or first fixed-fee payment is almost always *not* the total cost of the case.

If the client balks at the retainer or first payment, they aren't going to be a suitable client. They will not be able to afford the divorce (or they will be able to afford it but be unhappy). We know from our data that even the cheapest divorce cannot be completed for less than a typical retainer. As of this writing, divorce lawyers in our area are accepting anywhere from $1,500 to $10,000+ for retainers, with a common amount being $3,500. The retainer creates a number fixation similar to a payment amount for a car loan. A low payment might be a worse deal, where higher interest and a longer payment schedule mean that it's a bad idea for you. Similarly, once you realize that the retainer is just the ante to get started, you should think about a couple of things: Why does this lawyer ask for such a low retainer? If they are this bad at selling themselves, how are they going to sell my case to the court or negotiate for me? And how is a low retainer any guarantee that the total cost will be low or lower when we are all done? Consider that they have to ask for the low retainer (and usually offer a free consult) because they have trouble getting new clients. If a firm has been around for five or ten years and they are any good they won't be lowballing the retainer or first payment. They will have great reviews, raving fans, and a strong referral network and will be able to set their prices and retainers where they see fit.

5. **Ethics complaints and licensing issues.** It is always important to check the disciplinary records of any lawyer you are considering to verify that they are licensed to practice law, that their license is in good standing, and that they have a clean ethics history. In Illinois, you can check this on the Attorney Registration and Disciplinary Commission of the Supreme Court website.[4] A license "suspension" means the license is suspended for a period of time, and the attorney cannot practice law during the suspension period. If the lawyer is "disbarred," that means their license has been revoked, and they cannot practice law at all. Ethics and disciplinary records are typically available on state bar websites. These include ethics complaints, the responses filed by the attorney, and any hearing information about ethical violations, including the punishment given, if any. A Google search of the attorney's name and law firm's name may reveal more useful information.

6. **Bad online reviews or too few of them.** As discussed earlier, you want to be able to see a wide variety of opinions from former clients. If you see a high number of negative reviews or an average rating below four stars, buyer beware. If you

---

4   www.iardc.org.

see too few reviews yet the firm has been in business for a long time, the firm is not asking clients for reviews. Why not?

7. **No website, poor website.** In 2000, this was not a deal-breaker. But with tools available today that allow anyone to build a good-looking website in minutes, this indicates a lack of tech knowledge. It is likely they won't comprehensively scan documents, won't have a client portal for you to upload and view your case file, won't have e-signing, and likely have had struggles with office processes. Our law firm is 100 percent remote—we never missed work or sent people home during the 2020 pandemic due to illness. Once the government ordered a lockdown, we all went home and remained remote. There is no reason why lawyers should rely on paper or be tied to a physical office. Slow, outdated paper systems cost you in billable time. For example, many years ago, we mailed copies of court orders to our clients with a cover letter following each court appearance. We billed clients to prepare the letter and review the draft, and that was common procedure among law firms. (And for some, it still is.) Why bother, when we can just allow the client access to the folder where scans of all new documents are posted or email a copy in about a minute?

8. **Poor billing practices.** Lawyers have an ethical duty to charge reasonable fees and to keep clients informed about their billing. For hourly billed work, the statements should be:

   a) *Detailed.* You should see who did the work, a description of what was done, the rate for that person, the amount of time spent, and the total charge per item. You won't see a narrative description of the work done, but a reasonable description might be "Phone call with client regarding alimony modification."

   b) *Monthly.* Modern billing software makes it easy to track billable time. If you aren't getting monthly bills, more than likely the lawyer is not recording their time in a contemporaneous manner. They should be recording the time worked on your case right after that work is completed—otherwise, the billing is guesswork.

Without these elements, you can't know the ongoing cost of your case and weigh that in connection with future costs to make an informed decision about any settlement proposal. Poor billing practices are an indicator that the law firm has other problems with its operations. If they can't send bills out on time, they aren't getting paid. If they aren't getting paid, what other parts of their business are below par? How can you trust them to take care of your case if they aren't even able to send bills out?

9. **Oversize team.** Some law firms assign a too-large team to your case. This is especially true if you are a person with a net worth of seven figures or more. The law firm considers this a "big" case and insists that they assign a team of multiple lawyers and paralegals. On occasion, this might be warranted—in a complex case with extensive business assets. However, most cases don't require more than one attorney for day-to-day handling. Even clients with a high net worth might not have a complex asset structure. That is, a retiree with a seven-figure retirement portfolio might have a couple of 401(k)s, a post-tax investment account, and a home. These are dollar-denominated assets and don't require complex analysis. Just because your bank accounts have more zeroes does not necessarily mean you must have a large team working on the case. I know of one firm who routinely sent two lawyers to every status hearing and charged the client travel time and mileage for both lawyers to attend. There was no reason for both lawyers to be at that type of routine hearing.

10. **Jack-of-all-trades.** The lawyer or law firm does not concentrate in divorce. Divorce is a specialized practice area (as many states recognize with their certification programs) and requires specialized knowledge. Lawyers who dabble in divorce leave their clients at a distinct disadvantage, simply

because they have a limited knowledge of the constant changes in family and divorce law. My favorite example is from a pretrial conference I attended. At the time, Illinois child support law required that support payers pay a straight percentage of net income for child support. At that time, one child equated to 20 percent of net income, two children were 28 percent, and so on.

At the conference, I said to the judge, "Of course, we're looking for twenty-eight percent of net income for child support, which is X dollars."

The other lawyer, incredulous, blurted out, "I don't know where you come off demanding twenty-eight percent of my client's income; that's outrageous!"

The other lawyer blushed when the judge pointed out that state law mandated the 28 percent.

11. **Bad-mouthing and name-dropping.** A lawyer who bad-mouths other clients or lawyers or divulges any information about other clients (example: name-dropping famous/wealthy clients). These are obvious red flags. The lawyer is trying to curry favor with you by talking trash about your prior attorney or your spouse's lawyer. Perhaps they are trying to impress you by telling you that they have represented well-known athletes or businesspeople. Or they are talking negatively and disparaging your spouse. If they lack the discretion to keep their mouths shut to someone they just met at a consultation, what will they do with people they know? This kind of lawyer lacks the objectivity and discretion required to do a good job for you. What's worse, you'll be the next person they tell their friends and colleagues about. The "no comment" style of lawyering is best. It is an attorney's ethical duty to keep attorney-client relationships confidential, so lawyers should never discuss their clients with anyone outside the law firm staff.

12. **Talking down.** The lawyer talks to you like you are a child. This can be connected with the next item on this list as well.

This lawyer acts like they are the only person in the world who can "save" you. The lawyer takes a "Don't worry, we'll handle your evil spouse and protect you" tack. Sexist, stereotypical, and not helpful. Expect this is how you will be treated during the representation. You want a lawyer who treats you with respect, like an equal partner, not one who is a boor.

13. **Overpromising/tough talk.** The attorney makes statements in the consultation that seem too good to be true. "You'll get permanent alimony" and "I'll make sure you get sole custody" are examples. Connected with this, tough talk like "We'll get that so-and-so for you" or "We'll make him pay for cheating" may sound OK at the consultation, but there is no way even a skilled, experienced divorce lawyer can realistically assess your chances at a consultation without seeing a substantial amount of evidence. This kind of happy talk from the lawyer will lead to your disappointment later.

"You're going to win" is an overpromising red flag. Nobody wins in a divorce. It's about losing, but better. Nothing is black and white. Divorce will cause you damage, but you want a controlled landing that you get out of it in the best shape possible.

14. **Putting themselves first.** Avoid lawyers who don't value you as a client.

Jack Newton, the founder of Clio, a law-practice-management software package, wrote a book, *The Client-Centered Law Firm.* In it, Jack stresses the importance of attorneys putting the client at the middle of everything they do in the law firm. This is not a new idea in business outside law firms, but believe it or not, this is pretty radical stuff in the law business.

The practice of law is a monopoly and is one of the few industries that is largely self-regulated. In some states, like Illinois, the state supreme court regulates attorney licensing, and in others, the state bar association governs lawyers. There are steep educational requirements that secure that monopoly. The smallish supply of lawyers before the 1990s meant that the monopoly had extensive price control.

Also, without the internet, clients had virtually no way to compare one lawyer to another, to check the attorney's disciplinary records, or to learn about divorce law in general at all. That knowledge was locked in the law libraries of larger law firms and courthouses. Similar to this, real estate agents once tightly controlled home listings until the advent of the internet. This was a way to protect information to effectively cement real estate agents' monopoly in home sales. (I recall shopping for my first house in the late 1990s and not being allowed to have paper copies of the listings for homes I wanted to visit.)

With clients mostly in the dark about the subject matter of divorce and with no way to compare one to the other, bad lawyers could get away with a lot. If an attorney could afford big Yellow Pages ads, they could get clients. Negative experiences were largely only spread by word of mouth, as was praise. Lawyers with poor client service were able to continue working without much difficulty.

As a result of the internet and the ease of access to information, those days are rapidly coming to a close. Lawyers have been among the last professions to be affected by the internet. We've seen real estate agents, travel agents, booksellers, shoe stores, and even car dealers affected by these changes. The changes brought by technology have already hit the law business and will continue to move things in the client's direction.

Unfortunately, some lawyers still haven't gotten the "memo," so to speak. They think the good old days are still here. Some of them still act like the job would be a lot easier if the pesky clients wouldn't call all the time. This is the "library analogy." The way I imagine it, librarians don't like people coming in to check out books because they mess up all the neat shelves, don't return books on time, and generally cause chaos. I bet the librarians think, *This place would be great if these people would stop coming in and checking out books all the time.* (Apologies to any librarians reading this. I love the library!) But too many lawyers still act like this about client service. In law school, lawyers are not taught how to run a business or deal with customer service. We're taught about the law, legal research, how to handle evidence, and so forth. So at the outset, attorneys think that the legal work is what the client is purchasing, but in reality, the client is purchasing a result. As it turns out, the important distinction to make is that clients don't want a *divorce lawsuit*; they want *to be divorced.*

Thanks to the increase in the number of licensed attorneys in the United States and the spread of information on the internet (reviews, legal information in general, books like this one), competition is higher, prices are lower, and clients are in general much better informed consumers. So we have to be better at taking care of those consumers. Law firms that treat clients poorly begin to get bad reviews, the word gets out over time, and people start avoiding them. Bad firms and lawyers can no longer hide from an unsuspecting public. These changes are all positive for a firm willing to focus on client goals and satisfaction like ours. It becomes a tremendous business advantage and makes clients satisfied and much more likely to pay our bills and refer friends and family.

Divorce attorneys, due to the nature of the business, generally won't make clients "happy." No one is happy to be divorced in general. But divorce attorneys can make the best of a bad situation for the client. The objective is to provide great service, be responsive, and listen and help the client meet their goals efficiently.

DEVIL ON YOUR SHOULDER

Divorce is the intersection of all that people hold dear: children, love, sex, and money. This ratchets up the emotional stakes in divorce cases. Therefore, lawyers hold a position of power with clients, similar to the role of psychologists and counselors. The client naturally places substantial faith and trust in the attorney, and an ill-intentioned lawyer can take advantage of this. When the client asks the lawyer, "Do you think he has a girlfriend?" the attorney has a choice. They can say, "There is no evidence of that, but once we review all the financial records, we should see any major spending," or "Generally speaking, guys don't get divorced unless they have a girlfriend." The first statement is true and points out the absence of evidence. It does not ratchet up the acrimony between the divorcing people. The latter statement is a truism:

a throwaway claim that is not based on evidence but serves to ramp up the level of discord in the case. The next thing that happens in that case is the client tells the kids, "My lawyer says Dad probably has a girlfriend." See how just a few poorly chosen words can dramatically impact a divorce case? Lawyers can (even unintentionally) crank up the level of anger with subtle suggestions like this.

1. **A cheerleader.** When you hire a lawyer, you want an objective advocate, not a cheerleader. There's an important difference between an advocate and a cheerleader. Your lawyer must be an objective advocate who looks out for your best interest, including things you might not want to hear. Leave the cheerleader role to your best friend and your parents. When your lawyer acts like a cheerleader and lacks objectivity, you don't get honest advice. Cheerleaders tell you to "go get 'em," and they back you no matter what. The crucial and practical cost-benefit analysis is lacking and, you as the client might unwittingly drive headlong into expensive trouble. It's easy to cheerlead a client, but it's not the best course of action for a professional advocate. The cheerleader problem is often intertwined with the difficulty of having a "yes man" lawyer . . .

2. **Yes women (or men).** The hardest thing to tell a client is no. When a client is upset about something or says that they feel like the case is taking a long time (and it can feel that way at times in nearly every divorce case), it is easy for a lawyer to fall into the trap of simply doing whatever the client wants. The easy way out for the lawyer is to just say OK and take some action—any action. But lawyers have options in case handling. We can push the gas pedal or not take action, as discussed above. However, the available tools for action are limited (as I explain below). And aggressive action may not be the best solution. Sometimes, waiting or not taking action is the best strategy in the long term when taking the cost-benefit analysis into account. The best advocate should

tell you things as they see them, not as you wish they were. Sometimes, the best advice is "Let the ten-thousand-dollar problem go because it will cost fifteen thousand dollars to solve." You're hiring a good divorce lawyer to tell you things you may not want to hear, and that's a good thing. The objective should be to keep you out of trouble and simplify things to make your life better so you feel better sooner. We're not robots; we shouldn't just do what you say. Good lawyers analyze the evidence, listen, and advise you on the best course of action to obtain the ultimate goal of an efficient divorce with an acceptable outcome, taking all aspects into account.

3. **Lack of energy.** The flip side of experience. Look for the right balance of experience and energy. Be aware of the attorney's overall energy level. Do they have what it takes to keep up with a demanding case? Attorneys who have been in this line of work for decades might not have the energy required to keep up with the demanding world of civil litigation. There are some exceptions, of course, but sometimes too much experience is not a good thing. At some point, attorneys may keep working when they should retire from active practice or at least slow down and move away from intensive litigation. Law practice, especially family law litigation, is physically and emotionally demanding. Divorce lawyers aren't out playing golf during the week. Most work at nights and on the weekends. As an important note, however, older attorneys might be perfectly capable of handling mediation and ADR/collaborative practice cases as the time demands are more modest, and their long experience can be extremely valuable in those contexts.

4. **Poor communication.** Avoid lawyers who are poor communicators. Communication with you, your spouse's lawyer, and the judge or mediator are all crucial to having a good outcome in a divorce case. It is important to realize that

divorce lawyers only have two tools to work with to solve your case.

TALK   LITIGATE

Figure 4. Divorce Lawyer Control Panel

Those two options are shown in Figure 4. The "buttons" on the control panel are "Call Lawyer" and "Go to Court." That's it. Communicate or litigate., both require good communication: one with the other lawyer and, in turn, your spouse and the other with the court, which is a form of teaching.

First, clearly worded calls and written communication with the other lawyer/spouse are vitally important. Calls, email, letters, text messages, or perhaps a meeting on Zoom or in person can be used to exchange ideas and reach mutual understanding. The chances of success for this depend on the communication skills of your lawyer and the other lawyer and the willingness of your spouse to talk outside court. Therefore it is critical that your attorney be a skilled communicator. It is usually far more efficient to work directly with the other lawyer than through the court to accomplish something in a divorce case. The other option, of course, is to seek help from the court by filing a motion; taking action in discovery, like a deposition (a sworn statement of a witness); or sending a document request to someone. Of course, court action requires clear and concise communication as well, this time with the court itself. Other than direct contact with the other attorney and court action, there are no other magic tricks to get things done in a divorce case.

Unfortunately, you can't pick your spouse's lawyer, and you might get one who either does not believe in direct communication and likes to use the court for everything or is overwhelmed and practicing law reactively, so you only hear from them at a court date for the case. This is, sadly, all too common.

The only ways to assess the communication skills of your attorney are via reviews and getting a sense of the lawyer in the consultation. Do they talk over you, fail to listen to points you make, or talk down to you? If they are doing this in what is, at its root, a sales call, expect they will act this way during the case.

5. **Communication but via the wrong medium.** Poor communication is a major problem in divorce cases. It is the culprit in a number of difficulties that can develop. Negative or misinterpreted communication leads to ratcheting up negative emotions, increased acrimony, and a breakdown in mutual understanding. It makes the signal-to-noise ratio worse. It also leads to attempted mind reading as the lawyer or client struggles to determine what was intended by a message, typically taking it in the worst way possible. This can cause serious damage to your case.

Communications are often mishandled. Lawyers, especially younger ones, hide behind their keyboards. They don't pick up the phone. We teach our attorneys that in person, video, or voice is the best form of communication and to use other forms for less important messages. We've learned the importance of a good signal-to-noise ratio in handling divorce cases.

Therefore, the best order of priority for communication in divorce cases (and probably in life) is:

in person > video > phone > email > text

Person to person is always best for a serious, complex exchange of ideas. For example, discussing settlement. We are emotional creatures and have a lifetime of accumulated intelligence based on sensing cues given by body language, tone of voice, and more. The more you can see and hear, the better you can sense all the cues. Therefore, video is second best, phone calls third, and written communication last.

Lawyers should avoid texting a client serious information or bad news: "We lost the motion. Now I need you to do this . . ." They should pick up the phone. Inevitably, the client will have questions and ask for an explanation. Also, there is no need for attorneys to forward nasty emails from obnoxious lawyers. The lawyer should filter messages to the client so they get the important information without the invective. This is another subtle way lawyers can ratchet down the negativity in communication between the parties while still fully informing the client about what is going on in their case.

One of my favorite tactics to disarm an overly aggressive lawyer is to say, "I want to hear what you have to say. Tell me about facts that I might not know. Educate me about the law if there is a case or statute that would change my point of view." Which is genuine. I do want to know the other point of view. If there are facts or law that would affect the case outcome for my client, you can bet I want to know about it!

Sadly, most lawyers can't write simple letters and emails. Many devolve into combative eye poking. Writing short and simple emails and letters is an art form. Sadly, many emails from divorce lawyers say things like this:

Dear Mr. Lawyer:

Your client, John Doe, lost it and swore at the children on Tuesday. Your client is also running around town with his girlfriend. Your client needs to stop being disrespectful to the children and stop rubbing my client's nose in his affair. You need to get control over your client. If you don't get Mr. Doe to stop this by the close of business tomorrow, I will have no choice but to file a motion with the court.

Govern yourself accordingly.

James. J. Attorney, III, JD, Esq.

It's all about "you, me," "your client, my client"—and frequently contains an order ("Get control over your client" and "get him to stop this"), as well as a threat ("I will be forced to file a motion"). The threat can only be one of two things: "See you in court," or "The deal's off the table; see you in court."

This is not helpful.

The fact is it's the parties' divorce, not ours. There is a better way to communicate. For starters, it would be best to have a phone or video conference about sensitive topics. But we will move on to the content of the email.

First, the email assumes everything is true. Even a first-year law student knows there are two sides to any story, and the other party is likely to have a different perspective. At the least, admit you've heard this from someone. This makes it clear that you take it with a grain of salt, especially if you have not investigated the facts yourself.

Second, personalizing everything with the "you" and "your" stuff drags the lawyers into the case. There's no need to make this about the lawyers.

Third, referring to "your client" and "my client" makes the human clients out to be generic robots. They are individual adults and are in charge of their own actions.

Finally, threatening another lawyer with court action is not effective. Lawyers understand the consequences of inaction. First, divorce lawyers who handle litigation generally like court. (This should come as no surprise.) We're comfortable lawyering there. It's like threatening a kid who likes ice cream with a Blizzard as a punishment. It gives us justification to go to court, do more work, and make more money. It also gives our client the moral high ground as they end up looking like the victim or at least the innocent party.

If I forward this nasty email to my client, it's going to needlessly aggravate everyone, and the case devolves into a fight. "How dare that *%&!*& tell me what to do!" Lawyers can choose to ratchet up the negativity or keep a lid on it. Best to take the pressure off and simply discuss the facts. We're all grownups, and we need to act like it.

Lawyers should keep written communications short; avoid assuming truth by stating that the information is from another source; not drag the lawyers in and personalize the situation by using "me," "my," "you," and "I"; humanize the clients by using their names; and avoid demands or threats.

The best practice is to write the email this way:

Dear Mr. Lawyer:

Susan told me that Dave swore at the children on Tuesday. Also, she has seen him around town with his new significant other. I wanted to inform you about this and hope you can speak with Dave about it. Thank you.

Raiford D. Palmer

There is no need to lecture the other lawyer about what he should do or what the consequences might be. He already knows that stuff. In this message, I don't assert that the information is 100 percent true; I am simply saying I heard it from Susan. I don't personalize the message by making it about the lawyers since this is the parties' divorce. Finally, I ask nicely for the desired action at the close of the email.

No divorce client should have to go through all this trouble. Better to avoid poor legal representation in the first place. You deserve the best.

QUESTIONS TO ASK TO AVOID A SWAMP CREATURE

To avoid hiring an attorney who is a bad fit for you in the first place, ask these questions along with the screening items listed above:

1. **What is the best process for resolving my case?** Here, think ADR (mediation, arbitration, or collaborative practice) or litigation. This tests the attorney's knowledge of ADR methods and whether they might be court-is-the-only-option lawyers. You are looking for flexibility and not a one-size-fits-all approach. Their discussion of the methods and how they might suit your case should give you an idea of their thought process.

2. **Who will be directly responsible for my case?** This is important to know. The lawyer handling the consultation might not be the lawyer who will run the case.

3. **Who else will be handling my case?** You want to know the team assigned to your matter, including paralegals and other lawyers.

4. **How can I best reach you?** You want to have the cell phone number and email address for anyone assigned to the case and know when you can talk with them.

5. **Who do I talk to if you can't be reached?** It is important to have a backup plan in case the lawyer is sick or simply unavailable, and you need help right away.

6. **What are your billing practices?** You want to know how they bill, what the minimum charges are, whether they bill hourly or on a fixed-fee basis, what the rates are, and whether they charge more for court time or emergencies than for out-of-court time. Also, who to contact with questions about bills.

7. **Can you tell me what you heard about my goals and concerns for the case?** (This ensures they were listening.)

If you've been working with an attorney but think it is not working out, you probably have a sinking feeling in the pit of your stomach right now. You've spent a lot of money and time and don't feel closer to a resolution than when you started the process. You may feel like you're sinking, and the high hopes you had for your case have been dashed. You're in damage-control mode. You feel out of control. The best thing you can to regain it is to carefully evaluate the situation and make a change.

WHEN IT'S TIME TO FIRE YOUR LAWYER

1. **Your calls aren't being returned.** Being responsive is a lawyer's number-one duty to a client. Keeping you informed about your case is an ethical duty for lawyers. One ethics rule all lawyers must follow reads, "A lawyer shall explain a matter to the extent reasonably necessary to permit the client to make informed decisions regarding the representation."

2. **The lawyer blows court deadlines.** Keeping court deadlines is a bedrock function of any law firm. If multiple dates are missed, the case might be dismissed entirely. If your lawyer can't show up to court dates, your case is in jeopardy. Run, don't walk away. The lawyer's systems are either nonexistent or broken (or the lawyer is overwhelmed). If they cannot maintain a simple calendar, you need a new attorney.

3. **Your lawyer does not know the basic facts of your case.** This seems elementary, but a lawyer who does not know the information about your case cannot represent you well. Do they know how many kids you have? What your asset structure is? That you own part of an LLC, not a partnership? The lawyer need not know every detail at any given moment, but they need to have a handle on your situation to properly represent you. If they do not know that information, they are overwhelmed, not communicating well, or worse.

4. **The lawyer does not deliver on promises.** This is similar to number two and is a sign of worse things behind the scenes. Does the lawyer check in when they say they will? Get that draft document done within the promised time? If things are getting done on time, it is a sign that the lawyer's and the firm's systems are in order and things are running properly behind the scenes. If the attorney never follows through, get a new lawyer.

5. **You're getting bad advice.** Sometimes the advice and guidance you receive may simply be incorrect or wrong for your situation. If your gut instinct is that the recommendations from your lawyer aren't correct or aren't suited to you, it is a good idea to get a second or third opinion (described in the next section) to see whether or not you are on the right track.

6. **You argue about goals.** You disagree over the ultimate objectives of your case. The attorney is in charge of tactical decisions in your case, but you are in charge of the ultimate goals. This is another ethics rule attorneys must abide by. If you and your lawyer are constantly butting heads, you probably need a new one. Don't confuse this with getting advice you don't like to hear—you may have an excellent lawyer who is simply telling it like it is. But if you are sure that the attorney does not have your goals in mind, and his handling of the case is taking it in the wrong direction, move on. This is another time when a second opinion can be helpful.

If, as you read this list, you feel it is time to make a change, do not officially part ways just yet. There is a cost to changing horses in midstream. It is only time to fire a lawyer when you have brought up your concerns, and they go unheard. So before you fire your lawyer, give them the opportunity to make things right. Here is how.

WHAT TO DO BEFORE YOU FIRE YOUR LAWYER

1. **Think before acting.** Think over your issues and concerns about your attorney and the case. Write them down. Review them after a day or two, and see whether you missed anything. If so, add the missing issues.

2. **Get a second opinion.** If you believe some of the advice you are getting is incorrect, consult with another attorney or two about your concerns before confronting your lawyer. You won't have to tell your attorney that you talked to someone else, and the consulting attorney has to keep your information confidential, so it never hurts to get a second (or third) opinion. Check your feelings versus objective information. You don't want to fire your lawyer just because you don't like what they are telling you—it may be the absolutely correct advice.

3. **Schedule a meeting** to discuss your concerns with your attorney. Face to face is best (video is fine), and phone is second best. Do not have this discussion by email or text. It is too important (see priority of communication above).

   Send your list of concerns to the attorney in advance, with enough lead time so they can prepare for the meeting.

4. **Discuss your concerns at the meeting systematically.** Go item by item, from your list.

   Ask why the problems are occurring. "Why was the document late?" "Why did you miss the court date?" Don't be accusatory; use a "just the facts" approach. Write down the responses for your consideration later.

5. **Ask about the plan of action for your case** and a timeline for the plan. When will the planned action take place, and when can you expect to see results? Some of this will

naturally be in the form of estimates, which is fine. Again, take notes on these items.

6. **If communication is a problem, ask how the lawyer can be reached**, and discuss your desires about communication. Do you prefer text messages? A phone call? A Zoom meeting? Is there a staff person you can call when the lawyer is not available? Does the lawyer want you to schedule your calls and meetings ahead of time?

7. **If you are concerned about bad advice, ask questions based on your second opinion** to probe why the lawyer thinks their way is the proper course of action. Again, take notes.

8. **Reiterate your goals for the case** and the representation. Let the attorney know your expectations, and make it clear that if your requests aren't met, you will get another attorney.

9. **Don't make promises at the meeting.** Instead, say you will think it over, and set a date (in a week is fine) to decide on your course of action and follow up with the lawyer.

10. **Decide whether to keep your lawyer.** Take time, review your notes, think over your concerns.

11. **Contact the attorney to let them know your decision.** Confirm it in writing.

If you decide to get a new attorney, follow these steps to do so tactfully.

HOW TO FIRE YOUR LAWYER

1. **Have a new lawyer hired before you do this** to ensure a smooth transition. The new attorney can help you terminate your existing lawyer—they can handle the entire process if you wish.

2. **Email your former attorney that you are terminating the relationship**, like this:

Mr. Old Attorney:

I am terminating our attorney-client relationship, effective immediately. Please make my entire file contents available to Ms. New Attorney at newattorney@newlawfirm.com, phone 123.456.7890, as I have hired Ms. New Attorney to represent me in this case. Please call me or Ms. New Attorney if you have any questions. Thank you.

Inform your new attorney by copying them on the email. Call the new attorney to follow up in a day or two.

3. **The new attorney should file an appearance and a substitution of attorneys** (or similar document) officially informing the court of the change in lawyers. The new lawyer will also handle any transition of file materials and will need to review the existing case documents to get up to speed. This is an expense you will have to bear. (Some attorneys may waive this expense.)

4. **Don't worry about how it "looks" to your spouse, the judge, or whomever.** This is a common concern, but people change attorneys all the time, and it is not held against them by the court. The exception to this rule is in the event you have fired two or three lawyers; the judge (and future lawyers you might want to hire) will think *you* are the problem, damaging your meta case, discussed in detail in Chapter 8.

5. **Your new lawyer should pick up where the former one left off** and run with the case.

Firing a lawyer is hard, but keeping a bad one is worse.

ALEC'S STORY, CONTINUED

We were able to transition Alec out of the swamp and onto dry land, where we could calmly sort out his case with his wife and get it resolved.

We resolved the case via collaborative practice, outside court, saving Alec tens of thousands of dollars in fees and two years of litigation. His wife agreed to put the litigated case in "neutral" and try to resolve the case through collaborative practice. (Recall that Alec would have had to pay his wife's attorney fees as well and keep paying all the marital bills during the lawsuit, all for a short marriage.) All property earned during the marriage, up until the divorce judgment enters, is marital property, so you literally are handing your spouse half (or perhaps more) of your marital property as each day goes by in a divorce case.

The settlement wasn't perfect, but it was acceptable for Alec. Alec wanted sole custody due to his concerns about his wife's fitness as a mother—but again, it was unlikely he would be able to convince a judge to award him that. We ended the divorce case quickly with a minimum of fuss and little additional expense. In this case, having a custody fight the client was not going to win entwined with the financial case (especially for a short marriage) made it a case to settle, and quickly. For Alec, it was best to get the financial case done, get a decent result on parenting, and have the option to revisit the parenting issues later.

He spent $75,000 with his downtown lawyer and much, much less with our firm and was divorced. As a postscript, Alec's ex messed up a couple of years later, and he was able to get custody of their daughter. But this time, with the divorce behind him, Alec could isolate and address the parenting issues alone and deal with them in court. Because of our advice, he did not have to pay her fees for the later custody litigation.

CHAPTER 5

HOW TO BE A
SAVVY CLIENT

C olin is one of my favorite clients. He is at the same time the most
intense and most chilled-out client I've ever worked with. Before
his divorce, Colin was a Fortune 500 senior exec and avid surfer—in
his fifties! He also survived a life-threatening illness and realized life
is much more than work. Luckily, his hard work paid off, and he had
a large nest egg. After Colin's epiphany about work/life balance, he
wanted to live the life he had put on the shelf in exchange for work.
Unfortunately, Colin's wife was not interested in travel and adventure.
He went off to exotic locations, and she stayed home. He wanted to
spend his money on his bucket list, but she wanted to spend it on . . .
nothing. His wife was satisfied with life at home. Colin simply could not
be—not after facing death.

Years went by. Colin and his wife drifted apart. They tried to work it
out, but Colin felt like they were going through the motions—that they
weren't lovers or life partners anymore. A divorce felt right to both.
They weren't angry, just disappointed and sad.

Colin's case could have exploded. The wrong lawyer might have advised Colin's wife to do a deep dive into his entire financial history. They might have stirred up doubt and concern between the two of them. The traditional court approach could have cost them both a lot of time and money.

Fortunately, Colin found me. Also good, he and his wife got along pretty well. Neither of them want revenge; they just wanted to get divorced with an acceptable result. He wanted to take care of his wife and kids and get the case over with efficiently. These were their goals, so they were mine as well. I told Colin that avoiding litigation was the best way to resolve his case, and he gave me the impression he would take my advice.

I wish every client could be like Colin. Most divorce lawyers probably do. You can be that client, too—even if you and I don't work together. Following a few simple rules will make you the best client you can be. In turn, your attorney will get you much better results more efficiently.

Over the next few pages, I'll give you step-by-step instructions to prepare for working with a lawyer, becoming an informed client, and saving time and money.

TO BE A SMART CLIENT, DO ALL THIS

Here are twenty-six tips I've shared with clients over the years that are worth including in this book. They'll help you reduce the friction of divorce by aligning you and your lawyer to get you the best possible result.

1. **Gather evidence.** Getting the data set right is often one of the big obstacles to reaching a settlement. Providing the correct information in an organized way and conveying that to your spouse and their lawyer can be a big task. Getting to the point where both sides agree on the data is a major accomplishment. You can help accelerate this from the start

of your case. You have the opportunity to collect the documents and information you will need for your case. These typically include:

a) Tax returns (with all schedules and exhibits)
b) Bank statements for all accounts (even closed accounts if closed in the last three to five years)
c) Statements for all 401(k)s and IRAs
d) Statements for all investment accounts (Schwab, Ameritrade, etc.)
e) Mortgage statements (current)
f) Auto loan statements (current)
g) Pension statements showing current benefits
h) Loan agreements (auto loan, home loan, etc.)
i) Current pay stub
j) Financial records for any business interests (profit and loss, balance sheets, audits, account statements for all accounts, 1120-S tax forms, Schedule K-1s)
k) Other records for any business interests (corporate books and records, stock certificates, stock transfer ledger, stock purchase agreements, shareholder agreements, LLC operating agreements, partnership agreements)
l) Life insurance records (declarations page, policy itself usually not needed)
m) Information about the inheritances, if any
n) All 529 and similar college accounts
o) All statements for accounts held for children (UTMA and UGMA)

Scan all these documents and organize them in a folder. You can use any number of online storage options, like Google Drive, Dropbox, or Box. Be sure to use good password security and two-factor authentication to keep your information secure. Offline backup on a portable hard drive, kept in a secure location and password secured and encrypted, is also a good idea and inexpensive.

2. **Keep a diary** for custody cases. If you have a custody dispute or think you may disagree over the division of parenting time, keep a diary of when you were with the children, as well as what communications you had with your spouse about the kids. Having this information later beats trying to recall how much time you spent with the kids. Documentation like this is admissible as evidence to show the time you spent with the children, and your involvement with the kids will be key to showing you deserve substantial parenting time. This is essential with cases where you seek fifty-fifty parenting time.

3. **Tell your lawyer your goals and fears.** Telling your lawyer what your concerns are and being clear about your goals is critical. That way, we can represent and advise you properly and let you know what your expectations should be. If we don't know what you want or what you are afraid of, we have a hard time doing our best job for you. Goals can be on a large or small scale. For example, a goal could be to keep the family intact as much as possible in terms of the children. Minimizing disruption and not bad-mouthing each other to the outside world can also be good goals. Your goals may be for the divorce case, such as keeping it within a certain timeline or managing the costs. They can be small (but important) goals, like making sure you get your family heirlooms or get copies of photos of the children.

4. **Be honest about everything.** And don't hold back. Many times, we've had clients who were afraid to tell us what they thought were embarrassing details, only to have them catch us by surprise when the other lawyer raises the issue in court. You should never keep information from your attorney. I represented a person about whom the other lawyer continually brought to light embarrassing and damaging information in front of the court, and the client had given me no warning about it, leaving me looking stupid in front of the court on more than one occasion and making my client look bad as

well. For example, I learned from the other lawyer, in court, about the following claims: my client's alleged trips to Las Vegas with girlfriends, paying for a condo in another state where a girlfriend lived, and allegedly paying to fly two women from Europe to meet my client in Las Vegas, all on the marital dime. I—and my client—lost credibility in front of the court. Pretty soon, the judge did not believe anything my client said or anything I had to say on his behalf. I had no choice but to fire the client as he continued to keep information from me. Lawyers cannot represent you properly if you won't disclose facts about your case. Attorneys should never hear it first from the other lawyer. If your attorney knows all the facts, they can best prepare to deal with them. Just like an accurate diagnosis is key for a doctor to treat a patient properly, so it is with lawyers knowing about all the dirty laundry. All these details are part of what I call the "meta case," which we'll return to in Chapter 8.

5. **Pay your bill.** Do you work hard for someone who doesn't pay you? You'd be surprised to know the number of people (even with money) who somehow think attorneys should work on their cases for free. These people will pay doctors, dentists, and accountants without question, but for some reason, they will delay payment to their lawyer who is handling their divorce, the most important legal issue most people will ever address in their lifetimes. Pay your bill in a timely manner. If you are paying your bill, you stay top of mind, and the lawyer wants to make sure you get good service. Forget to pay your attorney, and your attorney is naturally less excited to deal with your emergencies and call you back quickly. Also, keep this up, and pretty soon, they will fire you as a client, and you will be forced to find another lawyer and lose progress on your case. That's not to say you should not review your billing. Be a smart customer. Review it promptly, and be sure to ask questions if you don't understand something. But do pay your bill on time.

6. **Know the difference between mental health and legal issues.** Many times, our clients call with concerns that are emotional or communications based. They aren't legal questions. (Recall the 90/10 rule from Chapter 3.) The court can't fix these issues. For example, clients complain that their spouse bad-mouths them to their children, their parents, or family friends. We, of course, give them some common-sense advice—for example, don't buy into it, ignore it, don't engage—but we then have to bill the client for that time. Also, we are trained as lawyers and legal counselors, not psychologists or professional counselors. Counselors have the formal training to deal with issues such as communication with children, spouse, and family in divorce; how to deal with emotions that naturally flow in these situations; and more. We can give advice, and we will try our best, but we may not be the best tool for this job. Recognize that ahead of time, and you will save yourself time and money. See Chapter 11 for more on how to choose the right counselor or coach.

7. **Listen to your lawyer.** Lawyers only want you to be satisfied with their service. We want you to have a good outcome so you are pleased, give us a great review online, and send your friends to us. There aren't many bad apples. Lawyers are disincentivized to take advantage of you or give you bad advice. Good lawyers who have been in business for a long time would not be successful for long if they were "out to get" you.

8. **Don't listen to friends and family**—at least, not on legal issues. Listening to your lawyer also means taking advice from friends and family with a giant grain of salt. Well-meaning though they may be, family and friends are not much help in terms of high-quality legal advice for your divorce case. They are there for you, but they lack objectivity and perspective, as well as legal training and experience. They will always side with you. What's worse, even with the best

of intentions, they can ramp up your anger and upset at your spouse, clouding your judgment. That one friend who had a bitter divorce is not the best one to give you objective advice. They tell you to "take them for all they're worth" and "not let them see the kids." This is not going to be helpful in resolving your case as a whole. Your buddies at the club complaining about their exes are similarly of little value. The problem is that your friends and family may simply raise the level of acrimony in the case, and they likely do not understand the cost-benefit complexities involved. This is emotional "noise" for you and clouds your judgment.

9. **Avoid getting friends and family too involved.** A corollary to avoiding legal advice from family and friends is involving them in the case. A girlfriend or best friend may insist on being present at your discussions with your lawyer, like an adviser in the king or queen's ear. Even with the best intentions, this can backfire. Perhaps a younger person is getting divorced, and their dad insists on "helping." Maybe Dad's even paying the attorney's fees. But the attorney-client relationship remains with the client, not the person paying the fees. You don't have to allow the person paying the bills to communicate with your lawyer, but don't be surprised if they demand to talk to the lawyer as a condition of payment. The trouble is that some friends, significant others, and family members can be positive influences, but many can be horrible influences. I had a post-divorce case in which a mother wanted to move her children out of Illinois to another state. My client had a long-term live-in girlfriend who continually injected herself into the case, and she had an impact on my client's decision-making, which interfered with my role as his attorney. At one point, I did not know she was on speakerphone during one of our conversations, and she started to jump into the conversation and argue with me. I told the client if that happened again, I would terminate the representation. One final note is that allowing a third party to

participate in an attorney-client conversation waives attorney-client privilege. The third party could be asked under oath in a deposition or at trial what was discussed between you and your lawyer, and nothing would stop that person from answering.

10. **Cooperate with your spouse** as much as possible. You need to find a way to co-parent with them during the case. You want to show you can parent responsibly and be a team player if you seek joint custody and substantial parenting time. Fighting constantly, being a jerk, and causing problems show the judge you can't be trusted and taint the rest of your case. This brings up the meta case, which is not the case itself (i.e., your incomes, the kids, the house, alimony, child support)—again, more on that in Chapter 8. The case is the judge, the other lawyer, your spouse, your lawyer, and how everyone treats each other during the case. This "vibe" of the meta case has a profound influence on the outcome of your actual case. If the judge thinks you're a jerk because you did something nasty early on in the case, the judge won't forget that at your trial. If anything is in the balance, it will be decided against you.

11. **Cooperate with the guardian** *ad litem* **(GAL)**, child representative, or attorneys for your children. These are professionals (usually attorneys) appointed by the court to evaluate what is in the children's best interest in custody cases. For the same reason you should cooperate with your spouse, playing nice in the sandbox with GALs is critical in custody cases. You want to do whatever you can to get in the good graces of the GAL or child rep. They are going to make recommendations to the court that will determine custody and visitation. Do you want to be on their bad side?

12. **Cooperate with expert witnesses** for the same reason you cooperate with the GAL. There are three types of experts: those hired by you or by your spouse to assist your case (such as business valuation experts, accountants, potentially

vocational experts) and those chosen by the court for a particular reason (e.g., evaluating parents in a custody dispute). You don't want the expert witness to be asked at trial, "Did Mr. X cooperate with your requests for information?" and have their response be, "No, they obstructed my investigation," or "They didn't follow my advice with regard to the children." This makes you look like a jerk and ruins your meta case. Also, cooperating with your own expert witness simply helps them get work done more quickly and efficiently, and you are paying for their time, so this means less expense for you.

13. **Comply with all court orders.** The court will enter various orders during your case for temporary parenting, temporary child support and alimony, and more. Follow the orders; do what they say. Failing to do that will land you in contempt of court; the other lawyer will bring a motion to tell the judge you violated the order. You will look like a jerk, be punished by the court, negatively affect your meta case, and possibly have to pay your spouse's attorney's fees in the bargain. Don't do it.

14. **Don't use "self-help."** Think changing the locks on the house and throwing your spouse's clothes out into the yard. When you have a divorce case ongoing, the court demands that you use the legal process to get what you want and not take matters into your own hands. Call your lawyer for help. Again, doing things on your own may seem like a shortcut, and your frustration about progress is real (more on that later in this chapter), but avoid self-help. Your meta case will thank you.

15. **Don't be a jerk** (to your lawyer, your kids, your spouse, the other lawyer, the GAL, the judge, anyone). This should go without saying, but it is an issue sometimes. Emotions run high, and people get understandably upset. But being a jerk to your kids and spouse, the attorneys, and especially the judge is extremely damaging to your relationships with

those people and the ultimate outcome of the case. Again, major meta case damage potential here.

16. **Read any court order or settlement agreement thoroughly** before you sign. This is always a must. Any agreed order or settlement agreement deserves a thorough reading before signing, and be sure to ask questions of your lawyer before you sign anything, of course. These orders will determine temporary or permanent issues in your case, so you need to understand them completely. If you don't read the orders and don't ask your lawyer questions about them, that's your fault, not that of the attorney.

17. **Ask questions efficiently.** Set a personal meeting or at least a phone call to discuss big issues. Group together your ideas and write them down in advance of any meeting or call. Avoid calling daily with one issue. Instead, keep track of your concerns and reach out perhaps weekly to get information. Otherwise, you are just ramping up legal fees needlessly.

18. **Don't talk to your attorney when you are tired, drunk, or high.** You'll say (or send) a rambling mess to your lawyer and cost yourself money in fees as they try to decipher it. Or worse yet, they'll answer a bunch of questions that you didn't need to ask but seemed like pressing issues at 1:00 a.m. You also won't be able to answer questions your lawyer asks or intelligently tell the attorney what you want.

19. **Review your attorney's bills carefully.** Be on top of what work is going on and what you are paying for. Watch your retainer balance if you have an hourly billing arrangement. If you don't understand a charge, ask about it.

20. **Have the right case mindset.** Approach the end of your marriage with a business mindset rather than a divorce mindset. If you handle your divorce case the way you logically manage your career or business—considering evidence and the prevailing conditions—you come out of the process sooner and with more of your money and mind intact. Too many people fall into the emotion trap, allowing anger at the

other spouse for an affair or hurt because of the other spouse leaving the marriage to guide all decisions. Recognizing that the emotions you are dealing with are powerful and can cloud your good judgment is invaluable. We will discuss the value of a coach or counselor to support you in this effort in Chapter 11.

21. Remain calm. Divorce cases are like airplane flights. The luggage is loaded, you find your seat, you secure your seat belt, and everyone gets organized. The flight attendant gives the talk about the seat belts and exits, the engines roar, and pretty soon you roll down the runway. You feel tremendous acceleration as you shoot down the runway. You lift off, and pavement and buildings drop away. You're pulled back into your seat as the plane climbs. Then at cruising altitude, the sound of the engine drops from a roar to background white noise. Not much seems to be happening. Now you are above the clouds. The plane is flying four hundred miles per hour . . . not that you can tell up above the clouds. Without a GPS, you would not feel like you were getting far. You can't see what the pilot sees. They are busy in the cockpit, flying the plane, and they see things moving quickly. Then, similar to takeoff, descent and landing bring more action. The crew bustles around the cabin. Fasten seat belts, lock your seat fully back, move your tray tables to the locked and upright position. Then you break through the clouds. Suddenly, the ground rushes up to meet you.

This is how the typical divorce case feels. At the outset, a lot happens. Lawyers prepare and file the case, gather information, and ask you pages of questions. But at "cruising altitude," you get the sense that the case has stalled. You don't hear from the attorney as often. There is less action in court as discovery progresses. Or in a negotiated case, the lawyers are exchanging records and gathering evidence, often without involving the clients. So it seems like the lawyers are twiddling their thumbs, even as they're busy on your case. Near the end, whether that is settlement negotiations or a trial, the pace picks up again. You find yourself talking quite often to your lawyer and their team.

Just like the plane flight, most of the action is at the beginning and the end. The middle seems relatively slow. When you feel like this, check in with your attorney so you know what is happening and can be assured of progress. In the meanwhile, please remain calm.

22. **Be cool and do nothing.** In the right case at the right time, doing nothing can be the best strategy. Taking action in a divorce case costs money. If time is on your side—for example, you are the spouse receiving temporary support, you are hoping to reconcile, or you're confident some important event will occur down the road—sitting tight makes sense. At some point, this strategy may conflict with practical considerations. Specifically, the court may lose patience and push deadlines or trial dates. This depends on your locality and your judge, as well as the opposing attorney.

When the other side starts World War III to spend you into surrender, the best strategy is to fall back. Spend minimal money and effort on the case while the other side exhausts themselves—and the willingness of your spouse to spend outrageous fees.

Water shapes its course according to the nature of the ground over which it flows; the soldier works out his victory in relation to the foe whom he is facing.

— Sun Tzu

To achieve the best possible outcome from your divorce, you may need to take Sun Tzu's advice and be like water.

23. **Keep the broader consequences in mind.** Being aggressive in litigation (and trying to drive a hard bargain in divorce)

have negative effects in all cases in which they are not warranted. If you have children, they will hear about the case one way or the other. Rest assured that your aggressiveness will get back to your children and reflect poorly on you, no matter who did what to whom or how you try to "explain things." The other parent will play the victim and have a willing audience with the kids. Moreover, long after the divorce is concluded, your spouse is going to be in your life. You'll see your ex at football games, weddings, and graduations. Those interactions can be pleasant—even when new partners or spouses enter the picture—rather than miserable. The kids will respect you if you can be civil together rather than sitting at opposite ends of the stadium like many divorced parents do.

24. **Let your go-getting get up and go.** You have had a successful career by setting your mind to solving problems and working hard to overcome them. You're a high achiever—probably a type-A personality, too. You're a person who manages risk well, and you try to control as many variables as possible. You get the last word because you earned it. And you adhere to the winner's rule that effort equals success.

Your divorce is completely different. You can "work the problem," but you still need to trust your lawyer to do most of it. Decisive action, which works in every other aspect of your life, rarely brings you what you want from your divorce. In divorce, the businessperson is out of their element. You don't call the shots here. The law creates guardrails or weather conditions for your case that you must contend with, like it or not. Also, you have to make a deal with your spouse or let the judge make the deal for you. You aren't entirely in control. You can't just fire your spouse and go with someone else. Your spouse's lawyer has a role, too, and that is to support your soon-to-be ex, not to look out for your interests. Finally, the judge, the ultimate decider of your fate and your case if you cannot settle it, is a "black box" beyond your reach. Divorce is challenging for go-getters since they aren't able to call the shots in every instance, and many times, too much action backfires.

You are used to getting what you want, sometimes by pushing people—your employees, your children, and yourself—to get things done. If you try to push your spouse, push them through your lawyer, or push the judge, expect to get the opposite of what you want. They'll dig in and refuse to negotiate, or worse, they'll cause trouble and make the case harder. Like pushing a rope, you won't get far trying to push your divorce case.

25. **Take the not-so-good deal when you can.** There is rarely a "win" in divorce, only an acceptable solution. We make our best efforts, but commonly, it is not possible to engineer an ideal outcome for both spouses. You are faced with a range of probable trial outcomes, and the cost-benefit analysis may make a not-so-good deal make sense. Here are five reasons why.

    a) You stop the bleeding (cut off the four costs of divorce, including attorney fees, increased ongoing living expenses, emotional harm to you and the children, etc.).

    b) You're in the swamp, and you need to get out. Cases don't age well like wine. Every day litigation continues, your expenses increase.

    c) You stop paying for your spouse's lawyer out of marital assets. The law requires that both attorneys are paid from marital assets during the divorce. Accepting an OK deal means stopping the drain of marital money for attorney's fees. After the divorce, any post-decree issues are paid for by your ex from their own money.

    d) You deleverage the case. Your spouse might be using parenting issues in the case to try to gain leverage with financial issues. Linking the issues is technically not allowed by Illinois divorce law, but it happens frequently as a practical matter. For example, settling most issues in the case knowing you can address the one negative item post-decree (most typical with parenting issues, as an asset division is forever) can make a lot of sense. In this manner, you can remove the leverage and get most of the case behind you, then resolve the last item in isolation.

e) You save time. Getting things done now is usually worth the trade-off. You might have a business deal in the offing, want to get remarried, and so on. These external positives may make a less-than-perfect deal the best option for you, rather than dragging a case out.

26. **Commit.** You've never bought or sold a divorce before. This isn't like a normal business deal with a vendor or purchaser. You can't walk away from even the worst deal. That's hard for an entrepreneur. Normally, you can kill a deal and move on to another vendor or find another customer. But in this case, you're stuck with your spouse. You have to make a deal with this spouse—or let the judge make one for you. So one of the biggest tools you have in negotiation is not available: the power to walk away from the deal and go somewhere else. This is important. It means being civil with your spouse even when you are angry. Listen to your spouse or their lawyer even when you don't want to, and if you don't have anything nice to say, like your mom told you, don't say it. Entrepreneurs who do the best in divorce put away their egos so they can get their ultimate goal. This means being willing to come back to the table. The only time you "kill" the deal is when there is no reasonable settlement offer available. The only guardrails to any deal in divorce are weighing the likely trial outcome with the cost of trial (remember, there are multiple costs; we will discuss this more later) versus the offer on the table. That's it. Nothing else matters.

If you want a controlled landing, you have to commit to making the negotiation work. It takes patience, time, and effort. You will be angry. You will want to walk away. You will feel like you are giving too much. (This is normal, by

I JUST WANT THIS DONE

the way, when you are the moneyed spouse.) The law looks at marriage like a partnership and does not care that you earned most of the money while the other person stayed at home. You are both equally entitled to the marital assets. A typical mindset (for both men and women who are the higher-earning spouse) is "I can't believe I have to give half my estate to that loser who sits at home all day." If your mindset is, "Screw it, I'll take my chances," you may be making a big mistake. Carefully consider any deal on the table. If the deal is somewhere near the potential trial outcome plus the costs of preparation and trial, it's a good deal.

COLIN'S STORY, CONTINUED

Colin had all his documents lined up and in order and had a spreadsheet of his assets ready to go. He was realistic about his chances in the divorce case. He did not want "revenge" and had a good idea about what was realistic in terms of potential outcomes in his case. He just wanted out. One of his goals was to take care of the kids with child support and payment of college expenses. Colin also had a girlfriend after he moved out but wisely kept her in the background, never making her an issue with his soon-to-be ex or the children. He was always prepared for our meetings, so they were efficient and to the point. Most importantly, he was willing to trade some money to buy goodwill and time. He was willing to make a deal in order to be done. He didn't need his "best" deal, just an acceptable one. And he got one.

We went on to settle Colin's case, which could have been a nightmare, in a relatively short amount of time and at modest cost because he treated it like a business proposition and was willing to be flexible with the deal and accommodate his wife's wishes. He also was responsive with providing information.

CHAPTER 6

DIVORCE MYTHS

Being a divorce lawyer at a party means you either stop conversations or start them. When people are chatting and ask what you do for a living, and you tell them "I'm a divorce lawyer," they either stop talking and try to change the subject, or they start asking questions. I imagine it is like being an undertaker or an oncologist. Some people want nothing to do with you, as if you are contagious, and some people inevitably want some advice or to share a story.

I want to tell you about Nick and Stephanie, two friends of mine. Nick is a kind, respected guy, and Stephanie is a gorgeous, successful woman. They have nice kids. I always thought they had it all. He and I have exchanged business tips over the years. (He was growing a software development business, and I managed a law firm.) Nick had heard me talk many times about the mistakes people make in divorce and the way that smart businesspeople seem to succumb to the same blunders time and again.

I was at a barbeque at a mutual friend's house over the summer when Nick approached me.

"Raif, I'm getting divorced. Stephanie wants out."

"What? I can't believe it!" The look of surprise was evident on my face.

"I know, I know. We're 'perfect,' right? Well, not so much. I took all the advice I've heard you give people over the years and stuff you've told me and have been working with her to get it resolved out of court. I do need a lawyer to finalize things, and she'll need one, too. We don't want any fighting; we just want to get it done quick, and we don't want to spend an arm and a leg on lawyers . . . no offense," he said with a sheepish grin.

"None taken. I'm glad to hear that. I will get you a couple of good lawyers' names. If you need anything more, let me know."

I referred them to a couple of collaborative lawyers I trust. Nick just thought I was too close to him and didn't want me knowing the details. Fine with me—I just wanted to stay friends with him.

Divorce lawyers themselves know the game and work to avoid the pitfalls. For example, I was in court one day a few years ago, and I saw a well-known divorce lawyer in the courtroom. This was an out-of-the-way courthouse, and I knew he normally did not work in that court, so this piqued my interest. He didn't notice me. Right at the start of the morning court call, the judge motioned to the lawyer, and he stepped up to the bench. He quietly proceeded to ask the lawyer the typical questions for what we call a "prove-up" or final settlement hearing. But the lawyer had no client present.

I realized the lawyer himself was getting divorced, out of his home county, away from people who knew him. He was representing himself. He handed up the divorce papers, answered several questions, and that was it. His wife wasn't there, either. (That is not required in my state.)

Nobody in the court even noticed. Totally legitimate but also totally discreet. Out of curiosity, I looked up the case on the court clerk's website. The divorce was done in weeks, not months or years. It took maybe fifteen minutes in court.

This divorce lawyer knew better from a career of hard-won experience and stayed out of the swamp.

It's the same with celebrities. Don't you wonder why most of the rich and famous people you know get divorced without a big public battle? They can't afford it. They get the best advice. They are advised by their counsel to avoid the common mistakes divorcing people make. They are smart enough to avoid the pitfalls. Successful divorce lawyers and superrich household names can't afford to slide into the swamp for months or years—or worse, have their personal business become public record.

GET DIVORCED LIKE THE SMART CELEBRITIES AND DIVORCE LAWYERS DO

Those who don't know any better accept one or more (or all) of these pervasive myths about divorce. Let's debunk them all right now.

"I Keep Giving and Giving and Giving"

I call this the loser fallacy. This works two ways. The primary income earner in the family feels like they are "losing" or "giving" because they understandably feel that the money is "theirs" to lose. The person primarily responsible for taking care of the children feels like they are "losing" or "giving up" custody because they feel like the children are "theirs." They are both wrong.

All the assets and income in the marriage are marital property. Judges don't see "your" money versus the "other person's" money; you are both equally entitled to an equitable share of the assets. No one "wins" and walks away with all the money, leaving the other spouse with nothing.

Similarly, neither parent gets to "keep" the children or block the other parent from seeing them. The law presumes that it is in the best interest of the children to spend time with and be parented by both parents. The only exceptions to this are when abuse or neglect is involved. Even then, courts want to see children spend time with both parents. The law dictates that money and children are shared during marriage, and the same is true after divorce. Any lawyer who leads you to believe you will "lose" the kids or have to give up "all" your money is a swamp creature.

"I'm Going to Win"

Many people are under the mistaken impression from pop culture that they can "win" a divorce case. The better mindset is that both people lose, but you can lose better, control the landing, and minimize damage. People think they can be tough, have their attorneys work harder than the other side, and do more, thereby "winning" the case. The bottom line is that the facts and the law decide the case, and as we discussed earlier, the court must use the principle of equity when making a ruling. This means that, with the wrong mindset, you wind up needlessly spending tens of thousands of dollars (and possibly far more—people have spent millions on divorce legal fees) and spinning your wheels with no net gain at the conclusion.

"I'm Better Off Taking My Chances with the Judge than Settling Out of Court"

Three things to know about court: first, judges are human beings, too, and subject to human frailties. Second, many courts are overloaded and slow. Third, the process of trial in and of itself is an inefficient and imperfect way to have your case decided.

Judges are human, subject to human failings. Did you know that judges are elected or appointed? I'd love to tell you that this means the smartest lawyers are elected as circuit judges, and that does happen sometimes. But, as in any other area of human endeavor, not every judge is great at what they do. Some are better than others. And judges are subject to human frailties.

In my state, associate judges are appointed rather than elected. Lawyers submit resumes to the circuit judges, and the circuit judges in a given county vote to appoint the associates. Again, I would like to tell you that the best and brightest make it. That is true sometimes but, unfortunately, not always.

Early in my career, I had a near-reverence for judges and assumed they were the best among lawyers. My boss and mentor at the time, hearing me talk about a judge in glowing terms one day, said, "You're a better lawyer than that guy, Raif. I've known him since law school." That certainly put things in perspective. Since that time, I've come to know many judges, many of whom are good, smart, hardworking people. I'm also old enough now to have known judges "when"—and to know they aren't the best lawyers or perfect people. I also know several who are political appointees, some of whom should have retired some time ago, and folks who just "phone it in," like in any other aspect of life.

Divorce court is slow. Judges are pressed for time. Courts are over-loaded. A Cook County (Chicago) judge once told me that he had over a thousand cases in his active caseload. In Cook County, for example, a case can take two to three years just to proceed to trial. In Dave's case in Chapter 3, the trial lasted nearly a year and would have exceeded eighteen months if we had not settled. I'd like to say that is an extreme example, but it is not. In fact, the long lead times and expenses have led many Cook County divorce lawyers to move cases to out-of-court mediation, ironically using retired Cook County judges to help decide their cases. It turns out this provides results much faster than using the traditional court system. If that does not tell you how broken the system is, I am not sure what else will.

Trials are messy. Current divorce law in the United States is at best a compromise. Our legal system is not the best way to deal with family issues. It is best for black-and-white, binary issues. Win/lose, guilty/not guilty. For example, our system does fairly well with criminal matters, personal injury cases, and even contract cases when the decision is essentially "yes/no" and "how much?" The challenge with divorce issues is that so much of what is involved in a divorce matter is in shades of gray.

The court is not a temple where judges get perfect, Oracle of Delphi–like insight into your life and all the relevant information about your family and finances. A trial is probably the least efficient way ever devised to educate a judge about the issues and facts in your divorce case and then ask them to make major life decisions for you. The rules of evidence are a filter governing what you can tell the judge and what documents can be examined by the court. The rules constrain what the court can hear from either you or your spouse. The lawyers have to present all the key information about your family and finances to the judge through that filter. What's more, the judge has never met you and your spouse and has a limited amount of time to listen to evidence and legal arguments and make a decision.

Even a great trial judge is at a disadvantage. They are only able to look at your life through a drinking straw. They only can hear short snippets of the facts of your case. The court only has several days (chopped into three- to four-hour blocks) to hear the evidence in your case. Many courts deal with their other active cases in the mornings and hear trials in the afternoons. The court doesn't know your family, doesn't know you, and does not know your situation. The net result of all this is that they (like all of us) put people and situations into familiar categories to help make decisions. This means your trial result is likely not perfectly tailored to your situation. The judge is going to decide major life issues for you, without knowing you and after hearing hours or maybe days of testimony from you, your spouse, and other witnesses and arguments from the lawyers. Everything about you is viewed through this filter. If it does not get addressed at trial, the court won't know about it. Because of the volume of cases judges hear, even good judges rule in ways that might not suit the people involved. Also, the confines of the law bind the solutions the judge can use, whereas people negotiating a settlement can arrive at creative, out-of-the-box solutions.

The bottom line is that if you have faith in the judge to efficiently hear all the important information in your case and make a great ruling (especially with a complex case), you are placing a risky bet with your future.

"The Court's Job Is to Punish My Ex"

A common misconception is that a divorce trial will be like the dramatic stuff shown in movies and on TV. The big day comes, a crowd is in the courtroom, and after dramatic arguments by the lawyers, the court pronounces one person "good" and the winner and the other person "bad." The reality is far from this. No one is awarded a halo, and no one gets hit by a lightning bolt in court. Divorce trials are far from exciting. There is no jury and usually no one in the courtroom except you, your spouse, the lawyers, and the judge. Much of a divorce trial is boring, involving recitations of dry financial information. There are few dramatic speeches by the lawyers at the closing argument. Fiction: the judge pounds the gavel and gives one person custody of the kids and all the assets, followed by a stern lecture to the "loser." There are rarely big revelations and big "wins." For clients, it's a big letdown to be awarded half the marital assets (and debt), get joint custody, and later get a bill from the attorney for tens of thousands of dollars to finish the trial. There was no vindication or dramatic punishment. Instead, it was boring and a little (or a lot) scary. You were on the hot seat. Strangers were asking you questions under oath about your personal business in a public forum. Better to get the best deal you can through what you can control in a negotiated settlement than to hope the judge will rule in your favor and give you all the money, all the property, and custody of the kids.

"The Judge Will Sympathize with Me"

Judges in my state make $180,000 per year. When you earn a seven-figure income, do you think the court is going to cry for you in your divorce case? Your complaining about your spouse's spending habits or demanding that they get a job is going to more than likely fall on deaf ears. I recall a case in which (against my advice) my client wanted me to argue that his wife had extravagant expenses in a pretrial conference. Specifically, he was upset that she had spent money on horseback riding—a hobby that cost her a few thousand dollars per month. The court was unimpressed, pointing out that my client earned $125,000 *per month* in ordinary income (not counting his other compensation, like restricted stock units). Acting cheap or acting like your spouse does not deserve an equitable share of the estate (or alimony) makes you look like a jerk and harms your meta case big time. On the flip side, judges might not have sympathy for the stay-at-home mom who chooses not to work, especially if the kids are older (think twelve-plus). In one pretrial, the lawyer representing the wife argued that the judge should not impute (assume) a minimum-wage income for the wife in the support calculations. (This is typically done when someone is capable of working.) My client was a mid-six-figure wage earner, and the family had mid-seven-figure assets. The judge said, "Why can't she work? My wife works; we have kids in school. She's a paralegal making forty-five thousand dollars a year."

"The Judge Is Biased"

The idea that the case is "rigged," the "fix is in," they're "out to get me," the GAL is "in the tank" for your spouse, and all this kind of stuff is ridiculous. Why would the court, the guardian, or other expert witness jeopardize their licenses and careers for *your* divorce case? These people aren't getting rich from your case. They need to stay in business after your case is done. Especially GALs—they are paid typically at lower rates than they could earn working on regular cases. In most places, GALs are working almost as a public service. Why would they "throw" the case for some lawyer or your spouse? This just isn't reality. While it may seem like the case is going against you, and things may feel "rigged" because decisions are going against you, I've never seen evidence of this being the case in twenty-five years of practice. I have seen cases go against a party because that party screwed up the meta case. That's not about the case being rigged; that is about the judge understanding (and maybe misunderstanding) who is the jerk and that perhaps affecting decisions that might otherwise have been "on the bubble."

"I'll Do Better with a Male/Female Judge or a Male/Female Lawyer"

These are the same issue. The concern is that gender matters in divorce. That the female judge will favor the wife, or the male judge will favor the husband, for example. There is a consistent theme about this one. In a consultation, I will inevitably be asked, "If I get a (female/male) judge, will they favor (insert spouse here)?" Or "You're a guy. Shouldn't I have a woman represent me so it doesn't look like we are ganging up on my wife?" In my two decades of practice in divorce law, I've never seen this matter. I've seen male judges be hard on men, I've seen female judges come down on women, and I've never seen the gender of the attorney matter in a material way in a divorce case. What determines the case are the facts, the law, and the meta case, which I've discussed elsewhere in this book. If you blow the meta case, you can best believe the judge will tilt against you, no matter their gender.

"The Case Will Be Done at the End of the Trial"

The trial is not necessarily the end of the case. Once the trial is over, typically the court takes time (usually four-plus weeks) to prepare a ruling. This may include the court asking the lawyers for written closing arguments: these are the final arguments the lawyers make using the evidence admitted at trial combined with the law. They can be done orally or in writing, and because of the scattered nature of family court trial practice in our jurisdiction (over days and weeks), many judges like to have the lawyers prepare written closing arguments to help the court review the entire case. Unfortunately, this is a time-consuming process and is expensive for the client. It takes several hours to prepare a written closing argument, multiplied by the number of hours consumed by the trial.

Even after the court enters a judgment order, the case is not final. After thirty days, the order becomes a final order, but it can be challenged by either party within that time, if one or the other thinks the court did not correctly apply the law, or some new evidence arises that will be determinative to one or more of the issues. This challenge is called a motion to reconsider.

Even after that, a party can appeal a trial court decision and seek for it to be overturned by an appellate court. This takes several months to a year or more and typically costs tens of thousands of dollars per person.

"I Deserve Sole Custody"

"Custody" is possessive, like keeping someone in "custody" in jail. Which is why, in Illinois, the term has been replaced with "parental responsibility." Because that is what we are talking about: who makes decisions and who is responsible for the children. Also, don't confuse "custody" with "visitation." They are two different concepts. One has to do with decision-making (custody), while the other involves the time spent by each parent with the children (visitation). In Illinois, the law has changed to call visitation "parenting time" as well because it was thought that "visitation" sounded again like a prison reference, and the idea that one parent was "visiting" diminished the importance of the time spent with children, which the law sees as equally important for both parents.

"I Deserve Equal Time with My Kids"

From the court's perspective, custody is not your "right"; the children instead have the "right" to be cared for and have a relationship with both parents. Think "our children," not "my children." Judges hate it when people talk in front of their spouses in court about "my kids," as if the other parent does not exist.

I call people who fight over days and nights and demand "equality" in parenting time "balance-sheet parents." I sympathize with divorced dads—I'm one myself. I understand the feelings of the groups of fathers pushing for equal-time legislation. A parent's desire to have equal time with the children is natural and shows the parent's desire to stay involved with the children. But what if the parent was not a hands-on parent when the family was together? How old are the kids? How much parenting do the children need? Do the parents have similar parenting styles? If the parties have a solid history of parenting during the marriage, the children are more likely to adjust to equal parenting time as they are accustomed to being cared for by both parents.

Simply proclaiming that equal time is the best solution and should be the default is short sighted and does not consider the best interest of the children in every case. How about placing the kids first? What do they want? What is best for them? Recognizing their needs is important.

The old parenting model admittedly needs reworking—the days of Mom staying home and Dad going to work are over. Now, in many families, moms work, dads stay at home, both parents work from home, parents hold multiple jobs and work different ways, et cetera. The trend with courts in my state is that (usually) fathers are getting more parenting time than ever.

Kids don't want to be jerked around. Some back-and-forth is inevitable in divorce, but think how much you'd like it if you had to change homes every two days. Not fun, right? This is what some parents do to their kids when they demand "equal" time. Kids need to spend time with both parents, and a lot of it, but as for scheduling, consider the quality of the time spent and the price paid by your children to travel between homes. During the marriage, parents never spend equal time with the kids, so why would parenting time be split equally automatically?

I often represent hardworking, type-A people who aren't with their kids all day or who don't have time to pay attention to them even if they work from home. Hiring a nanny to watch them during the day is not parenting time. If you were the child, would you want the nanny (or the new girlfriend, who isn't good with kids in some cases) to take care of you rather than Mom or Dad? You're not dividing an asset; you're raising young human beings. Fifty-fifty parenting time can work and can be in the children's best interest, but a "cookie cutter" application of an equal parenting schedule fails to consider the needs of the children.

When your kids are teenagers, a custody battle can only be a losing one. If you have children nearing age eighteen, custody litigation might be completed around the time they turn eighteen, or close enough. Once a child is eighteen, any parenting judgment is void as to that child. Also, unlike a younger child, a teenager is not going to follow a set parenting schedule. With school, activities, sports, and friends, they aren't interested in the artificial schedule you set up with your spouse. Better to be flexible and allow your teenager to live their life rather than grow up resenting one or both parents. A classic example: my son once dated a girl in high school whose parents were divorced. Her father made her come up to his summer home out of state every other weekend in the summer with him and his new significant other, even though she had no friends there and nothing to do. She hated it and vowed to never go there again after she turned eighteen. That is a perfect example of demanding parenting time simply to "check off a box" so you can claim you've had your time with your children. If your kid has a driver's license, do you think they will hang around with you all evening if they have things to do? When you were married to the other parent, the child was coming and going at will. Why would that change after divorce?

The only exceptions to this myth are when parents are abusive or using hard drugs, as a couple of examples, for obvious reasons. If that's the case, the court is more likely to side with the reasonable, sober parent than the cruel, drug-addicted one.

"My Lawyer Should Hate My Ex and Their Lawyer—and Show It"

Some clients think that their attorneys should personally adopt their animus for the spouse and the other attorney. Divorce lawyers are not paid enough to do that. "Wearing" your problems is unhealthy and keeps lawyers from being objective advocates. Lawyers engaging in verbal battles with each other outside court is cool in movies but is a bad idea in real life. The same goes for making nasty comments about the other spouse or, worse yet, talking to them in a condescending or rude way. It's massively counterproductive. It is far better to be cordial and professional. Attorneys must deal with the other lawyer and your soon-to-be ex for a long time and, at some point, will try to negotiate a settlement. A hostile relationship between you, your soon-to-be ex, and the lawyers is to be avoided. The better everyone can get along in the case, the easier it will be for the case to be resolved.

"My Lawyer Should Do Whatever It Takes"

No, they shouldn't. Lawyers have to preserve their reputations, and they won't ruin them for you. Lawyers have to deal with the court and other lawyers every day, for years before you came along and for years afterward. They need to retain their law licenses and their incomes. And the ethics rules rightfully constrain attorney conduct as well.

"The Lawyers Are in Cahoots"

Some clients from time to time ask me whether I am friends with the other lawyer. After seeing us in the hallway of the courthouse (before the pandemic anyway), they may say, "I saw you smiling and talking with the other lawyer over there. What's that about?" Sometimes, the lawyers discuss the case with each other. Other times, the attorneys discuss the case privately with the judge out of the presence of the parties. More likely than not, I will know the attorney on the other side of the case, and in many instances, I will know them well. I don't have many attorney friends—I do enough lawyer stuff during the day—but I am cordial with the people I work with. It may be natural to be concerned that we might get on the phone and "rig" the case or "make deals" you don't know about or that the lawyers are in a conspiracy to make money and screw the clients. Nothing could be further from the truth. I have no interest in sacrificing my license and livelihood to rig any case. Some assume we're both laughing all the way to the bank. No. We want those five-star Google reviews and referrals.

"My Lawyer Did It"

False. The client is the lawyer's boss. Always. Behind every swamp creature attorney is a client who approved the actions taken in the divorce case. So while we've done a lot of talking about swamp creature lawyers in this book, they are directed and paid by clients. The divorce lawyer makes recommendations, and the client either approves or turns down those recommendations. A typical claim is "The lawyer told me to say those things," or "The lawyer told me to file such-and-such." Not likely. While the lawyer may have suggested a course of action, the client always remains in charge. The client is typically required to sign the pleadings in divorce cases. Any claim that your spouse "didn't know about it" or "the lawyer did it" is nonsense. The client always has the ability to tell the lawyer to not jump into the swamp.

"I Need to Teach My Ex a Lesson. It's about the Principle"

When someone tells me that they are fighting "on principle," I tell them to get out their checkbook. They won't feel any better a year later, and litigation is probably the worst way to teach someone a lesson in divorce. First, they don't care. You're getting divorced. Second, when you attack with litigation, you spend double the money because you cause your spouse to spend marital money, which is 50 percent yours. It is literally cutting off your nose to spite your face. Third, the vindication people assume they will get in court is ephemeral. As described elsewhere in this chapter, there is no "movie moment" when the judge pronounces you the winner and your spouse the loser. If you are upset to this degree, you need to see a counselor. Don't try to get your revenge in divorce court.

"High Net Worth and High Income Equal Higher Legal Fees"

More zeroes does not necessarily require more litigation or mean more complexity. This myth leads clients to go to the "Big-Time Divorce Firm" and buy into the "You Need a Giant Team" concept. Just because you have a lot of money does not mean you need World War III. If you have a business, have substantial real estate and other investments, and so on, your case is more complex and will be more expensive whether litigated or not due to the complexity of your assets (the need to value everything, determine income, etc.). But if you are a person with, for example, post-tax investment accounts, large amounts in a 401(k), and perhaps restricted stock, options, and a high salary, big numbers don't mean the case has to be expensive or take a long time to resolve. At the core, accounts like these are easy to value and determine; they have price tags clearly attached to them. A person with a $10 million net worth who holds those assets in two homes, a brokerage account, and two 401(k)s might have a much simpler case than a business owner who owns a home plus a few pieces of rental real estate and has a net worth of $5 million.

"I At Least Deserve What's Fair"

"Fair" is another four letter-word. To quote my colleague, collaborative divorce lawyer James Lenahan, "Your 'fair' is going to differ from your spouse's 'fair.'" People have been taught about "fairness" since they were little children—usually starting in kindergarten, when they were told to share cookies. Fairness is freighted with your life experience and your biases. Courts, however, do not base decisions on fairness. Equity is the driving principle. And what is equitable may not seem fair to you. For example, if you worked and built a business, and your spouse stayed at home to raise the children and, after they went off to college, never returned to work, you may not think it is fair that they get a large amount of alimony and half the assets you worked hard to acquire. Or if your spouse had an affair and left you, giving them any assets and support will seem profoundly unfair (understandably so). But in divorce law, the marriage is treated as a uniform single entity like a business partnership, and the partners share in the assets.

"I Should Get More Because They Cheated"

Affairs are a reason to get divorced (a "cause" you can cite in some states; in Illinois, "for cause" divorce has been abolished). Adultery doesn't improve your chances of getting what you want in your divorce. The court typically does not care why you are getting divorced; they care about an equitable share of assets, support, custody, and visitation.

"We Kept Our Money Separate, so We Should Each Keep Our Own Stuff"

In divorce court, the judge does not care that you kept "your" income and your ex kept "their" income separate or that you both had separate expenses. The law considers income and assets gained during the marriage to be marital property (with exceptions for nonmarital property that I won't get into in this book because you can easily learn about them from a lawyer in your local jurisdiction or an internet search—there are local quirks). The bottom line is that people get wrapped up in counting expenses and worrying about who spent money on what. All the court sees is one pot of marital money. You are earning marital income, and so is your spouse. You are spending money on marital expenses, and so is your spouse. (There are also exceptions for dissipation and waste of marital assets, which is also googleable, and nuances exist on this in each state.)

"Whoever Keeps the House Gets the Kids"

Another common myth is that the kids "go with the house." We've seen battles over the former marital home based on this. Generally, there is a trend (at least in my state) in which parents tend to get equal time with the kids (or at least closer to it than before). If one parent was the person caring for the children primarily and the other parent is busy with work during the week, it is likely that no matter where the first parent lives, they will have more parenting time overall than the latter. The children are not attached to the house in a legal sense.

"I Can Retire Early and Not Pay Alimony"

Some people, especially those with high-paying, high-stress professional or C-suite careers may have contemplated an early retirement before divorce. Maybe they even discussed it with their spouse. They naturally would like to stick with those plans and might see divorce as a ticket to escaping the high-pressure work world and, in the bargain, avoiding alimony. I understand the resentment and the upset at having to give your ex money after you are divorced. So some think that the answer is to quit their career, sell their business, move to a beach town, and work at Walmart part time. No alimony, right? Wrong. The court will look negatively on your intentional avoidance of paying alimony and probably will require you to pay alimony as if you had kept your high-paying career.

Look at it this way: before you got divorced, your spouse had access to 100 percent of the money you earned, and you probably shared the assets equally. Post-divorce, alimony (at least in my state) will be one-third or less of your net after-tax income (lower than that if your spouse earns income). Quitting your high-paying job will deny you 66 percent of your income. So you are punishing yourself in that instance.

Another thing—what the court orders you to pay, you must pay. Verbal agreements to change or eliminate alimony or child support don't count. You need a court order to be safe on any agreement to modify or terminate support.

Another important thing to remember: alimony and especially child support are forever if you don't pay. Unpaid amounts become judgments that accrue interest (in Illinois, at 9 percent per year), and they will haunt you for the rest of your life. And you still have to pay unpaid child support after the kids turn eighteen. I once tracked down a guy who owed unpaid child support of $23,000 from the early 1970s. With interest, (and this was several years ago) it was $78,000. There is no statute of limitations on unpaid child support. The "kids" were in their forties by then! Plus, the burden is on the support payer to prove they made the payments, not on the recipient to prove nonpayment. Pro tip: keep *all* records of alimony and child support payment in a safe place for the rest of your life.

"I Can Protect My Assets so I Don't Lose Them in the Divorce"

A potential client called me a couple of years ago.

He asked, "Can you help me plan for divorce to prevent my wife from getting my assets? I've heard that Nevada LLCs can protect my assets."

"Is the property marital—I mean, did you accrue the assets during the marriage?"

"Yeah, but I don't want my wife to get any if we get divorced. So I want to put them into this LLC in Nevada to protect them from her."

"It doesn't work like that. LLCs will work against third-party creditors but not your wife in a divorce."

"Well, what if I put the assets into a trust, then into the Nevada LLC?"

"That doesn't work, either, I hate to tell you," I said. "You're basically talking about putting your assets in a box and putting that legal box inside another box. But the bottom line is that, as to your wife, it won't matter. You can put the assets into a thousand boxes, and she will be able to get her share."

Once you have marital property, it does not matter what clever ideas you come up with to attempt to shield the assets from your spouse. With electronic records of everything, these days it is easier than ever to track money.

If I knew of a way to shield assets from spouses in divorce, I'd write a totally different book. It would be one chapter and cost $1 million per copy—and I'd retire from law practice. It's cold fusion.

You've got a lot to lose. The IRS eventually catches up with people.

NICK'S STORY, CONTINUED

Nick knew all about these myths from overhearing me talk about them over the years. I'm just glad he listened. Instead of lawyering up and battling it out, Nick told me how he and his now-ex-wife sat down at the kitchen table for a couple of hours and all but settled their divorce amicably.

"We opened our laptops, went over our finances together, and sketched out a plan. Once we were both satisfied with it, we sent it to our lawyers to be finalized," Nick said.

I was proud of Nick. He did the right thing, and he and his family stayed out of the swamp.

I JUST WANT THIS DONE

CHAPTER 7

CASE
RESOLUTION OPTIONS

Remember Alec, the fortysomething professional who married a twentysomething party girl? He thought he needed a swamp creature to drag his soon-to-be-ex through a custody battle. Six months into the stalemate, he had spent $75,000 in legal fees. The lawyers were running things, not he or his estranged wife. Alec realized nothing would change until he did.

When Alec and I met, he was concerned that he'd have to spend another $75,000 before long with nothing to show for the investment. For a guy with an $800,000 annual salary, that was not going to bankrupt him. But what mattered to Alec more was the time and mental energy he was expending on the case, taking time away from his daughter and demanding career. His baby was now a little girl. He didn't want the child growing up with a mom who couldn't be counted on to stay sober during the day. Naturally, he wanted sole custody. As you know, the courts rarely give it. In fact, Alec had less of a chance than most people. I was the first lawyer to tell Alec how his wife's attorney would frame

Alec as a "rich, selfish guy fighting for custody just to punish the poor young mother."

Alec's only chance to get anything close to his desired parenting time was to call a cease-fire, get out of the swamp, and choose an option beside litigation. These alternatives, I told Alec, fall under the umbrella of alternative dispute resolution.

Although litigation is the most common way that divorces are resolved in Illinois, almost all cases ultimately settle prior to trial. For most people, it's better to choose ADR from the outset. ADR includes **mediation**, which is popular for parenting disputes, as mediators are used to help resolve parts of litigated cases and complete divorces. **Collaborative law**, developed in the 1990s, has become much more popular and widespread as a method of ADR and, in my opinion, is superior to mediation. **Arbitration** is still uncommon for divorce in my state, but it is used to determine complex financial divorce disputes in some counties.

One thing that is unique to the collaborative/ADR space is the frequency of referrals to another lawyer. For example, if a client hires me for a collaborative case, frequently they will ask me to recommend a collaborative attorney to represent their spouse. Since I have extensive experience successfully resolving collaborative cases with a number of attorneys, I know I work well with certain lawyers, and I can trust them. As a result, we get cases resolved more quickly and efficiently.

I'm going to explore alternative divorce methods for you in the same way I did with Alec. For each, I provide a description, the length of time each method takes, and the players involved. I discuss how information is gathered, the degree of involvement required by the parties, confidentiality, the legal effect of each, and pros and cons.

CASE RESOLUTION OPTIONS

Litigation

Definition: Litigation is resolving your divorce through a court process. In court, the case is decided by a judge (without a jury, except in a few states like Texas). Each party is represented by lawyers. There is no requirement that you have a lawyer, and people can represent themselves. This was once called "pro se" (a Latin term) but is now termed "self-representation." The attorneys file pleadings with the court to start the case, and proceed under the judge's supervision. Typically, the court wants the lawyers to check in monthly. State and local court rules govern the litigation process. If emergency matters or issues arise that cannot wait until the conclusion of the case, the court may hear them on an expedited basis. These include interim decisions on custody, visitation, alimony, and child support. The court guides the discovery process and resolves disputes over discovery. Eventually, the court has a pretrial conference to help settle the case by making recommendations to the lawyers about how the judge thinks this case might turn out based on the facts.

If the parties do not agree to a settlement, the court will have a trial in which the lawyers will present their clients' cases to the court. This is done by asking questions of the witnesses under oath, including the parties and other witnesses, such as experts. The judge decides the case and enters a judgment for divorce, which sets forth custody, visitation, division of property and debt, alimony, and child support.

If either party does not like the trial decision, they may appeal it within a set amount of time to the appellate court. The appellate court then reviews the court record, including pleadings and transcripts, to determine whether any errors were made by the court that are serious enough to warrant reversal of the trial decision in whole or in part, sending the case back to the trial court.

Time to completion: One to three-plus years. The trial itself takes from one day to multiple weeks, depending on complexity and the court's schedule. Some trial "days" are only afternoons, for example, and trials proceed a few hours at a time.

Players: Attorneys for both parties, the judge, potentially financial experts, guardian *ad litem* (or similar), child custody experts.

Information gathering: Known as "discovery" in litigation, this follows court rules. Mandatory disclosure of certain information, subpoenas for documents, possible depositions (sworn statements) of witnesses. The judge decides discovery disputes.

Party involvement: Parties will be in contact with the lawyers. They are not usually required to attend court hearings unless they require testimony, such as a temporary support hearing or temporary parenting. The parties must attend trials.

Confidentiality: None. Statements made in a court proceeding and documents filed with the court are public record.

Legal effect: The judgment entered by the court is appealable (in Illinois, within thirty days of entry) but otherwise is binding and final.

Litigation Pros:

- The court will decide the disputed issues in the case, both interim issues (before the case is resolved) and final issues at a trial (division of assets and debt, custody and visitation, child support and alimony).

- Court enforcement. If you have a high-conflict case with short-term or emergency issues requiring resolution, this can be important.

- The court can issue temporary restraining orders to halt improper conduct, seize computers to be copied if there is a fear of deletion of data, et cetera.

- Subpoena power. You can send subpoenas to compel third parties to provide documents, appear for deposition testimony, and appear to testify at hearings and trial. The court will enforce discovery orders and compel compliance with requests.

- Defined timeline. The court will help move the case along. Even this is not a guarantee, and depending on the jurisdiction, a party can slow down the process drastically. Eventually, the court will set deadlines and a trial date. This depends on the facts of the case, the local jurisdiction, and even the individual judge.

- Formality. State law and court rules bind the parties and the lawyers and limit the evidence that may be considered and the arguments that may be made by the parties. This can be a positive in some cases.

Litigation Cons:

- High expense. The court appearances and the discovery process, along with interim litigation, can gobble up money in legal fees. More time spent by lawyers equals more expense.
- Slow. Overall, litigation takes the most time of all case resolution options.
- The court system is not well suited to family problems, as discussed elsewhere in this book.
- The information-gathering "discovery" process is inefficient, as both lawyers gather basically the same data from different directions, and assuring the parties have the same data set is a huge problem. For example, one lawyer gathers stuff from their client, and the other gathers stuff from theirs, then they exchange the information and have to review all of it. Essentially, two law firms are duplicating work to verify the data. This can be the biggest obstacle to case resolution as neither lawyer wants to make a mistake based on incomplete or incorrect data. This process can "eat" the whole case as lawyers can use "zealous representation" to justify vast searches of data that may not be relevant ultimately.
- Formality. This can be a positive, as listed above, but also a negative as it can slow the process and limit the information the court can consider. This is highly case specific.
- Negative tone/tenor. Adversarial. No one likes a court fight.

- The result is less likely to be "owned" by the parties as they were less involved in the process of arriving at it. If the case is not settled, the court will impose a result on the parties.
- If the case is settled short of trial, the parties may feel rushed into a deal, depending on the circumstances of the settlement, or that the decision was forced on them due to lack of time. The parties may feel that they had no choice but to accept a deal based on a pretrial court recommendation that they may feel was incorrect or based on the wrong information or a lack of information.

Mediation

Definition: Parties work with a trained mediator to resolve a dispute. Mediators are usually lawyers, but that is not a requirement. Mediators act as neutral facilitators and guide settlement discussions. Mediation sessions can run two hours to as many as eight hours at a stretch. (Avoid these, as people typically burn out after two hours.) Mediation sessions can be held as often as required to resolve the issues, but typically, they are monthly, in order to give the parties time to digest the prior session and schedule a future session with the mediator. The mediator is neutral and will not provide legal advice to either party. Mediation can be in the same room (or virtual "room") or can be in separate rooms. (This is known as "shuttle" mediation.) Mediation proceedings are confidential and what is said in mediation cannot be discovered by a later court proceeding (for example, if negotiations break down and you end up in court).

The mediator does not "decide" your case. The mediator instead guides you through the issues and makes sure people play fair during negotiations. When the parties reach an agreement, the mediator prepares a "memorandum of understanding" detailing the terms of the agreement in writing.

A common misconception is that a mediator will "solve" your case and is the fastest and least expensive way to resolve a divorce. Mediators can be useful to resolve portions of divorce cases or entire cases but only with the parties supported by attorneys so they know their rights and responsibilities and understand the law and how it applies to the facts.

Time to completion: Three to nine-plus months.

Players: The parties, a mediator. Sometimes attorneys. (This is known as "attorney-assisted mediation.") Experts can be hired by the parties to assist (appraisers, business valuation experts) as needed.

Information gathering: This is done voluntarily. The parties exchange and share information. The mediator usually does not get involved in this process. This means that the mediator is not a judge and does not force anyone to turn over information. There is no subpoena power, so all document turnover is voluntary. There are no depositions of witnesses.

Party involvement: The parties attend sessions with the mediator. As noted above, they may or may not have lawyers directly involved in the mediation. They may consult lawyers before and after sessions but not have them present, or they may have the lawyers attend the sessions. Mediation requires the most involvement of the parties as they drive the process, using the mediator as a referee. Once they reach a tentative agreement, they need to work with lawyers to prepare settlement documents, review those documents, and make sure they understand them before signing.

Confidentiality: The statements made in mediation are confidential, according to the mediation agreement signed by the parties and the state mediation statute. Documents exchanged by the parties related to finances are not confidential and are subject to later discovery if the couple cannot settle the case and go to court.

Legal effect: The mediator's memorandum of understanding is non-binding and must be fleshed out into a full judgment for dissolution of marriage (marital settlement agreement and joint parenting agreement) and be entered by a court to have the force of law.

Mediation Pros:

- Speed. Typically substantially faster than litigation and can take less time than other ADR methods.

- Less expensive in general.
- The parties are in control of the process and will be more likely to take ownership of the mediated agreement.
- Convenience. The scheduling is driven by the parties and can fit with work/family life better.
- More amicable process.

Mediation Cons:

- The mediator is not like a judge or arbitrator and does not decide disputed fact issues. The mediator does not "decide" your case after hearing the arguments from both sides. The mediator facilitates the negotiations between you and your spouse and helps you understand the terms discussed by the parties.
- Interim and emergency issues must be settled by agreement. Therefore, this may not be well suited to high-conflict cases.
- The mediator cannot give legal advice. For example, the mediator, being neutral, cannot tell a party whether a deal is good or bad for them. That is the attorney's role. Some mediators will be hands off ("nondirective") and will not provide potential solutions to a given issue while others may help generate options. This means that, in complex matters, the parties are left wondering what to discuss since, without lawyers, they are not sure what to ask for. They are not educated in the law and, therefore, are in the dark when negotiating.
- There is no way to force disclosure of information by parties or third-party organizations (no subpoena power), so this is not a great option if a party suspects concealment of assets, dissipation (waste) of assets, or concealment/misrepresentation of income. However, a party can refuse to negotiate or enter into an agreement until the other party provides relevant information, and that may be enough to motivate compliance.

- The mediator will not draft a settlement agreement. (As stated above, the mediator prepares a "memorandum of understanding" with notes about the agreement reached by the parties; then a lawyer must prepare the settlement documents.)
- There is no way to force a case to conclusion. If one party wants to move slowly, they can delay the process. The only thing motivating the parties is their desire to get divorced and their fear of the case going to litigation.

Arbitration

Definition: Arbitration is a process that is more like court than the other ADR processes. Arbitration was the original form of ADR, tracing its origins back to England in the eleventh century. In arbitration, a neutral arbitrator adjudicates the case in a quasi-judicial abbreviated proceeding, subject to the rules set forth in the arbitration agreement signed by the parties. Many arbitrators are former divorce judges or experienced divorce lawyers. Arbitration organizations like JAMS and Endispute exist to facilitate arbitrations. Arbitration was first commonly used in commercial disputes and was later used in all types of legal disputes, including divorce matters. With arbitration, think "court lite," with a faster, more tightly focused process. At the conclusion of arbitration, the arbitrator will hear evidence presented by the parties' attorneys and will consider legal arguments made by the parties, similar to those in a trial.

Time to completion: Three to nine months.

Players: The parties, attorneys, an arbitrator, expert witnesses (potentially).

Information gathering: This follows the rules of the arbitrator or the organization hosting the arbitration. These rules commonly include mandatory disclosure of information, voluntary exchange of documents, and even depositions. The arbitrator supervises any discovery disputes and works to ensure compliance with arbitration rules. Discovery timelines are much shorter in arbitration cases than in typical litigation.

Party involvement: The parties will be in contact with the lawyers, and they may give depositions and attend arbitration hearings, which are similar to a trial.

Confidentiality: The arbitration agreement makes the statements of the parties confidential.

Legal effect: The arbitration award is binding and not appealable, but it still must be entered with the court as a judgment.

Arbitration Pros:

- The arbitrator will decide disputed fact issues and the outcome of the case.
- Speed. You aren't tied to the court docket, and the arbitrator has a much smaller number of cases to deal with than a divorce judge.
- Convenience. You schedule dates that work for you and the lawyers with the arbitrator.
- Cost. Generally less expensive than litigation but more expensive than the other ADR options. Arbitrators and the related facilities can be pricey.
- Finality. Binding arbitration is final and prevents further litigation. Arbitration awards are not appealable.
- Privacy. The proceedings are not public record.
- More informal. Less tied to rules of evidence and court rules. This frees up the parties and can make the process more efficient.

Arbitration Cons:

- Can be more expensive than mediation and collaborative practice.
- The parties have less control over the result. Since the decision is in the hands of the arbitrator, the parties may not feel they "own" the result.
- No appeal process as in litigation. Once the decision is made, it is final.

Collaborative Practice

Definition: A fusion of mediation and traditional negotiation methods, Collaborative practice was invented by Minnesota divorce lawyer Stu Webb as described in his book *The Collaborative Way to Divorce.* The Collaborative Law Model Act has been passed into law in twenty states and is pending passage in several others. In the collaborative model, the parties negotiate their case with the help of their attorneys in a series of meetings (in person or via video), at times with the help of other professionals, such as financial neutrals and divorce coaches. At the conclusion of the negotiations, an agreement is reached, and the divorce matter is filed in court to finalize. This team approach is unique to collaborative law. Also, in the pure collaborative model, if either party terminates negotiations and proceeds to go to court, both lawyers are fired, and the parties need to find new counsel. This keeps the collaborative lawyers motivated to settle the case and ties the financial interests of the lawyers to the success of negotiations; they make less money if they threaten litigation and "blow up" the deal. It also keeps the parties interested in making a deal because there is a real price to pay if they proceed to court—they have to start again from scratch with new lawyers.

The financial neutrals are unique to collaborative practice. They are financial professionals, usually financial planners or accountants. They are trained in collaborative practice just like the lawyers. The neutral's role is to gather the financial data and analyze it for the collaborative team. They provide a central gathering place for all the documents and data and provide financial reports such as a balance sheet as well as models for child support and alimony, all from a neutral/unbiased viewpoint. This saves the parties substantial money as only one person is collecting the financial data rather than both lawyers, and getting a unified data set is much simplified. The neutral's rates are also lower than those of the lawyers, so there are cost savings there as well.

The use of divorce coaches is also unique to collaborative practice, but other case resolution options are starting to use coaches as well. Divorce coaches are typically counselors or psychologists who work with the parties in a facilitative role rather than a traditional therapy role. As I explain it to clients, they aren't here to help you with your rough childhood or to understand what went wrong in the marriage. They are present to help you communicate with your spouse, your kids, and the attorneys and understand what is going on in the divorce case. A good coach can be a real asset in a divorce case, just as poor ones can be a detriment. Choosing them carefully if they are needed is a worthwhile investment of your time.

Neutrals and coaches are all collaboratively trained, so they understand how the process works and understand how divorce cases work. This provides a tremendous resource for clients seeking guidance. Many of the questions and concerns clients have are emotional and communication related rather than legal, and the divorce coaches are less expensive than lawyers and trained in these areas specifically.

Time to completion: Three to nine months.

Players: The parties, the attorneys (possibly divorce coach, financial neutral, and other experts as needed).

Information gathering: Entirely voluntary. Agree to cooperate by the terms of the participation agreement. The lawyers exchange information and, in many cases, choose one of the lawyers to be the repository of all the information, using a secure shared drive on the web where all can upload and download the case documents in one place.

Party involvement: The parties will be in contact with the lawyers and will attend team meetings, where they set forth their goals and concerns; identify the key issues; discuss assets, liabilities, income, and expenses; and negotiate the terms of the divorce with the assistance of the other professionals. Typically, one or both parties are required to participate in the final hearing where the court grants a divorce, but, at least in some counties in Illinois, even this remote appearance on video is not required, provided the parties sign an affidavit attesting to the key facts of the marriage and the divorce, and that they understand the agreement.

Confidentiality: The participation agreement signed by the parties and the Collaborative Law Act (state law governing collaborative practice, where in force) make the statements made in a collaboration confidential. Any draft settlement agreements or discussions are not admissible in a court proceeding and remain confidential. Documents produced to the parties are not confidential, however.

Legal effect: The agreement reached by the parties in collaboration is not binding until it is entered as a judgment for divorce in the appropriate court. The collaborative practice lawyers prepare the settlement documents and enter them with the court to make them binding as a matter of law.

Collaborative Practice Pros:

- Speed.
- Lower expense.
- The parties have control over the process and are included from the start. Therefore, they have a high degree of "buy-in" and understanding of the resulting settlement agreement.
- Convenience. Two-hour sessions are scheduled when the parties and attorneys are available.
- No time pressure. No court threats, no court pressure of trial.
- Creativity. Collaborative professionals try to accomplish what is best for the family and, while informing clients about the law, aren't bound by it in most cases and can form custom solutions.

Collaborative Practice Cons:

- No court assistance. If an emergency arises—for example, in a high-conflict case—there is no court to turn to for help or to decide a disputed fact issue as in mediation. You must work with the collaborative team to solve issues that arise. As an example, if the spouse in control of finances cut off the other, the court cannot assist unless the other spouse quits the collaborative process and starts a case with the court, which will take time to get rolling.

- No one is present to decide disputed fact issues, like a judge in litigation or an arbitrator in arbitration. You need to negotiate a solution.
- No subpoenas. If documents are not voluntarily disclosed, there is no way to obtain record requests directly from the providers (banks, credit card companies, etc.). However, the parties can sign record request authorizations to secure records.
- There is no way to force a case to conclusion. If one party wants to move slowly, they can delay the process. Good collaborative lawyers can keep the case on pace by making sure meetings take place monthly or at a similar regular interval. But ultimately, the only thing motivating the parties is their desire to get divorced and their fear of the case going to litigation.

Your circumstances will dictate which alternative dispute resolution method is best for you. Note that you may not have a choice since your spouse gets a vote as well. For example, if you want mediation but your spouse won't agree to mediate, you are stuck with the court process. The same is true with the other ADR methods.

ALEC'S STORY, CONTINUED (AGAIN)

After I laid out these options for Alec, he chose collaborative practice. He realized that he had little to no chance of winning the custody battle at the time, and he and his wife were burning up huge sums of cash on legal fees. Weighing that against the likely expense in time and money, collaborative practice made sense. My first item of business was to get Alec out of litigation and redirect his wife to a collaborative lawyer, which worked. Because I told Alec to *ask* his wife to meet with the new lawyer one time, not *demand*. I trusted that lawyer, of course, so I knew what would happen next. Alec's wife fired her first lawyer, hired the collaborative one, and worked with Alec to bring the marriage to a much cheaper, much quicker end.

In the process, we sorted out all parenting and financial issues in only three meetings between the parties. Six hours total. Alec and his wife surprised each other—they worked well in the collaborative setting and reached an amicable settlement.

If you too carefully consider your options, alternative dispute resolution can help you make a better choice for your family.

I JUST WANT THIS DONE

CHAPTER 8

THE META CASE

Sometimes, the outcome of a divorce case is not driven solely by the facts and the law. Often, the meta case—the stuff surrounding the case—substantially affects the result.

I once represented a woman named Cheryl in a divorce case who had multiple medical issues that weren't readily apparent. She and her husband Amir had been married a long time but had no children. Cheryl was an adjunct professor working part time at a local university. Her medical issues limited her ability to work full time; she told me part-time work was the most she could do. We'd had a brief conference with the court about settlement, and the judge was leaning in the direction of the husband. Amir's lawyer argued that my client didn't need her soon-to-be-ex-husband's money. She was fine and could easily work full time, he said. Why would she be entitled to alimony?

It was at that point Cheryl asked for my help. From the start, we made little progress. The judge still believed the other lawyer over me. The court bought the narrative of the other attorney that my client was just lazy and could increase her income if she wanted. They were trying to push my client into a bad settlement that would leave her unable to take care of herself financially, and I couldn't let that happen. As I thought about the human dynamics in play, I realized that if we could win the "meta case," we'd win over the judge on the actual case.

WHAT IS THE META CASE?

So what is the meta case? The meta case includes all the players and circumstances surrounding a case—excluding the evidence and the law—that ultimately influence the outcome as much as, if not more than, the evidence and the law. Lose the meta case, and you'll likely lose the actual case, even if the facts and the law are on your side.

In my first job as an attorney, my boss (now Judge) Jim McCluskey taught me the importance of the meta case. When I told him about a new case, he'd always ask me, "Who's the other lawyer?" I didn't understand why. I'd tell him, a little puzzled, and he'd grab the *Sullivan's Law Directory* to look up the other party's legal representation. He'd say something like, "Oh, he works for so-and-so and has been a lawyer for only three years. Don't worry," or "This guy is experienced, so watch out." He'd also always ask, "Who's the judge?" We knew the "who" was just as important as the "what."

In law school, I had thought cases were decided based on evidence and law, not the lawyer and the judge. But Jim taught me that the other lawyer and the judge have almost as much impact on the case as the facts themselves. It turns out that, in divorce cases, the parties have a major role in the meta case, too.

I've always told clients there are three major factors that affect the outcome of a case. I call them "weather conditions." As in, you can't control them. These are the judge, the client, and the opposing lawyer. If all three are easy to work with or at least not bad, you'll probably settle the case reasonably quickly. If one of the three is not good, it'll be tough to get what you're hoping for. If two or even three are problematic, you'll end up at an ugly trial.

Since my first job as a lawyer, I've learned that the players have a significant impact on a divorce case's outcome. Here they are:

FACTORS OF THE META CASE

You: How you conduct yourself in the case can be more important than the facts of the case. If you are a jerk to your spouse and kids or the other people involved, this will eventually get back to the judge and affect you negatively. When a decision in the case is on the bubble, how do you think the judge will react when making the decision if you've been a jerk? Exactly. It won't go well for you. On the other hand, if you've done well and played nice, and you've cooperated, you will do better. In most divorces, the judge who hears the trial is the judge who handled the case from the beginning, so they get to know who is involved in the case and how they behave. And, like Santa Claus, they know who's been bad and good, so be good, for goodness' sake! The good thing about your involvement in the meta case is that you *can* control your actions and have a positive impact on the outcome of your case. The other elements are largely out of your control, so make the best of your own behavior to reap the rewards later.

    Your spouse: This may be obvious to you—your spouse is out of your control. What they are dealing with, how they react to stress, the issues in their life all play into whether the case moves toward a reasonable settlement or spirals into litigation. They are dealing with all the things you are dealing with as well. They may be scared about the future, worried about finances, concerned about how they will manage relationships with the kids, nervous about what family and friends will think, and so on. Having an appreciation of how they are feeling can go a long way toward understanding what is happening and make negotiation and resolution of the divorce case easier.

    Your impact on your spouse. How your spouse acts may not be within your control, but their behavior is within your influence. How? By the way you treat them. If you're nasty, don't expect sunshine from your spouse. If you're understanding and you behave yourself, you are likely to have a better outcome. Reserve the snark and nasty comments for later (better yet, keep them to yourself).

Spouse as a positive influence. Each of you has a significant amount of control over the case. If your spouse is willing to exercise control, they are in charge and can tell the lawyer what to do. As mentioned earlier, the lawyer is not the boss; the client is. So be leery any time your spouse says, "The lawyer did X," or "The lawyer filed Y." Notice that your spouse's signature is at the bottom of any court filing. They are fully aware of what is going on, and if they say they aren't, they are intentionally ignorant, or they are lying to you. I had a case a couple of years back in which the other party was a lawyer in a large Chicago law firm, and she wanted to be divorced quickly and cleanly. She was a strong influence on the speed and cadence of negotiations, and she kept her attorney on track throughout the settlement negotiations to make sure the case was resolved amicably and promptly. Had the spouse been weak willed, the case might have been sucked into the swamp.

Spouse as a negative inf uence. Conversely, it almost goes without saying that an angry or vindictive spouse can mean a major war, extensive litigation, and tremendous expense. Doing your part to mitigate the hard feelings present in most divorces and being as pleasant and agreeable as possible with finances and the children will go a long way to help in this area.

Your kids: Whether they are doing well or poorly, whether they have health issues or mental health problems, et cetera all factor into how the case works out, aside from custody and visitation. How they feel about the way you treat their other parent is important. The way they interact with you and your spouse plays a role. The kids are always watching, and they absorb what is going on. They also influence the the Guardian ad Litem and thus the judge.

Your parents and family: Your family has a huge impact on your case, as does your spouse's family. They love you; they support you; they want to be there for you. They will listen to you and your concerns. They are your family, and so you are stuck with them. You know your family. They can be a help or a huge hindrance in your divorce. There are some concerns, however.

They are paying for your fees. If they are paying your fees, they will naturally think they should have some control over the case. Legally, they aren't the client even though they are paying the bills. Your lawyer has no obligation to talk with them—your case is confidential, and your conversations are protected by attorney-client privilege. In fact, by including family in discussions with your lawyer, you technically are waiving the privilege, and those communications could be discovered. (As in your family could be asked about what you said in a deposition or at trial. Parents paying for a divorce can be intrusive and cause all sorts of problems in a case. Even if you don't let them talk to your lawyer, they will potentially pressure you into doing things you may not want to do. Beware that money often comes with strings attached.

They have a financial stake in the divorce. (For example, a loan to the couple, family-owned business, estate/will distributions, promise to pay for college). This can cause real complications. Frequently, this arises when the parents contributed money for a down payment or purchased a home for the couple. Later, the parents try to claim that the money was not intended as a gift but was a loan to the parties. Without proper loan documentation, the court will find the money was intended as a gift if the property has a mortgage. Also note that title companies and lenders require a "gift letter" at the time of closing to confirm that the financial contribution was intended as a gift and was not, in fact, a loan. (The lender does not want any other claims on the real estate in the event of default.) In situations in which the parents of one party transferred a business interest to a child during the marriage, this can create marital property and a potential ownership interest of the soon-to-be-ex in the family business. Perhaps a generous in-law offered to pay for college for the children, and because of some other issue in the case, they now are upset and threaten to refuse to pay (true story). Worse yet, one party was slated to inherit a substantial estate, but since they are getting divorced, the family threatens to "cut them out" of the estate or withhold distributions. There is not much that can be done to change these things, but being aware that they all affect your case helps you navigate the situation intelligently.

They love/hate your spouse. This seems obvious, but if your family hates your spouse, this might, at the outset, seem like a positive, but it can be a bad thing. First, they want you to "win" and will encourage potentially punishing litigation and push you to drive for objectives that might not be realistic. Also, this can blow back on your children—you will have events like graduations and sports and other activities where the grandparents will interact with you, the kids, and your ex. A high degree of acrimony does no good here, either during the case or afterward. On the other hand, if they love your spouse, they may see your decision to get divorced as crazy and wrong and will be in your ear, trying to convince you to stay married.

Some advance communication with parents about an impending divorce is important so people aren't blindsided, and they can see things your way. Too much communication, on the other hand, as discussed in a later chapter, may lead parents to dislike the other person to the point where reconciliation is impossible, and even civil communication with the ex after divorce becomes extremely difficult. If you have young kids, this becomes a major problem with school events, holidays, et cetera.

Your spouse's lawyer: This person can make or break a case. Let's look at your options.

The swamp creature. Get a swamp creature on the other side, and no matter how nice or agreeable you want to be, you are in for a war, especially if your spouse is not assertive or thinks they will get some kind of vindication or punishment out of the case (in short, the ideal client for the swamp creature). This lawyer will push your spouse into WWIII; urge them to leave no stone unturned; and subtly (or not subtly) suggest you have been stealing from the marriage, cheating on them, and more. All with "maybe" or "it's possible" attached so they can back off those statements later.

Here's a swamp creature horror story. Several years ago, we had a high-net-worth case with some business interests that could have been settled reasonably. The other attorney's law firm was known for being aggressive and made this a selling point on their website. The minute I learned who it was, I told the client, "We're going to trial in this case." This lawyer typically settled at the last minute and demanded terms very disadvantageous to the other spouse. In essence, this forced a trial (or a bad settlement) in every case. This scorched-earth litigation style can get results, but the price is high in terms of fees and acrimony. And it is all so unnecessary. Sometimes, out of weariness and desiring to just be done, clients will agree to terms they perhaps should not. And this lawyer knew this. Which is why the only way to deal with this kind of person was to fight and get ready for trial.

Opposing attorney as positive influence. Alternatively, a lawyer you trust and a person who is reasonable can make a huge positive difference in the case. Does the lawyer tamp down trouble, smooth things out, or raise the level of acrimony in a case? The kind of cool-headed lawyer I like to work with makes the case 100 percent easier and results in faster settlements and happier clients.

The import of expectation management. A lawyer's expectation management is important here. Did the lawyer do a good job managing the other spouse's expectations in the case, or did they promise them the moon? Unrealistic expectations cause major problems when you're trying to negotiate. If a potential agreement (even a reasonable one) deviates from what the client thought was promised by their lawyer, they have a major problem. This can force hearings when normally a hearing is not required, just so the lawyer can blame the failure to deliver on the judge and "luck" instead of simply saying their advice was wrong.

Client control. An attorney's ability to control their clients is important beyond just expectation management. If a client is misbehaving in a case—for example, texting nasty messages to the spouse—a lawyer telling the client to quit it and behave well can have a strong positive impact on a case and avoid needless court action.

The judge: We did a lot in Chapter 6 to address the frailties of judges and the court process. But what is important here is to realize that the judge is human and is, in fact, judging people and assessing credibility all during the case. It is not just about the trial itself, but about how the court perceives you during the entire litigation. Does the judge think you're telling the truth? That you are generally well intentioned? Has the court entered multiple orders to rein in your misbehavior? Did the court hear you testify at a hearing and now think you aren't credible? Have you or your spouse violated a court order, resulting in sanctions from the judge? Or, also as important, has your lawyer made a good impression on the court? If you've treated your spouse and the kids poorly, played games with discovery, or cut off financial support to your spouse, the court will remember these things when making important decisions about your case.

Judge's biases. Also, the judge comes into the case with all their past experience and biases. All this affects the outcome of your case. This is why it is helpful if your lawyer has some familiarity with the court and their nature. I will say that, overall, most judges work hard to be unbiased. Some might favor one party over the other or have rules of thumb for handling certain situations, and that might adversely affect you. What has taken place in the meta case can poison the well—for better or worse. Does your lawyer have a good reputation with the court? Does the other lawyer? These factors can play into your ultimate outcome in ways that may be quite subtle but no less important.

Judge's scheduling issues. In one case I described earlier (the one in which the trial went on for a year), the judge only would hear the trial for a few hours per day, which clearly had a huge impact on the case. In contrast, other judges might hear a trial daily until it's complete.

Failure to provide guidance. Judges who waffle and give weak pretrial recommendations are a negative factor for your case. Some judges don't give strong recommendations to settle a case in a pretrial conference, which can easily lead to a trial that might not have been necessary had the judge simply been clearer about their opinions on a likely outcome. Note that some types of cases (such as custody matters) may depend on the credibility of the witnesses, and the only way the court can assess that is by having a trial. At least a good judge can narrow the issues by providing guidance on some items while perhaps leaving others open.

Good guy/bad guy stereotypes. Also, I have experienced a few judges who take things personally or place too much weight on the meta case and base too much of the outcome on who they believe is the "good guy" or the "bad guy." These judges can place substantial emphasis and bias against the "bad" person, and unfortunately, this can seriously influence their decision-making.

Judges and custody cases. Another factor important in custody cases. Bad behavior that would upset you and me relative to the children (yelling, some physical discipline, name-calling) does not generally motivate divorce judges to take action. Think about the context. Judges see a cross section of society. They deal with serious child abusers, drug addicts, alcoholics, and worse. The bar is therefore unfortunately pretty low for what is considered acceptable parental behavior by the court. So what seems like terrible parenting to you may not be considered "abuse" by a divorce court judge as a practical matter. Proving more subtle misbehavior on the part of a parent is also tough. Therefore, it is difficult to get court action on those items.

Stereotypes. Judges are busy, and they have limited time to hear cases. Keep in mind that, just like the rest of us, judges put cases and people into mental "boxes" when thinking about them to help process what is happening and guide them to come up with solutions. You don't want to be "the rich guy who tries to control his wife and make her miserable." Overcoming the judge's stereotypes and biases can be a daunting task. For example, if you are a working dad and your wife is a stay-at-home mom, it is just not realistic to think you will be the primary parent with the majority of parenting time at the conclusion of the case, without strong evidence suggesting that result is warranted.

The mediator: Mediators are both appointed by divorce courts and hired privately to try to resolve divorce disputes. Some mediations are limited to parenting issues, and others deal with the entire case. Mediators are typically experienced divorce lawyers, and all receive about one week of specialized training in mediation and negotiation techniques. Just like anything else, there are good and not-so-good mediators. When they are appointed by the court, the judges typically know and respect the mediator. A good mediator can make a big difference. It is important to make a good impression and bring your A game to mediation.

Be prepared. Know what your goals and concerns are for the mediation. Get legal advice in advance so you know what you want and, more importantly, what is realistic in terms of outcomes. Have notes about the relevant topics so you can intelligently discuss the issues.

Be reasonable. Being reasonable with the mediator is important. If the mediator perceives you as reasonable, the things you are asking for will be seen in that light. If you are disagreeable, the reverse will be true.

Listen to your spouse and the mediator. When your spouse speaks, let them talk. Listen, and do not interrupt. This also goes for the mediator. *Don't argue.* You can convey your thoughts and concerns without being a jerk. You can politely disagree. When you raise your voice and get angry, you instantly lose the debate as you look unreasonable. Calmly expressing your opinion is the best way to convey your ideas.

Avoid personal attacks. This is not the time to attack your spouse for their perceived failings. You will not convince them to see things your way by denigrating or disparaging them.

Avoid getting "historical." Who did what to whom, why you are getting divorced, and all the perceived wrongs your spouse is guilty of have no place in mediation. Again, you will not convince anyone by digging into the past.

Behave yourself and come prepared to mediation. Discuss the case in advance with your attorney so you know what to ask for and you know what is reasonable. Listen and do not interrupt the mediator or your spouse during the session. Avoid arguing, and instead present your thoughts when it is your turn to speak. You can disagree with your spouse without appearing angry or unreasonable. Behaving well in mediation improves both your chances of success in settling the case and in making a good impression on the mediator (and your spouse).

While the mediator simply reports to the court that you and your spouse reached an agreement or did not reach an agreement, it is a possibility that word gets out from time to time of a person acting unreasonably, and it's also possible that a judge gets wind of this. Or your spouse tells their lawyer that you did not behave in mediation and were mean and nasty and therefore unable to reach an agreement. Either way, the mediator has a major impact on your case.

The expert witness: Expert witnesses are used in a number of roles in complex divorce cases: for forensic accounting (tracing money and figuring incomes), business valuation (to appraise and value business interests), real estate appraisal, and child custody evaluation. (This is usually done by a psychologist or psychiatrist.) These experts typically interact with the parties and solicit information from them in the course of their work. For the financial experts, contact with the client is required to secure information about business and personal finances. For child experts, interviews are conducted with parents by the experts, and psychological inventories and testing may be performed to aid in determining parenting issues. These experts will generate reports and potentially testify in depositions or the trial of the divorce case, and their opinions carry substantial weight. They also will testify in general about how cooperative the parties were in their investigation. It won't look good if the expert tells the judge that party A did not cooperate and made the investigation more difficult. (This could also factor into a potential fee award against the uncooperative person.) So cooperation is important. Transparency in providing documentation and responding to requests for information is key. Being nice to the expert witness, even when they are hired by your spouse, may be critical in positively influencing the expert's opinion of you. Why risk making it worse?

The GAL or child representative: GALs or child representatives are chosen by the court to investigate child custody and visitation issues in your divorce case. Their impact on your case cannot be overstated. The judges rely on and put great faith in them (or people in similar roles in your state) when determining child custody issues. These people will interview you and your spouse; meet your kids; and interview others such as school administrators, counselors, and family members to help decide the custody dispute at issue. They make recommendations to the court about the outcome of custody and visitation disputes, and they also may testify at trial or make evidence-based legal arguments for some position about custody and visitation in your case. Advice:

Pay your bill to the GAL. Do you think the GAL will think highly of you if you aren't paying them? Better to keep them paid than to annoy the GAL and the judge.

Be courteous to the GAL and reply promptly to requests for information. As with the expert witnesses, hiding the proverbial ball won't look good and may bias the GAL against your position.

Don't argue with the GAL when they advance an idea about custody. Give the person a full opportunity to speak, then express your thoughts. Arguing with them has no benefit. Telling them your evidence-based concerns about your spouse is valuable, but just arguing with the GAL and bad-mouthing your spouse without evidence can damage your case. *Follow the GAL's recommendations during the case.* I represented a person in a custody case, and he disagreed with many of the things the GAL wanted him to do for the children—see a counselor jointly with his ex, avoid having his girlfriend around the kids for a while, and more. Instead, he disregarded the GAL's advice, and this factored into their recommendations against my client ultimately. Moreover, the court heard testimony that my client was not cooperating with the GAL. Bottom line: the GAL is a person to work with, not against.

Your friends: Similar to the impact of family, the bias and prejudices of friends can be a benefit or a hindrance. Also, a friend telling you about their divorce and using it as a yardstick for your divorce is not only not useful; it can also be extremely misleading. Here are the ways their case can differ from yours: 1) Different state. Divorce law varies from state to state. What happened in Florida has no bearing on an Illinois divorce. 2) Settled in the same state even a few years ago. Divorce law changes frequently. In Illinois, since 2015, the legislature has completely overhauled child support, alimony, and parenting law. It is a completely different situation than it was even a few short years ago. So your buddy telling you he paid X dollars in child support and Y dollars in alimony is unhelpful. 3) You don't know all the facts. Every case is different, and cases are decided and settled on their own merits. You have no idea what was at work "under the hood," so it is impossible to compare apples to apples. Incomes of the parties, nonmarital assets, medical conditions, inheritances, and more all play into the ultimate outcome, and too frequently, people fail to get into the "weeds" to tell you the details.

Also, as with a significant other or a parent, their own biases and dislike for your spouse can affect their relationship with you and the things they say to you. Be careful to keep your counsel and avoid disclosing a lot of information about your case to anyone. It is just generally better that you keep things on a need-to-know basis, or everyone will get involved in your personal business. And if you decide to reconcile after you've disparaged your spouse to your friends, putting your predivorce life back together can be nearly impossible. In some cases, a trusted friend can help you evaluate choices in your divorce or help you understand issues in the case. Conversely, a friend can end up confusing and misleading you about the case. Bottom line: leave the legal advice and guidance to your lawyer, and let your friends be your cheerleaders.

Your significant other (SO): Your girlfriend or boyfriend can either be a big help or a big hindrance. Sometimes the new SO upsets the other players: your spouse, your kids, your family. It is vitally important to understand how the SO can affect the meta case positively and, most important, negatively.

The SO as an influencer. Typically, your SO wants to get involved in your case, either for positive or negative reasons. They might want to be involved in discussions with your divorce lawyer and may inject themselves in decisions surrounding the divorce. If they are dating you, they have (or think they have) a vested interest in the outcome of your divorce. They might want to get married to you, so they see the financial outcome of your divorce as important to their future. They may like your kids and envision themselves as a future stepparent. They might want you to hurry up and get divorced so they can marry you. (And they can stop hearing you talk about the divorce and your spouse all the time.) This all can lead to the SO telling you things about your case and trying to influence your thinking in the divorce. They may tell you (and believe) that they are looking out for your best interests, but they cannot separate out their personal interests and are not an unbiased observer.

The SO wants to be a stepparent. In one case I handled, my client was devoted to his long-term GF, who did not have children. The GF wanted badly to be the "stepmom" for the children, even though she was not yet married to the client. She continued to inject herself into the case, insisting on being involved in attorney-client discussions between me and my client. She insisted on being present for parenting time with the children, even though it was a bad idea, and the guardian *ad litem* (and I) advised against it because the children were very hostile and disliked her.

Your SO can be a positive influence. The SO can be a positive influence as well, helping you understand what is going on in the case, helping you stay focused and positive, and giving you emotional support.

The GAL, experts, and judge get wind of your SO's involvement. In a case I had some time ago, the GAL was well aware of the demands made by the SO on my client related to the children. Worse yet, the client and his SO got into a verbal altercation in front of the children, leading to the kids calling the police. The GAL got the impression that the SO was more important to my client than his children and relayed this to the judge. Naturally, this was bad for my client's position in the custody battle. Once people have these negative impressions, they are hard to unwind.

Beware of letting your relationship with your SO have too much impact on your decision-making and the outcome of your case. Think long term. There is a reason counselors and psychologists recommend not getting involved with a new SO until your divorce is completed. Understandably, life is not that simple, which is why I give this advice. SOs may come and go, and ultimately, this is your divorce, not theirs. Their motivations may not be 100 percent aligned with yours. The best practice is generally not to involve your SO in your divorce and keep the divorce case and related decisions to yourself.

With all these players, you can see how they influence the meta case and in many cases what you can do to positively influence them to achieve a better outcome. Ignore the meta case and the players at your peril.

CHERYL'S STORY, CONTINUED

Cheryl needed alimony. The judge was leaning against it. She didn't have a lot of money for legal fees to have a long battle with depositions and medical witnesses. I decided to file a motion for temporary alimony. This would be a mini version of the alimony hearing if we went to trial. We would have an abbreviated hearing on the central issue in the case at much less cost, and both my client and her husband Amir would testify. I felt confident from reading over Cheryl's medical records and talking with her that she could testify credibly about her medical conditions. I hoped that the court would see this and realize that alimony was warranted based on the facts.

I was right. I brought a pile of medical records that I knew would not be entered into evidence but that I could use to "refresh her recollection." The giant stack itself would lend credibility to Cheryl's story without even having to put the documents into evidence.

Cheryl was great on the stand. She looked the judge in the eye when answering questions, and he was convinced she was telling the truth. Meanwhile, Amir disparaged her from the stand in his testimony and tried to make it sound like she was a hypochondriac. It sounded like sour grapes rather than reasoned testimony. The hearing turned the tide. Not only was Cheryl awarded temporary alimony, but she also received a very favorable asset settlement.

Cheryl won the meta case as much as Amir lost it.

I JUST WANT THIS DONE

CHAPTER 9

THE FOUR TRUE COSTS
OF DIVORCE

Remember the story about Dave in Chapter 3?
The attorney's fees were huge in that case, even before I got involved. Dave's wife, Carly, was angry and vindictive, and she continued fighting about every single issue. We had depositions. Carly's lawyers demanded endless volumes of documents. Carly was in contact with Dave's estranged brother, who was also Dave's former partner in the family business. He had only bad things to say about Dave, which Carly immediately told their kids. Carly also disparaged Dave's girlfriend to everyone in their social circle.

Dave received a huge settlement as a result of the family business's lawsuit against his brother. He was receiving payouts on an annual basis, totaling a couple of million dollars.

Meanwhile, Carly made no effort to find a job. She spent Dave's temporary alimony of $12,000 a month and ran up credit cards on top of that. She bought high-end clothes and traveled to exotic destinations with no regard for spending. Not to mention the huge legal fees both parties were spending.

Late in the case, Carly and her attorneys manufactured a custody case out of thin air. Custody issues had already been settled prior to trial. They claimed Dave was addicted to prescription drugs. The accusation caused the court to appoint an expert to verify that Dave did not have an addiction.

Dave was terribly distracted by all the trouble, so he had a hard time focusing on work. He didn't want to start a new business during the marriage only to have Carly's lawyers claim that it was a new marital enterprise and that he would have to share it with her. The case was a nightmare for him.

Carly made one major mistake. She failed to recognize that Dave was not a bottomless pit of money. She did not recognize all the true costs of the divorce. Divorce cases have multiple costs that must be weighed, not just the cost of attorneys. In this chapter, we'll examine the four actual costs of divorce and how to calculate my go-to cost-benefit equation.

THE FOUR COSTS OF DIVORCE

The Emotional Cost

This is not a financial expense, but it comes first for a reason. This includes the emotional cost to you, your children, your extended family, and your friends. This may well be the most significant expense to you and your family. The emotional cost may ultimately be more valuable to you than any money. The emotional impact can have a direct impact on your health and that of your family and friends through lost sleep, increased susceptibility to illness, and worse. Health problems, addiction issues. Depression and anxiety. Self-harm. Suicide. During my own divorce, I developed high blood pressure, which dropped substantially after the divorce was final.

The emotional toll any divorce, even an uncontested one, takes on you and your family is substantial. Divorce is a stressful life event, second only to the death of a close family member. The longer the process takes and the more vitriol between the spouses, the higher the emotional toll.

Children may show effects from the divorce immediately or have delayed or subtle reactions no one notices until it's too late. Divorce always affects the kids. It's only a matter of how and when. Generally, the sooner the parties can resolve the legal portion of the divorce, the better. Let your family recover as soon as possible.

Family and friends are burdened emotionally, too, as we so often call on them for emotional support. No one likes to hear bad news, especially on a prolonged basis. It's difficult to support a friend or family member who is suffering from serious stress and pain for a prolonged period. Again, the sooner you can reach a conclusion, the better for this group of people as well.

Weighing these costs on yourself, your children, your family, and your friends is important and should not be overlooked. Sometimes, the best settlement is one that costs a little more money but concludes much sooner. The money can be replaced more easily than the harm to your health and the impact on others you care about.

The Legal Fee Cost

Legal fees in a divorce can range from modest to astronomical. Thousands of dollars to hundreds of thousands of dollars. The fees vary, depending on the nature of the case; the issues involved; the parties to the matter; and, frankly, their attorneys and the process taken by the parties to resolve their divorce.

Alternative dispute resolution, including collaborative law, mediation, and arbitration, tends to be less expensive than litigation. The issues in any case may add complexity and expense. In collaborative law, use of a child specialist, divorce coaches, and financial neutrals will add to the expense but can usually be justified with lower legal fees due to the help provided by these professionals.

In litigation, parenting disputes can add substantial expense, as the courts in disputed cases may appoint a guardian *ad litem* or child representative. The GAL or child representative is an attorney and is paid by the parties in addition to their ordinary legal fees. In protracted parenting litigation, the parties may seek additional expert witnesses to give opinions about the parenting skills of the other parent, adding from several thousand dollars to tens of thousands of dollars in expense.

Use of outside experts to value assets such as businesses, real estate, and vehicles adds expense. Protracted discovery and fact-finding, including depositions, will add attorney time and therefore legal fees to the tally. All these things must be weighed against the ultimate goals you are seeking.

The Cash Burn Cost

An additional cost that most people fail to consider is the spending done by the parties themselves during the case. You and your spouse are not only spending money on attorneys; you are also spending a lot of money on yourselves. Your spouse may be furnishing a new apartment, buying new clothes, meeting with counselors, and going out to eat more, and this cash is being spent out of the marital estate.

In a recent case, the family had a sizable marital estate of approximately $2 million. One of the significant factors in motivating the settlement was the cash burn rate for the parties. They were spending $16,000 to $20,000 per month, and the primary wage-earning spouse had recently lost his high-paying position. Not only were the legal fees going to be high to proceed to a trial in the case, but the cash burn rate was also quickly consuming the assets that were in contention to begin with.

In that case, the difference in the divorcing couple's settlement offers was about $200,000. Setting aside the legal fees, we estimated the trial would take place in six months, and the parties' cash burn rate was roughly $20,000 per month. By the time we even got to trial, the parties would have had $120,000 less in assets just due to their living expenses! That projected spending added to the cost of the litigation made it clear that an immediate settlement, even one that wasn't "ideal" for either party, was still a far better deal than going to trial over $200,000. The projected attorney's fees plus the cash burn rate eclipsed anything that the parties were fighting about.

The Business and Career Cost

When you are involved in a divorce case, your thoughts naturally turn to the case much of the time. You are talking with your lawyers, obtaining documents, reviewing material provided by your lawyer, and spending time thinking about it and dealing with it. You're emotionally drained as well. All these things take a toll on your work performance. You are spending time on the divorce and not your business. You are therefore not going to pay as much attention to your business and career as you should, and this impact mounts over time.

THE COST-BENEFIT ANALYSIS (AND HOW TO MAKE ONE YOURSELF)

Until you assign price tags to them, the costs of a divorce case are theoretical and hard to visualize. That's why you should do a cost-benefit analysis in your case. Now that you know the financial, emotional, and practical costs of divorce, compare potential settlement to a likely trial result. What deal should you offer? What's the deal already on the table? What's the cost of just getting this done versus fighting tooth and nail?

First, Assess the Proposed Deal on the Table

1. **Compile an accurate data set and understand it.** Make sure you understand the assets and liabilities. To perform a useful cost-benefit analysis, you need accurate data. Current balances for all assets and liabilities are needed. (We will discuss dissipation or waste of marital assets below.) These should be input into a spreadsheet or dedicated divorce

financial software like Family Law Software. Every value should be tied to a statement or screenshot to confirm that the number is accurate. Data will change over time as balances change, or the stock market fluctuates, but you will be able to update all figures right before the final date of divorce. The key is whether the data are accurate enough to analyze.

2. **Determine the proposed asset splits on the table.** List your proposal compared to your spouse's proposal. For this example, assume a $5 million marital estate.

> Your proposal: 50/50 = $2.5 million per person
> Their proposal: 60/40 = $2 million for you, $3 million for your spouse
> The difference ("delta") = $500,000. That is, their deal is $500,000 worse for you than your proposal.

3. **If you disagree about asset values, factor in the delta between those numbers.** For example, with a business valuation by two expert witnesses, there will be two opinions of value submitted to the court. Business valuation is an art and a science, and there are many methods used to value a business. This is discussed in much more detail in Chapter 12. The important takeaway is that the valuation is rarely just "book value" or a simple "assets minus liabilities" balance sheet calculation. Valuation can include intangibles like goodwill and can be based on sales of similar businesses or cash flow. Typically, the court will go with one expert's opinion or the other and will not split the difference. Be honest with yourself. Spend time discussing at length with your lawyer and valuation expert the strengths and weaknesses of their opinion of value versus the other expert's number. This could increase the "delta" between your proposal and theirs even more.

Using the above example, we will add in a dispute about business value. Assume one of the assets is a business, and assume both experts are equally qualified. The following happens, which is quite common:

> Your expert values the business at $800,000.
> Their expert values the business at $1.2 million.

Neither you nor your spouse knows for sure which expert the court will agree with (or find more credible), but you can have some confidence it will be one or the other number. (In Illinois, there is case law requiring that the court select one of the numbers and not split the difference.) If you settle, you could use one or the other of these values, but more likely, you would compromise and choose a number between the two.

You now have two things affecting the delta in this case. First, following our scenario, your spouse wants more than half the estate. Second, they think the overall estate is worth more than you do. So using the example, you think the estate is worth $5 million, and you want a fifty-fifty split, yet your spouse thinks the total estate is worth $5.4 million and wants a sixty-forty split (with 40 percent to you).

In this scenario, the delta becomes

40% of $5,400,000 = $2,160,000 to 50% of 5,000,000 = $2,500,000, for a total delta of $340,000.

Important note: One of the real problems here is the cash versus business value problem. If you are the primary business owner, the court will award the business to you in the divorce. The court will not force a divorced couple to own a business together. Therefore, you will have to exchange cash and other assets for the business. If the court assigns a higher value than is reasonable, especially one based on intangibles like goodwill, you are trading real assets for intangibles. For example, if you think the business is worth $800,000 in this scenario, but the court finds it is worth $1.2 million, that $400,000 difference means you will be giving your spouse

$200,000 more in real assets (in a fifty/fifty split). This issue can also arise with real estate and similar valuations where asset values are disputed. The one advantage with real estate is that if the parties cannot agree on a value, the court typically orders the property sold and the proceeds divided. A court will not force the sale of a business.

4. **Consider your realistic chances of success at trial.** Consult with your lawyer on the expected range of outcomes. You should look at a best case, worst case, and a most likely "middle" case. What are the dollar values you reasonably expect from the asset-liability split at trial? There may be other issues to consider here, such as alimony. Is there a disagreement about whether your spouse would qualify for alimony in the first place? A debate about incomes that would swing the alimony number? How long will you be expected to pay alimony? Another consideration is dissipation or waste of assets. What are the chances that your spouse will prove dissipation of assets and in what amount?

   The best case for you will be a fifty-fifty split of $5 million, or $2.5 million for you; the worst case will be a high of a sixty-forty split of $5 million, or $2 million for you.

   Two outcome ranges: 50/50 or 60/40 of $5 million or 50/50 or 60/40 of $5.4 million.

   Trial outcome range 1: business valued at $800,000 = either $2.5 million (50/50) or $2 million (60/40 with 40% to you)

   Trial outcome range 2: business valued at $1.2 million = either $2.7 million (50/50) or $2.16 million (60/40 with 40% to you)

5. **Consider the fees required to get to trial from today.** The fees you've paid already are sunk costs. For this example, let's figure that going forward, you will spend $100,000 to finish discovery and try the case. Recall that the fees need to be approximately doubled because your spouse's fees

are paid from the marital estate as well. So the attorney fees number is $200,000 in this example.

6. **Consider the cash burn-excess living expense spending.** This is your and your spouse's extra monthly expenses during the divorce for however many months to get to completion. Again, prior cash spent is a sunk cost and not worth examining at this point. Assume, for this example, six months to get to trial, and you are spending about $10,000 per month more than normal. Total excess cash burn is $60,000.

7. **Add the legal fees to the extra expenses over the time required.** This is the total cost to get to trial. This is a "hard" number. You will spend this amount for sure if you go to trial, win or lose.

    Projected fees + excess cash burn = $260,000

8. **Add the additional expense total to your projected trial outcome (your best-case to worst-case scenario range), and compare that to settlement deals on the table.**

    Trial outcome 1: $5,000,000 - $260,000 x 50% (50/50) = $2,370,000

    Or: $5,000,000 - $260,000 x 40% (60/40) = $1,896,000

    Trial outcome 2: $5,400,000 - $260,000 x 50% (50/50) = $2,570,000

    Or: $5,400,000 - $260,000 x 40% (60/40) = $2,056,000

    You can see that your soon-to-be-ex's proposed settlement offer of $2,160,000 for you is within the range of potential trial outcomes when you subtract attorney's fees and cash burn. And we haven't even included lost productivity at work or emotional cost in this analysis.

9. **Consider the probability of an appeal filed by you or your ex, plus the attendant cost in time and money.** Sometimes, a trial court decision is binary (win/loss), such as with custody litigation. Think relocation of children out of state or a ruling that a valuable piece of property is marital

or nonmarital, which could dramatically swing the value of the marital estate. In that case, it's likely that one of you will file an appeal. It's difficult to estimate the chances of success for any appeal at the pretrial stage because you have no idea what the basis of the appeal will be at this point.

Regardless of reason, estimate that the legal fees for an appeal will be $25,000 to $50,000 per side and will add six months to a year to the total time.

10. **Consider dissipation of marital assets.** Depending on your state law, you or your spouse may have a claim for dissipation of marital assets. These claims are demands for reimbursement to the marriage of money improperly spent outside the marriage (for example, on a significant other). In my state, these claims are tightly circumscribed by state law. Illinois basically has a statute of limitations on these claims. Courts don't like them, and they are hard to prove anyway. If there is a claim, assess the amount of the claim and the likelihood that it will be proven. Then remember that a dissipation claim is reduced by the final split of the assets. For example, in a fifty-fifty split, a dissipation claim of $50,000 that is successfully proven against you will cost you $25,000, because half the money spent was already "yours." Consider the value of these claims and probability of success.

11. **Consider alimony.** Depending on your state, alimony might come up in the case. In Illinois, alimony is computed using a formula. State laws on alimony vary widely. Based on your state law and the facts in your case, determine the probability that alimony will be ordered, consider the amount (or range of amounts) in question, and add that to your calculations. An alimony buyout might be on the table as a settlement option. If that is the case, weigh the total amount of potential alimony over the length of time it may be ordered (e.g., $50,000 per year over ten years), then run a present-value calculation to establish what that stream of income is worth today. The discount rate is a frequent bone of contention here;

it can make a big difference in the present-value calculation. A discount rate is calculating interest in reverse: for example, $100,000 paid today is worth more than $100,000 paid over ten years, which is why lottery winners are paid much less when they opt for a lump-sum payment. Then consider a "fudge factor" for things going wrong. As in what if the alimony payer gets fired or dies, or the payee gets married, or alimony otherwise would terminate? This adds a discount to a present value buyout as well. Generally speaking, if longer-term alimony is a possibility, the payer does not want to buy out the payee, as too many variables make this a risky course of action.

DAVE'S STORY, CONTINUED (AGAIN)

As you can see, it's critically important to take the four costs of divorce into account and keep them top of mind. When making decisions about your case, consider legal fees and litigation expenses, the cash burn rate, and the emotional cost of divorce, as well as the impact on your business.

Carly realized this too late. We settled the case after she finally understood those other costs beyond fees. She was previously insulated from those costs. Dave was "paying" all the fees, and Carly did not realize the marital assets were being spent at an alarming rate.

After the divorce, Dave rebuilt his life and started a new business. He's been successful, and he's happily remarried. Carly, on the other hand, is still paying off the credit cards and owes her lawyers over $200,000. Unfortunately for her, she lost sight of the big picture and this cost Carly in a big way.

I JUST WANT THIS DONE

CHAPTER 10

STAGES OF GRIEF AND THE DECOUPLING MINDSET

I felt dejected. I sat alone in a huge conference room at the opposing lawyer's fancy downtown law firm. I stared down at Lake Michigan. It was a gorgeous view. Ripples on the water in the harbor and on the Chicago River reflected the late afternoon sun. The yachts bobbed rhythmically at anchor in the harbor. Sailboats traced glowing wakes near the horizon.

I wished I could have been anywhere but sitting in that room. My fingers drummed the glass table. My notes screamed up at me.

Kill the Deal?

I could see my client, Tom, and his divorce coach through the ten-foot high glass conference room walls. Tom was standing in the hallway, head down, wringing his hands and talking quietly with his divorce coach. Tears streamed down his cheeks. We had just reached a tentative settlement in Tom's collaborative divorce case, and Tom was freaking out. It was one of the best deals I'd ever seen a divorcing spouse offer.

In this case, the one who had decided to leave the marriage was Tom's wife, Susan. They had been married for twenty-five years. Susan was a successful corporate C-suite executive and made a huge salary with nice benefits. She traveled a sizable portion of the year for work. Tom had quit his career as an insurance salesperson to care for their children when Susan's career took off. They had amassed an investment portfolio worth multiple millions. Susan's 401(k alone was worth over $1.5 million, and their first house and their vacation home were worth a combined $2 million.

With only one child still in college, Tom and Susan had been looking at spending their golden years alone together. Susan cringed at the idea. Tom played golf every day, worked on his tan, refused to return to the workforce, and argued with her about little things like household chores. Susan was the breadwinner and felt like her husband was the "bread loser." To Susan, Tom was an unequal partner. She earned; he spent. Sure, he was a nice guy and a good father, but she wanted more from the person with whom she would spend the rest of her life. Tom was a good man, but he was emotionally paralyzed.

What Tom and Susan both had going for them was a collaborative "full team." Both parties had divorce coaches and a financial neutral: a certified financial planner who reviewed all of the key financial records, prepared a balance sheet, modeled alimony, and guided everyone through the financial portion of the divorce. Everyone could have faith in the figures because the financial neutral did not work for either party's lawyer. In collaborative cases, having these professionals can be a huge benefit, making the case move much more smoothly toward a resolution and in less time, offsetting the additional expense.

Together, we made progress. Several meetings in, we understood the financials and agreed on asset division and alimony. We reached a verbal settlement agreement. Tom and I discussed at length scenarios about how he would live. We looked at Tom's bills and compared them to the alimony amount and his portion of the marital assets. It would all work out fine for him—his wife was more than fair.

We went over the terms again with the team present in the glass conference room. This was slated to be our final meeting to wrap up the case. At the outset, Tom was in good spirits. He'd been exercising and eating right for the first time in years. As the meeting progressed, he furrowed his brow, twisted the balance sheet and alimony calculation worksheet in his hands, and nervously glanced around the room. I asked for a break and pulled his coach aside.

"Please talk to Tom—he's melting down," I whispered.

The wife, her attorney, the other coach, and the neutral left the room. Tom dragged himself into the hallway behind his coach. I scribbled on my notepad the costly decision I couldn't believe Tom was about to make—killing the best deal his wife could have offered.

In divorce, emotions are everything. But they're not all things to all parties. Typically, one divorcing spouse is "ready" to leave the marriage. The other may not be. Certainly, they're further behind. That was Tom. Susan would have been happy to cut ties after the first meeting. Write up the settlement, sign the paperwork, and be done with it. As soon as possible.

Tom was stuck in neutral. He was the "slowest common denominator." Because you're reading this book, you're probably the Susan in your relationship. You just want this done. Your soon-to-be-ex doesn't want this over or at least, not yet. They're coping with the past, and you're looking to the future.

It's rare that two divorcing partners are in the same emotional position at any point. Typically, one person has been thinking about the divorce for a longer period of time and has decided to move forward after much deliberation. Maybe they have had a counselor or therapist; maybe they have talked with friends and family. They are emotionally prepared for the divorce case.

The other person, however, is not as prepared. Maybe they understand the other spouse wants a divorce, but they are scared about the situation and refuse to deal with it.

Fear of change mirrors a concept you've heard of before—the stages of grief. Psychiatrist Elizabeth Kubler-Ross in her book *On Death and Dying* addressed the five stages of grief: denial, anger, bargaining, depression, acceptance. She theorized that everyone goes through these stages when the near and dear pass away. Since publication, her theory has been broadened to other emotionally challenging life events, including divorce.

No two people grieve the same way. Kubler-Ross emphasized that not all people go through the stages in the same order. Some may cycle back and forth between stages or even skip a stage. In divorce, one person has usually proceeded through all the stages (likely well before the divorce was even filed). The other spouse has not had the chance to process their emotions. Therefore, it takes time for the "later" spouse to make it through the stages of grief. This can cause divorce cases like Tom and Susan's to stall. Or worse, collapse into expensive and unnecessary litigation.

Visualize a bridge. In divorce, one person is farther across the bridge to post-married life than the other spouse. When the two are far apart on the bridge, things don't go well.

Can the "slower" spouse delay—or stop—the divorce?

DIVORCE IN STAGES

Every divorce includes the grieving stage known as denial. Some people believe they can prevent the divorce for any number of reasons. They genuinely want to stay married. They are afraid of how the kids will react. They are comfortable with the family and financial situation. They don't want change—and people in general don't like change. So they may try to delay a divorce case through litigation. They might instruct their lawyer to take their time and not move quickly with the case, filing documents on the last day, not providing responses to discovery quickly, and generally dragging their feet as much as possible.

But a divorce case cannot be stopped unless the person filing stops the process. If one spouse wants to get a divorce, it will eventually happen. The judge won't allow the case to drag on forever.

In my experience, the person who did not choose to file for divorce eventually realizes they are, in fact, also fine with getting a divorce. They have gone through the stages of grief, come out on the other side, and are emotionally ready. One question I like to ask when talking to the grieving person is "Why do you want to be with someone who doesn't love you?"

If you have taken the time to research lawyers online or talked to people to get a referral, called a law firm, and visited with a lawyer for a consultation, chances are you are going to get divorced. Many times, people will come in to talk with us, and they are "just looking into" getting divorced. By the time someone has gone to the trouble of thinking about it and had a consultation with a divorce lawyer, it is only a matter of time. To make the effort takes quite a bit of thought and means you have come a long way across the bridge, perhaps to acceptance. You may well cycle back to one or more of the stages of grief, but odds are if you are "kicking the tires," you are highly likely to get a divorce.

THE SLOWEST COMMON DENOMINATOR

Remember that no matter what you want, divorce goes as fast as the slower partner making their way across the bridge. They have to wrap their heads around getting divorced in the first place and secondly, any potential settlement. This can be the result of a less trusting person needing an extensive investigation into assets and income—the less financially knowledgeable spouse, for example, may want their attorney to do a detailed investigation into family finances while the more financially savvy spouse thinks such an investigation is a waste of time and money. The bottom line is that the "slower" person needs to satisfy themselves that they are getting a fair deal before entering into any agreement. When a party is moving slowly, it is useful to try to determine why that may be. It is also possible that you or your lawyer are delaying the process by not providing needed documents, for example.

DON'T PUSH THE ROPE

This is what happens in divorce cases when the client asks, "Why can't we just move this case along and get it done?" Sometimes, pushing a divorce case is like pushing a rope from one end: you pile up the rope and make no progress. Whether a divorce process is negotiated or litigated, it takes a certain amount of time. If you are in court, the court will allow time for the process to take place and generally will not hurry the parties to a trial. This is because of the concept of equity (fairness) overarching divorce proceedings, making the court want to be sure that each party is treated fairly, that all the issues are considered at trial, and all the relevant evidence is presented. The trial judge also wishes to avoid appeals, where finality of a divorce is delayed, and parties spend more time and money trying to rectify a mistake (real or perceived) in the process. No trial judge wants to be second-guessed by an appellate court and have their decision reversed, especially if the reversal is based on a claim that the court did not consider all the evidence.

Trying to accelerate the process is difficult at best and sometimes has a rebound effect that delays or derails progress. The other party may not be as far along on the "bridge," and they may attempt to block progress consciously or subconsciously. Understand that pushing the gas pedal requires energy: to push a settlement meeting, file a motion or petition with the court, request and take depositions, and schedule the case for trial. These actions cost money. It is important to balance the potential benefit of accelerating the process (and realistic chance you will succeed in speeding up the process) with the associated costs.

ADOPT THE CONSCIOUS UNCOUPLING MINDSET

If you adopt the "conscious uncoupling" mindset (made famous by Gwyneth Paltrow in her divorce from Chris Martin) you are likely to do better, and so will your children. Katharine Woodward Thomas coined the term "conscious uncoupling" in 2009 and began teaching her mindset about divorce to students. In 2014, when Paltrow was getting divorced, she found the concept useful. She wanted to avoid the worst outcome for her children, which was she and Martin not getting along. She wanted to minimize the negativity and acrimony that can happen between parents in divorce. The concept is to see divorce on a continuum with marriage, and the goal is to maintain mutual respect between the couple and keep the best interests of the children front and center. Understanding that marriage as a lifetime thing may not be possible or realistic and that you can respect your former spouse and have a good relationship with them is good for you and your children. You are still a family with your children, even though you are getting divorced. This is not always possible, of course, and you can only control the way *you* approach the divorce, but the way you deal with it has a substantial impact.

The sooner you are able to detach and uncouple from your spouse but maintain a good relationship, the sooner you will be on the path to healing and progressing through the stages of grief. And if you are self-reflective about your part in the marriage (and its failure), you have a much better chance at a more fulfilling long-term relationship in the future.

It takes two people to get married, and it takes two people to get divorced. It is a rare case in which one person is 100 percent at fault for a divorce. Keep things in perspective. Be realistic. Understand and acknowledge your role both in the marriage and in the divorce. Knowing that will help you uncouple more smoothly, temper harsh judgments about your spouse, and shape your future relationships in a healthy way.

WHEN EMOTIONS TAKE THE WHEEL

If everybody was perfect, divorce lawyers would be out of a job. But people are not. They are emotional creatures. Many people latch onto things based on emotions, rather than logic. This is why some trials happen: not because it makes sense from a cost-benefit standpoint but because emotions are driving the bus. Some people are not willing to concede things that aren't objectively important but that they hold on to for emotional reasons.

Divorcing spouses also fight over sixteen-year-old children with regard to parenting time, when the sixteen-year-old can drive and has a mind of their own. I once resolved a settlement when two people were fighting over furniture by offering to cover the $150 gap myself out of my wallet. Embarrassed, they gave up and settled.

If people used cost-benefit analysis and looked at the true differences—considered what was acceptable rather than what was fair (as fair is a relative concept)—more cases would settle sooner, and the four costs would be much lower.

When you are scared, upset, angry, or otherwise emotional, your animal brain is working, not your logical brain. Things that otherwise make perfect sense are overlooked or ignored. Clients ignore a good deal that may be staring them in the face. People make dumb decisions when they aren't able to think straight. It is always best to view your case rationally and switch your mindset from the "animal brain" to the logical way of thinking.

WALK IN THEIR SHOES

For a moment, imagine that you are your spouse, and try to look at the case from their point of view. Shifting your perspective will help you dramatically in negotiations. I routinely ask my clients about their spouse's personality, motivations, needs, and wants. Since they've been married a long time in most cases, people have a good idea of these things about their spouse. Are they linear thinkers; are they creative; are they stubborn, accepting, emotional, or practical? Understanding how your spouse sees things and knowing their personality type and motivations can go a long way in understanding how they will react in negotiations and in litigation.

CAN YOU FIND THE MIDDLE?

One of the most rewarding aspects of negotiation is finding a creative way to meet the needs of both parties. This means figuring out how to locate the settlement in the sweet spot of the Venn diagram, in the space where the circles overlap. Can the result be acceptable to both people and also meet their goals? Many times, a creative solution can be engineered that will reach a happy medium between what both parties need. Solving the problems of both people while meeting their goals in a reasonable way is the best outcome.

CREATIVE SOLUTIONS TO KEEP THE HOUSE

For example, many times one person wants to "keep the house," and the other person wants to sell, or there is a debate about the correct value of the home. Perhaps one parent wants the kids to stay in the house for a period of time, and this is why they want to keep the home. This can be a major obstacle to a settlement.

People often latch onto the house because that's where the children grew up, even though keeping the home would mean financial hardship. They fight over furniture even though the actual cash value of the fifteen-year-old bedroom set is negligible now. The mortgage is not the only cost. Upkeep, physical work required, taxes, roof, HVAC, et cetera. Memories are in your head, not your house. Have you considered the value of the freedom to move? Many divorcing people are at or near a life crossroads anyway (kids going to college, etc.), and taking the opportunity to downsize makes sense.

A creative solution may be to keep the house until the youngest child graduates high school and then agree to sell it at that point. You can work out the details of joint ownership prior to sale and determine in the settlement agreement how the property will be sold. This meets both parties' goals in that the home will be sold, getting a market price and releasing both from the liability for the mortgage while giving the children a smooth transition since they don't have to leave until they are done with high school.

NONVIOLENT COMMUNICATION MIGHT HELP

Nonviolent communication (NVC) was pioneered by Marshall Rosenberg in the 1960s, as explained in his book *Nonviolent Communication: A Language of Life.* The concept is to avoid arguing by expressing your desires and needs in a way that does not make the other party feel attacked and defensive. It is a book worth reading and a technique I find useful.

I first learned about NVC in a seminar related to collaborative practice. It is a communication process that is useful in negotiations and in talking with anyone where a conflict might arise. The basic idea is that all human emotions come from needs being met or not met. More importantly, all humans have the same needs (at different times), and therefore emotions are universally shared by all people, generally speaking. For example, if you have a broken window, you have a need to feel safe, so you might feel worried or insecure thinking that a burglar might enter your home.

In a negotiation, people have a need to be heard and understood, to be respected. If the other party is not listening or is talking over them, the speaker feels disrespected and not heard and is not likely to respond well or be willing to negotiate. The key is empathetic listening: hearing what the other person says without judgment, snide comments, or nasty looks. It also involves expressing your thoughts using facts, not opinions. ("Your annual income is eight hundred thousand dollars" instead of "You made a stupid amount of money last year!") Then expressing your requests (which are open ended and leave room for the other person to say no) and explaining them in the context of your needs and feelings. "I would feel much more secure financially if you were able to pay me six more months of support. I am feeling vulnerable right now since the ongoing expenses are X, and my income is only Y," as opposed to "You *need* to pay me six more months of support." With NVC, you are more likely to smoothly move through difficult conversations. I've used NVC techniques successfully in many settlement negotiations. I have also coached my clients in NVC to help them better speak with their spouses.

TOM'S STORY, CONTINUED

Tom talked with his coach about the proposed deal and his fears about being on his own. The coach calmed him down in the hallway, and they came back into the conference room. We talked again about the settlement proposal. I showed him how he would be able to cover his expenses with the income from investments, alimony, and even a small part-time job and not touch any investment principal. We talked about the costs of divorce, especially if he went to litigation, and I told him that the possible outcomes in court were worse than those on the table at that time.

Once he had calmed down and was able to use his rational brain, he saw that the deal was as good as it was going to get and more than acceptable. We settled the case.

I JUST WANT THIS DONE

CHAPTER 11

THE VALUE OF
DIVORCE COACHES

Krissy was beside herself. She'd just found out that her husband, Marc, had spent a week at the family vacation home in Florida with his girlfriend . . . without telling her. She only learned when the neighbors texted her about a strange woman they didn't recognize cavorting around with Marc, playing loud music and splashing around in their pool.

Marc couldn't explain himself—in fact, he acted surprised that Krissy was upset about it. (One of the issues in the marriage was Marc's difficulty with empathy.) What was the big deal? To Marc, it was *his* vacation home. He was a senior executive for a multinational manufacturing company; Krissy was a stay-at-home mom. The family certainly wasn't going to be using the place anytime soon again, Marc figured. His cavalier attitude only made Krissy more angry. She was upset because she had caught Marc cheating on her with the same woman. The Florida place was supposed to be their retirement home, before all this happened.

The divorce case had reached a critical stage in negotiations. I represented Krissy in what had been a collaborative divorce. After dividing up assets, we were about to discuss alimony and child support. Marc spending time with his girlfriend at the Florida place where many family memories were made caused Krissy to be angry all over again. Understandably, Krissy was in no mood to talk about alimony. She wanted to reverse the progress we'd made and sue Marc in court. To punish him.

I feared the deal we'd worked hard to put together was about to fall apart. I was talking with Krissy to calm her down, but we also had divorce coaches involved like we did in Tom's case.

WHAT'S A DIVORCE COACH?

The American Bar Association defines the role of divorce coaches. Their website states:

> Divorce coaching is a flexible, goal-oriented process designed to support, motivate, and guide people going through divorce to help them make the best possible decisions for their future, based on their particular interests, needs, and concerns. Divorce coaches have different professional backgrounds and are selected based on the specific needs of the clients. For example, some divorce coaches are financial planners, mental health professionals, lawyers, or mediators who have experience dealing with divorcing clients.[5]

Divorce coaches assist the parties with communication with their attorneys, each other, their children, and others. They help the parties like Tom and Krissy deal with their emotions and the stages of grief.

---

5   "Divorce Coaching," The American Bar Association, www.americanbar.org/groups/dispute_resolution/resources/DisputeResolutionProcesses/divorce_coaching/.

They help resolve concerns the parties have with the divorce process and misunderstandings that may occur with their attorneys.

People from many professions provide advice to those going through divorce, and that advice can be very valuable. Accountants, estate-planning lawyers, business attorneys, and other such professionals can provide valuable divorce-related advice.

However, such advice is different from divorce coaching services. Trained divorce coaches can help in any divorce context, whether before, during, or after and whether the case is in litigation, mediation, or collaborative practice. They help with concerns about communicating, future-casting, and visualizing life on the other side. And they can help people like Krissy and Tom get unstuck. Not every coach is perfect, so be careful to choose good ones. Bad ones can be a bad thing, just like a bad lawyer.

Divorce coaching arose out of the collaborative law movement. Coaches quickly found a valuable role in divorce, helping clients process their feelings, work through the grief, adjust to changing family dynamics, and understand the divorce process and translating "lawyer speak" for their clients.

I respect qualified divorce coaching professionals. They're incredibly valuable to the Toms and Krissys of the world and their spouses who don't understand what they're going through. A spouse's inability to manage emotions during a divorce can drive litigation.

Despite the nature of their work, coaches are not "shrinks." They are not treating psychological issues, providing therapy, or prescribing anything. Their role is specific and directly linked to the divorce. Coaches help people move from point A to point B in the divorce to get it done. The coach is an advocate for their client but also teaches them to be realistic.

For example, a coach may have an extended discussion with a client afraid of moving out of the family home. The coach might talk about options—where the person might live, how that might feel, and what the kids would think. This is not legal advice yet is still a valuable contribution.

My experience with divorce coaches has revolved around them in the collaborative model, so I concentrate on that here. In collaborative practice, there are a few ways coaches work with the clients, families, lawyers, and other professionals involved.

Not all coaches are great. Just like choosing an attorney, make an effort to find the right coach by getting personal referrals and checking reviews.

COACHING MODELS IN COLLABORATIVE LAW

The two-coach model. Each party has a coach. In the "full team" model, the coaches come to every team meeting where the parties are present. They help the parties process what is going on and are there to move the client out of the room in case of a misunderstanding or an emotional outburst. (Remember Tom?) In some cases, the parties might not feel they need to have the coaches at every meeting, so they only come to the most crucial meetings.

The one-coach model. In this model, the parties agree on a shared coach. Since they are not receiving therapy but coaching, this can work well for people who have communication issues and difficulties between them. They can have meetings with the coach present, or the coach can talk with them on the phone or on video to help them deal with problems that inevitably arise. Sometimes both people want their own coach, so a shared coach may work best with couples who still have a working relationship. Again, the coach may come to all or some of the meetings.

The "fire extinguisher" model. I borrowed this term from my good friend, collaborative divorce lawyer Theresa Kulat. The parties contact coaches and interview them to find one they like but have them on standby in the event that either person melts down or the parties get stuck. In this model, no coaches appear at the meetings unless the parties feel that it is necessary.

As you saw in Tom's case, the coach was critical to salvaging what was a good deal for him. Coaches can help you and your spouse in this manner, too. They can also help you understand what your divorce lawyer is saying and build confidence in your lawyer's advice. You have another pair of eyes and ears listening to the critical parts of the case. And because they're not emotionally invested in the outcome, they can process the information better than you can. Qualified divorce coaches are a valuable resource.

KRISSY'S STORY, CONTINUED

Krissy needed to be helped through the anger she felt about her husband rubbing her nose in his affair. Her coach—and the husband's coach—spent an hour before every collaborative meeting with the clients, working on these issues.

The coaches helped Krissy and Marc work through the issues with the girlfriend and the children, and they were able to make progress and be productive in the settlement meetings. Without the coaches' involvement, the case would have ended up in court. Instead, happily, the case was settled out of court successfully.

I JUST WANT THIS DONE

CHAPTER 12

OWNING A BUSINESS: WHAT HAPPENS WHEN SHE (OR HE) WANTS OUT?

B usiness law and family law overlap when one of the parties to a divorce owns part of a business and the marriage ends. A perfect example of this situation is the story of Ron and his wife, Kristi.

"There is *no way* I can afford to buy her out! The divorce will bankrupt the company!" Ron said, the strain crackling over the phone.

Ron owned a multimillion-dollar manufacturing business, which he'd started five years into the marriage. We were in the middle of settlement negotiations, and he was concerned for his financial future. He knew he would have to pay his soon-to-be-ex alimony. I had just explained to Ron why he would have to pay her for her share of the company.

"But her name is nowhere on the business! I've done all the work!" Ron said.

"I know, but the business is a marital asset, just as if it were a house you bought during the marriage. The law says she is entitled to half."

Ron fell silent. I heard a table saw slice through wood in the background on the phone. An air wrench made a high-pitched whine, like when pit crews change race car tires.

"Your wife's lawyer knows what the law says. That doesn't mean a judge can bankrupt you. They can't. Her lawyer just wants to make sure she gets her half of the value. Nobody wants to ruin the business. Your wife needs the business alive and thriving, or neither of you gets anything," I said.

"What's your suggestion?" Ron asked.

I addressed the fears of every business owner in the midst of divorce. "No, you don't need to sell your business, and, no, you won't lose majority control either."

The best tactic for a business owner in this situation has two parts: collaboration and transparency.

Collaboration in this instance is the business owner, accountant, bookkeeper, and business attorney working to help the divorce lawyer understand how the business has operated historically and the financials behind the business. The attorney must understand how the business works in order to properly handle the issues related to it in the case. It also means early and close coordination with a business valuation expert.

Transparency means providing the financial data for the business as soon as possible, not holding anything back. Don't think you can hide anything or limit disclosure. This only gets the other attorney excited—and ready to charge your separated spouse more for more work, and the marriage pays both lawyers. The sooner you provide company documents and data, the better.

Your spouse's lawyer will be energized, not upset, when you try to resist producing documents. This means the lawyer can justify big fees to your spouse and an even more intense examination. What's worse, you start losing the meta case. If the other lawyer can tell your spouse you can't be trusted with the business documents, what else might you be hiding? So be forthcoming. Make your employees available to the other attorney. Be an open book—otherwise, you risk going into a months-long discovery spiral. If you just want this done, help by getting your part of disclosure done. If you obstruct the investigation, this will just fuel the fire, and the opposing counsel will run to court asking for more and more information. They can even make you pay for it out of your pocket, as opposed to the fees being paid with joint marital assets.

Also, cooperate with any questioning. If counsel retains a business valuation expert, and they perform a full valuation rather than a calculation of value (defined shortly), they will need to interview you and any applicable senior officers (e.g., CEO, COO, CFO). The sooner you agree to sit down for a management interview (or consent to having your team meet with the valuation expert), the faster the expert's analysis will be complete. Preparation for this meeting is smart and should be done with your attorney and your own valuation expert in advance.

What happens to your business following divorce depends on whether it is a marital or nonmarital asset. Recall that only marital property is subject to division. Many times, a business interest is preexisting when the marriage begins. In that case, the business is likely nonmarital property (unless you added your spouse as an owner at some point) and thus not subject to division. If you have a prenuptial agreement, this will likely govern how a business is handled in the event of divorce. Even without a prenup, if you started or obtained your ownership interest in a business before the marriage, it is more than likely nonmarital property and not subject to division. Note that your specific situation may vary. If you acquired the ownership interest before marriage but paid for a portion of it during the marriage with marital property (e.g., income or other marital assets), then you will likely owe at least reimbursement to the marriage for those funds.

WHAT HAPPENS WHEN YOUR SPOUSE IS ALSO A SHAREHOLDER?

When your spouse is a shareholder, look at the facts. Did your spouse have their interest before the marriage, making it potentially their nonmarital property? Did you give partial ownership to your spouse, or did they purchase a share? If your spouse acquired their interest during the marriage, it's typically marital property.

Here's an example. Lilly forms a business before marriage. After marrying Pedro, she decides to make him a 50 percent owner of the business. She transfers 50 percent of the stock to him in a paper transaction. They split all distributions and dividends in following years. The business is 50 percent Lilly's nonmarital property, and the other 50 percent is Pedro's nonmarital property as it was gifted to him. Therefore, the business is owned equally by the couple.

Here's a slightly different scenario. Let's say Pedro used marital assets to buy his 50 percent share from Lilly. His portion is still marital property, but his 50 percent is subject to division. Therefore, in an equal-asset-split scenario, if Lilly were to keep the business, she would need to buy Pedro out of 25 percent.

In no scenario will Lilly, Pedro, or anyone be forced to continue working with their ex-spouse. Courts seek finality in divorce and don't want to make divorcing parties work together in a business. In the vast majority of cases, it is clear which spouse is the active business owner, and the court prefers to award the business to that person and require a buyout of the other spouse's ownership.

If your separated partner is employed by the company, keep them employed during the case if at all possible. If you terminate their employment, you might create the basis for an employment law claim, and you will certainly motivate the spouse to seek temporary alimony and child support. You also look like a jerk and damage your image in the meta case—and possibly your brand in the marketplace. Better to leave them on the payroll until the case is resolved or the job situation is otherwise sorted out. If you can't get along, or you don't trust them, place them on a paid leave of absence. Obviously, this depends on the cost-benefit analysis. If they are in a key role or have a large compensation package, the best decision may be different.

VALUING YOUR BUSINESS

Business valuation is complex. Entire books exist on this one topic. For the purposes of this book, the following is a 36,000-foot overview for the business owner going through divorce.

There are professional business valuation experts (similar to real estate appraisers) who have certifications and training in this field. They perform two distinct levels of analysis regarding valuing businesses: calculations of value and business valuations.

A **calculation of value** is an estimated value based on a document review. It is faster and less expensive and provides a good overall idea of value. The person hiring the expert determines the approach and method the expert will use to value the business, and the expert applies that method to arrive at a calculation of value. A calculation of value can be useful in a case in which the parties already have a fairly good idea of the value but want to double-check or are looking for a "ball-park" estimate. The calculation uses easily available financial records but does not include management interviews or a deep dive analysis into financials. It is less expensive and faster. At the time of this writing, a calculation might cost $5,000 to $10,000, while a full valuation might cost $20,000 to $30,000, for example. Since a calculation of value is more of an overview and less precise, many valuation professionals will not testify to a business value using a calculation, although they have been admitted into evidence as probative of business value in divorce cases in some states and other types of cases in federal court. A calculation of value report is not an independent appraisal report. This is one reason a calculation of value report may not be viewed credibly by the court. However, it can be useful for nondisclosed settlement discussions or getting a "ballpark" estimate as discussed above.

A **business valuation** involves a far more in-depth analysis of the company's financials, including source documents such as ledgers, bank records, and more. Significantly, the expert is permitted to determine what valuation approach and methods they see fit to apply to the given business, rather than this being dictated by the hiring party. The valuation includes management interviews and sometimes a plant/office visit to verify the existence and extent of facilities, equipment, and inventory. While more expensive and time consuming, this is the level of analysis required if you expect to offer a solid valuation opinion into evidence at trial. Some valuation experts will refuse to testify at trial regarding calculations of value, believing that they are not created for the purpose of litigation and are not precise enough. While calculations of value have been admitted into evidence in divorce matters (and other cases, such as commercial litigation), they lack weight because of the limitations of the underlying data and the narrow scope of analysis and are therefore subject to attack by the other party on those grounds.

Use of calculations versus full valuations involves the "weight versus admissibility" issue with evidence in court. Just because a court allows evidence to be admitted and will consider it does not mean it thinks the evidence is convincing (has "weight"). This is why you must consider how the evidence will be used in a case before engaging the expert. If a trial opinion is needed, it is best to spend the money and effort needed to secure a full valuation.

THE BEST TACTIC: DETERMINE BUSINESS VALUE *AND* ATTACK THE OTHER EXPERT'S CONCLUSION

When engaging an expert, carefully define the scope of work and be sure that the expert is aware that their opinion will be used in litigation. The care and attention paid (and the cost) will increase, but it will be worth the trouble to ensure good results for settlement negotiations or trial, should that be necessary. Also, be sure that the expert is engaged to critique the other expert's report and that there is ample time in the case discovery and disclosure schedule for them to perform this critique and to prepare their own report attacking the conclusions. Otherwise, it is likely that the court will not allow your expert to opine about any failings of the other expert's work at trial. It is important that you, as a business owner in a divorce, work with your attorney as soon as possible to discuss the needs of your valuation expert. The more time your business valuation expert has, the better they will be able to articulate a sound argument for their opinion of value.

HOW BUSINESSES ARE VALUED

There are three approaches to appraising a business: the asset approach, the market approach, and the income approach. The asset approach is useful to value holding companies and companies that have marginal or negative earnings. The other two approaches are generally considered for going concerns (i.e., profitable businesses).

The **asset approach** is based on your company's balance sheet, assuming an orderly liquidation or realization of those assets into cash. The net value after paying all third-party debt constitutes the company's value.

The **market approach** compares your company to either publicly traded companies or purchases of companies within your industry. In both instances, the appraiser will adjust for the larger size of the public companies or the nature of the transactions within your industry.

Finally, the **income approach** will either capitalize the business's current earnings or forecast earnings a few years out and discount those earnings to present value.

One or more approaches may be best, depending on the nature of the business and the availability of comparable sale data for a similar business. One of the issues in your case will be the approach and methods used by your expert as opposed to those used by the other expert and the pros and cons of each. Also, the assumptions made by each expert when arriving at value become important in determining the quality of a valuation opinion. These underlying assumptions (such as assuming continued revenue at a given level when the market is declining) can reveal weaknesses in a valuation opinion that can be exploited by a smart expert and sharp opposing lawyer at trial.

UNIQUE CONSIDERATIONS: ALLOCATION OF YOUR COMPANY'S GOODWILL

Many service businesses such as law firms, accounting practices, medical practices, and even small manufacturing businesses are reliant on a substantial amount of personal goodwill for their value. The personal goodwill is the value the owner/operator uniquely brings to the business. Without the principal, there would be no business. Or the principal is unique to the customer, industry, and vendor relationships that they possess so the appraiser needs to analyze the extent of personal goodwill. Personal goodwill is *not* a marital asset. Because personal goodwill is not a marital asset, the analysis determining personal goodwill (as opposed to the company's enterprise goodwill) is an incredibly important part of many business valuations in family law. There are many factors that go into determining the allocation of goodwill in a business. You will want to discuss with your attorney and the retained business appraiser who the primary operators of the business are and what relationships they have in operating the business.

Many times, we end up resolving the division of service businesses with a nominal or zero value due to a determined high level of personal goodwill.

THE IMPACT OF RECENT SALES

As you might expect, despite valuation experts and data regarding sales of similar businesses, there is nothing like a recent sale of part of your own business to establish value admissible into evidence. For example, say you own a business with five other people. One of the five retires and sells his interest back to you and the other owners. You negotiate and work out a deal six months prior to filing for divorce. More than likely, this evidence will be more persuasive than any expert analysis or comparable study as to value, unless business performance has dramatically changed in the interim.

PREDETERMINED VALUATION FORMULAS IN OPERATING AGREEMENTS, SHAREHOLDER AGREEMENTS, AND PARTNERSHIP AGREEMENTS

Recent purchase/sale data in your own business can also come into play when the debate is whether to use a predetermined formula to determine value as set forth in an LLC operating agreement, partnership agreement, or shareholder agreement. If the business has used the formula to buy and sell ownership interests (the more recently, the better), then that is strong, persuasive evidence that the formula is an accurate way to determine business value.

Capital Accounts in Large Partnerships and LLCs

In large businesses, such as consulting firms, large accounting firms, and large law firms, the owners have a set capital account along with retirement benefits and usually a set retirement plan. The company is required to purchase the interest of a departing partner in exchange for the capital account and usually some discretionary retirement assets. This provides a steady transition for the departing owners and for the business, prevents constant disruption in the business from new and departing owners, and keeps fresh blood moving through the business, preventing stagnation at the top. Typically, there is clear evidence that these entities use these agreements multiple times over a long period of time, and thus, in this case, it is fairly easy to determine the value of the ownership interest. It is not a fraction of the entity's market value; it is the predetermined amount sitting in the partner/member's capital account.

Discounts

One thing to know is what discounts are applied in certain valuation approaches. Depending on the approach used, experts will add discounts to the value of the ownership interest. A couple of major ones are discounts for lack of marketability (DLOM) and discounts for lack of control (DLOC). If you have a privately held or small business, obviously, it will not be as readily salable as a publicly traded company; hence, the application of a discount for lack of marketability. Similarly, if you hold a minority interest in the business, you lack control of the business, so the value of your minority interest is lower than if you held a majority interest. (Someone would be less interested in purchasing a minority interest since they would lack control.)

Income Analysis and Add-Backs into Income for Support

Aside from the business valuation issue, a challenging thing can be valuing the stream of income coming from a business. If you are an owner, you likely don't just earn a salary; you receive distributions and dividends, and the entity pays expenses for you, such as insurance, auto, and phone (perhaps more). It is common for these items to be debated in cases involving a business owner. For support purposes, when you are a business owner, the income reported on your 1040 is not necessarily your income as calculated for support purposes. Untangling your actual income from reported income can be challenging, and an attorney who understands these issues is essential to protect you. For example, in a pass-through entity with an S-corporation election for tax purposes, you will report your share of your business income, despite not receiving it—funds that remain in the business will be charged as income to you for tax purposes but will not go into your pocket. Knowing the difference between business income and earned income is important to accurately reflect your income for support purposes.

Retained Earnings

Retained earnings are the remaining net income left in a business after it has paid dividends to shareholders. They may be retained for many reasons. For example, retained earnings may be funds that are held in the business to pay future expenses, finance an acquisition, pay for growth, or pay down debt. Retained earnings have two impacts for a business owner in divorce: they increase the value of the business, and they might be added back in as income for the business owner for purposes of support. Also, in a nonmarital business, a tactic for the business owner may be to "stuff" the business with cash and intentionally undercompensate themselves. The owner then claims that the retained earnings in the business cannot be divided, attempting to shield the retained earnings from the marriage. If a savvy lawyer (or expert retained by that party) reviews the financials and sees outsize retained earnings, especially in the few years leading up to the divorce, an argument can be made that the owner was undercompensated and was intentionally leaving money in the business. The undercompensation argument usually requires evidence of compensation for officers in comparable positions. The undercompensation retained earnings "stuffing" argument is only effective if the owner has control over compensation. If the person in question is a minority shareholder and has no control over compensation, this argument is mitigated.

FINAL THOUGHTS ON THE BUSINESS APPRAISER EXPERT

The most important result you can have when utilizing a business appraiser/financial expert is a credible one. Every owner in a divorce wants his business's value to be zero, and every nonoperator spouse wants the value to be incredibly high. However, if your business appraiser asserts an opinion of value that is not credible, it will set you back further as a litigant in the meta case. The court won't take your expert seriously; your soon-to-be ex-spouse and their counsel will likely also see that the appraiser has taken an untenable and unsustainable position, which will only invite more litigation and delay meaningful resolution. So hire your business appraiser at the outset of your divorce, discuss the topics unique to the business, include any factors demonstrating personal goodwill or not, and get the expert motivated to do a credible analysis on your behalf. In the end, a quality result is about credibility.

HOW TO ACCOMPLISH A BUYOUT WITHOUT BREAKING THE BANK

Courts will not intentionally break up or bankrupt a business, and no divorcing party would agree to settlement terms that would destroy a viable business. The judge does not enter a judgment that destroys a business that generates income for the family. It is not in the other spouse's best interest to see that happen, either. Income for support, payment for insurance, and payment for college expenses, all flow from the successful continuation of a business after divorce. Therefore, the most common solution when a business is retained by a divorcing party is to have a buyout: with present available assets, if possible without overly depleting the marital estate, or on a payment plan, if ready cash or other assets are not at hand. This type of plan funds the purchase of the interest over time, sometimes as long as ten years, and is self-financed. Typically, the parties negotiate a modest interest rate for the financing since it will be paid over time. In this way, the current income of the business finances the buyout, avoiding crippling the business and allowing the business owner to continue to live with a reasonable income.

PROTECTING THE DEPARTING SPOUSE

A key provision of any settlement agreement in divorce is designed to protect the nonowner spouse from business liabilities. The person who retains the business also retains the business liabilities and indemnifies the other spouse from them. That is, in the unlikely event that the business owner's former spouse was sued for something related to the business, the other party would be required to reimburse them for any losses.

THE ISSUE OF COMPANY PERFORMANCE

A risk each party takes in divorce when a business asset is retained by one party is the risk that the business may increase or decrease in value over time. Divorcing parties agree on a fixed price for the business at the time of divorce, based on the available information and the opinions of the appraiser experts. It is certainly possible that the price might look cheap or expensive in comparison to actual business performance over time—a set value is only an approximation, and no one has a crystal ball with respect to business performance. Usually, the spouse more involved in the business has a better idea of at least near-term performance and, potentially, long-term plans that may not be readily ascertainable to the other spouse through typical discovery means. Those plans might dramatically affect value, but once a divorce judgement is entered, you are stuck with it.

THE IRS AND THE DIVORCE COURT

Business owners frequently ask whether the IRS will learn about anything that is going on with the divorce court. The court is not going to report anything out of the ordinary to the IRS or other government agency. As the business owner, you generally don't need to worry about the judge reporting you to the government. However, obvious tax shenanigans (such as reporting a tiny amount of 1040 income when your business has huge top-line revenue) will give you credibility problems and hurt you in the meta case.

Loss Carryforwards

Loss carryforwards are allowed by U.S. tax law. Carryforwards are when a business uses a current net operating loss to offset net operating income in future years, subject to applicable law. Carryforwards are typically "baked in" to the business valuation, so they should not be double counted and should accrue to the person retaining the business.

Tax Fraud and Innocent Spouse Exemption

A typical provision in a divorce settlement includes handling of future tax liabilities and refunds, as well as cooperating with any tax investigation or audit. In the event that a party (typically a business owner) is charged with fraud related to filing taxes, the other spouse may think they would qualify for the "innocent spouse" exemption from liability. The government understandably is not generous in granting innocent spouse relief from tax liability—the requirements are strict. If the person claiming such relief knew or should have known about incorrect data on a tax return, they won't qualify.

When You Are Married For Tax Purposes

For tax purposes, in the United States, you are considered married if you are married on the last day of the year. So if you are married on December 31, you are considered to have been married for the entire prior year and may file a joint tax return for that year with your ex. This may well accrue to your mutual benefit. (Talk to a licensed accountant for any tax advice.)

Tax Liability and Refunds

Trailing tax refunds or liabilities are not uncommon in divorce cases. Divorce settlement agreements address how to deal with trailing refunds or liabilities. The most common practice is to share the refunds or liability in the proportion you divide your assets. (For example, if you divided assets fifty-fifty, you should share any refunds or liability fifty-fifty as well.) This is because you jointly benefited from any underreporting of income (the reduced taxes accrued to the benefit of the marital estate and helped both of you) or your estate was jointly reduced by overreporting income, and therefore, you should share in any refund.

RON'S STORY, CONTINUED

We found a way for Ron to keep his business while maintaining compliance with the law so it felt like a clean break. In his case, that meant a ten-year buyout plan at 3 percent interest.

"This way, you can afford to pay for the fifty percent buyout over time, and if the company grows, so much the better for you," I said.

Ron liked the idea. We packaged it with an offer on alimony (the kids were now in college, so no child support) and made a written offer to the other lawyer. Kristi accepted the deal, and Ron was divorced without breaking the bank and was able to keep his business.

I JUST WANT THIS DONE

CHAPTER 13

CUSTODY: NAVIGATING PARENTING ISSUES (DOS AND DON'TS RELATED TO PARENTING)

B ill was at war. But he didn't know it.
Bill was a young, dynamic C-suite executive who did what it took to shoot up the ranks at a tech company. He had been married for fifteen years to his college sweetheart, Lorelei, but traveled four days a week for work. Bill was as confident as he was tech savvy. When we first met, he spent fifteen minutes showing me the features of his new iPhone.

In Bill's absence, Lorelei held down the fort at home. She was a college-educated, stay-at-home mom. They had two children, one in high school and one in grade school. In Bill's own words, the marriage was dead. They had not had sex in two years. He had a girlfriend, whom Lorelei knew about. Bill felt guilty about the ongoing affair and thought ending the marriage was the right thing to do. Lorelei took great care of the children and house, Bill told me. She'd earned a good living as a teacher before children. Motherhood came naturally to her, so Bill had no hard feelings. They even still lived in the same house.

That's why he and I both hoped a collaborative divorce would be smooth, agreeable, and quick. I sent a benign letter to his wife, our standard operating procedure when no opposing lawyer is yet involved. We approach almost every case from a settlement perspective, pivoting to litigation as a last resort (unless we know at the outset that the client has no choice). Normally, we get a call from the other lawyer and start talking about how we can work things out.

Not this time.

I received court papers from Lorelei's lawyer. They were *bad*. They made claims about Bill that were unnecessarily nasty and obviously exaggerated. The papers demanded sole custody, which was bizarre because Lorelei and Bill got along fine as parents, Bill never abused the kids, and he never did drugs. In Illinois, it takes a lot to get sole custody, and despite the bluster, no defensible case was made.

When I looked at the signature block for the lawyer's name, I understood. The pleadings were signed by a guy I'll call Sam Tsunami.

Sam is notorious in Chicago for hardball litigation. He's a skilled trial lawyer, a tough opponent, and a total swamp creature. There is never easy settlement with Sam. When Sam gets involved in your case, you had better get ready for war.

I called Bill to tell him the bad news.

"Sorry to tell you this, but your wife has hired . . . Sam Tsunami," I said.

"Who's that?"

"He's a tough customer. It means you're in for World War III," I said. "She's demanding sole custody."

"You're kidding! But we get along so well with the kids."

"I get it, Bill. I'm the weatherman. I don't control the weather. I just tell you what is going on."

"So what's this going to cost me?"

"Full-blown custody litigation in Cook County against Tsunami could easily cost you a hundred thousand dollars-plus and take two years, maybe more."

There was silence for a few moments.

"What should I do?" Bill finally asked.

"I'll think this over, come up with a plan, and call you tomorrow."

WHAT'S A CUSTODY WAR?

Custody may be one of the most fought over yet least understood battlegrounds in divorce litigation. People start World War III over emotionally charged words like "custody" and "visitation." (As an aside, many states are renaming these "allocation of parental responsibility" and "allocation of parenting time," respectively, at the urging of family lawyers. The reason is simple—the old terminology implies ownership. You "own" the children if you have "custody" of them. "Visitation" sounds like a parent is seeing the kids in jail. The terms alone foment conflict.)

Custody means decision-making about the child. The child's education, medical treatment, religious upbringing, and extracurricular activities are the key provinces of parental decision-making covered by custody.

Visitation, better termed "parenting time," is the sharing of time with the children between the parents.

The two concepts are not connected, although most people think they are. The general impression people have is that "sole custody" means one parent "gets" the kids while the other is locked out of their lives until they're eighteen. Incorrect. It's possible for one parent to have sole custody yet still have equal parenting time with the other parent. This is uncommon but still possible.

Misunderstanding how custody and visitation work, and feeling social pressure—family and friends who side with one parent who "deserves" the kids—trigger the majority of damaging, needless custody fights.

The two biggest BS threats in divorce are "I'll take you for everything you have!" and "I'll get the kids, and you'll never see them!" Both are wrong. The law requires judges to divide property equitably and address custody and visitation in the best interest of the children. This

227

"best interest" standard is the guiding principle for court decisions on parenting across the United States.

For example, judges don't grant "your" visitation rights with the kids. The children are the ones with the visitation rights, not the parents. Children *need* time with their parents; parents *want* time with their children. "I want *my* visitation rights!" sounds plain selfish in this context. It also reeks of "balance-sheet parenting."

Don't be a balance-sheet parent. Judges might treat a demand for equal parenting time at the outset of a case with skepticism in states where equal parenting time is not presumed by law. The court may be concerned that the parent is treating the kids like an asset to be split down the middle. (Please understand, I am *not* against the concept of equal parenting time, and several states now presume an equal time schedule at the outset by law.) In many states, a fifty-fifty schedule means reduced or no child support, and in states where equal time is not presumed, some judges may suspect people are asking for equal time merely to reduce or avoid child support. This is a great way to lose the meta case, to say the least. The best strategy in that circumstance is to spend a lot of time with the children, document that time spent, and have reasons to support the fact that equal time will be in the children's best interest. As an example, the court won't be thrilled to find out that much of the proposed "equal" time will have the children with a paid day-care provider rather than one of their parents.

Taking the higher road like this can help you avoid a costly custody litigation detour in the middle of the divorce. The expense is more than money. Remember the four costs, especially the irreversible emotional damage to your kids. Know your objective. Have a compelling reason to pursue custody litigation, if that's what you want. Valid reasons include abuse, neglect, serious psychological problems like a hard drug addiction, and criminal issues.

If you do dive straight into custody litigation, know what you're getting into. You'll be inviting total strangers into your family to decide how your children should be parented. The lawyers; the judge; potentially a guardian *ad litem*, child representative, or other court-appointed person in an investigative, advisory role; and possibly mental health and parenting experts can get involved in your case with life-altering consequences. They are well intentioned, but do you want them deciding how your children should be raised? You and your spouse working this out yourselves is almost always the best solution for you and your children.

WHAT IS JOINT CUSTODY AND TYPICAL VISITATION LIKE IN PRACTICE?

One of the big reasons people fight is they don't understand what joint custody and a typical visitation schedule look like in practice. On paper, "joint" or "shared" custody means that you are to share in all the major parenting decisions about the children. In practice, however, this means that the person who has been primarily handling these things will likely continue to do so. For example, if Parent A typically took the kids to the doctor, handled issues with school, dealt with sports signups and the like—since inertia is human nature and change is hard for people—it is 99 percent probable that Parent A will continue to do those things after the divorce. The other spouse might step up and take some responsibility, but these life patterns are set by the time most people get divorced. If Parent A wants to change primary care physicians, they might ask the other parent to agree first. If Parent A wishes to get elective medical procedures for the kids, they will be required to ask for permission first as well. But as for the operational day-to-day care and control of the kids, it will commonly, but not always, be up to the person with the majority of parenting time. With equal time, the parents will have to work out who has responsibility for each aspect of the children's lives, such as school, health care, extracurricular activities, and religious upbringing.

As for visitation, there is a trend in Illinois (and in other states) toward parents having equal parenting time. A fairly common parenting schedule is every other weekend plus two or three nights per week, with one of those being an overnight. Plus, the weekends are longer than they once were—running to Monday morning instead of Sunday evening and beginning Friday right after school. This matches demographic trends; with far more working women and work-from-home arrangements, many couples both work, so the work schedule issue is not as prominent a reason as it once was for the majority of parenting time to be with the mother (or the nonworking/less-working parent).

Litigation over visitation time is a tough battle. It is hard for the court to wrap its arms around why you think the weekend should run from Friday morning to Monday morning rather than the typical Friday afternoon to Sunday evening. You need some compelling evidence to get the GAL interested in your point of view and to ultimately sway a judge. What this means is if the only thing you're upset about with respect to parenting is the visitation schedule proposed by your spouse, take a long hard look at it, and try to negotiate the best you can. Be apprehensive about litigating that issue through trial.

There are entire books about custody and visitation schedules and what is best for children. I only discuss some schedules here to illustrate my point. As for equal time schedules, common ones include one week on, one week off (rotating seven-day blocks); 2-2-3 (two days for Parent A, two days for parent B, then Friday to Sunday for Parent A, and so on in rotation); and 3-4-4-3 (three days for Parent A, four days for parent B, four days for Parent A, three days for Parent B, and so on). Equal time parenting schedules require parents to live fairly close together in order to be functional.

HOW DOES SOLE CUSTODY LOOK DIFFERENT?

Sole custody means one parent makes all the parenting decisions for the children. Where they go to school, what doctors they see, extracurricular activities, and more. This does *not* mean that the sole custody parent "owns" the children. Sole custody may be awarded to a parent for a number of reasons. These include a lack of prior involvement with the children by the other parent, abuse or neglect situations, drug abuse, criminal issues, et cetera. I'm betting you don't see yourself on that list.

The thing you need to look out for in that case is a lack of ability to co-parent. The most common reason for a sole custody award in a case where none of the obvious "bad" factors apply: one parent is a jerk and consistently demonstrates an inability to cooperate and communicate with the other parent. For example, Mom sends an email to Dad asking whether Junior can get braces. Dad just does not respond. Mom sends another email a month later, with the same question. She offers Dad a choice of three local orthodontists. Dad blows it off again. Finally, she reminds him one last time, and Dad emails back, "We can't afford it." If this pattern of failed communication and cooperation continues during the divorce case, when the court and GAL have a microscope on the parenting, it may well end up as a sole custody situation, when that might not otherwise have been indicated by the other facts. This is where meta case bad stuff can blow up the entire custody case or practically create one out of thin air. Which leads us to . . .

THE IMPORTANCE OF BEHAVING WELL IN CUSTODY LITIGATION

This should go without saying, but it deserves emphasis here. You should work hard to behave well in any case, whether negotiated or litigated, in order to work toward the most efficient and best result with minimal friction. But emotions get in the way, people fall back on bad habits they had during the marriage, and tempers flare under tension in divorce. Take extra care to be cool. You are again being watched by your spouse, your kids, the GAL, the judge, and experts retained to examine the parenting situation. Things that might seem small in normal life (a meltdown during which you yell at your kids and swear at them, for example) can be blown up into a big deal, seriously damaging your meta case and making the GAL and judge think maybe you should have less visitation, and perhaps your spouse should have sole custody.

THE ROLE OF THE GAL

The GAL or similar professional appointed by the court to investigate child issues has a significant role in the custody case, and they have heavy influence on the judge's thinking. The GAL is retained by the court to investigate child custody and parenting issues and report back the investigative findings along with recommendations for resolution of the dispute. Courts appoint people they trust as GALs, and therefore the GAL holds a substantial amount of influence over the court with regard to custody. Normally, what the GAL says goes in terms of custody outcomes. That is why it is important to be cooperative with the GAL.

BE ON TIME

With pickups and drop-offs being potential sources of friction with visitation, being a few minutes early for pickup and drop-off is important. Keeping a schedule provides stability for the kids, respects the other parent's time, and lets people make plans and count on them. If you're going to be late, a quick text message is key to help people adjust. This is an important part of cooperating in joint parenting. Demonstrating that you are on time and consistent shows that you are good at co-parenting and can work well with your soon-to-be ex. It also removes a major source of stress for the kids. If you are the parent waiting for the other person to pick up the kids, be sure the kids are ready with their clothes, homework, and other essentials so they don't make the picking-up parent wait, causing the kids to rush and panic. Again, removing this needless stressor is important and builds a good cooperative relationship. This is along the lines of the old adage "Ninety percent of life is just showing up."

DON'T BE A JERK

We expand on this in a later chapter. Be nice. Be courteous in your text messages, voice mails, and emails. Be nice with the kids. Don't yell. All this stuff can be used against you in a custody battle. Don't create ammunition for your spouse to use against you.

AVOID PHYSICAL (CORPORAL) PUNISHMENT

No hitting or spanking, even if this was acceptable to your soon-to-be ex during the marriage. Just avoid it entirely. Many books exist about good methods of child discipline. Get one and read it. Spanking the kids, even when it was normal before, may create evidence to be used against you. And children tend to play parents off each other. They may tell the other parent about it just to gain some perceived advantage or favor.

HELP YOUR SPOUSE WITH *THEIR* PARENTING TIME

This is always a good idea. An example comes from an appellate case in Illinois, *Williams v. Williams*. In that case, the parties were divorced. The mother asked the father to help her with the kids when she needed to have emergency surgery. The father blew it off and spent the night at a concert with his girlfriend, in the local area to boot. Some time later, the mother brought a petition to move the children out of state. One of the key pieces of evidence she introduced at the relocation trial about his failure to co-parent was his complete failure to help her out during her scheduled parenting time when she had a legitimate emergency. The judge found it significant that the father was not supporting the mother when she needed it most. When your ex asks for help with the kids, give them help. You'll see your kids more often, they will be happier, and so will your ex. This is great meta case stuff for an ongoing divorce case—you are demonstrating the ability to co-parent well.

TAKE EVERY OPPORTUNITY YOU CAN TO SPEND TIME WITH YOUR KIDS

Offer to drive the kids to the gym, to Scouts, to wherever, even if all you do is talk to them in the car for twenty minutes. You'll help your ex out and see your kids more often, and that time in the car is quality one-on-one conversation time you won't get elsewhere. I used to pick up my youngest son from school and drive him to his MMA classes (fifteen minutes), wait for an hour, then pick him up and take him home, sometimes stopping for dinner. We had a lot of good conversations in the car and at dinner that I would not have had if I had stuck strictly to a parenting schedule.

SHOW UP TO SCHOOL, SPORTS, EXTRACURRICULARS

Don't miss out on these opportunities to see and support your kids. Knowing you are there means a lot and shows you care. Go to the sports events, concerts, and practices. They are only young once. If you care about them and want to show the GAL and judge that you do care, be there for them. This also opens up opportunities to spend more time with them, like ice cream after the game. The parent who claims to want more time with the kids but blows off the tennis tournament or spring concert will likely fail.

TAKE TIME OFF TO HAVE QUALITY TIME

Take time off from work when the kids have the day off from school. President's Day, Institute Day, et cetera are all chances to spend quality time with your kids. Plan ahead, take the day off, and offer to your spouse to take care of the children. Good stuff and more parenting time with you and the kids.

BUY SOME EXTRA STUFF (CLOTHES, TOYS, VIDEO GAMES)

Don't get into silly battles about the kids' stuff. This is a totally avoidable trap some parents fall into. They get into a tug-of-war over toiletries, the Xbox, and clothes. Stay away from these disputes. Just go buy them duplicate things so they have them at your place. This makes the kids comfortable, they don't need to shuffle tons of junk back and forth, and it avoids the "Why didn't you give me the kids' clothes?" arguments. Keep their toiletries and medication at your place so they don't worry about forgetting things. They are not "visiting." They are your children, and you should treat them like they are at home.

AVOID THE POSSESSIVE WITH THE KIDS

They are not "my" kids; they are "our" kids. Your spouse had the children with you. Keep this in mind: even though you are divorced, you are still a family and will be for the rest of your lives. Few things are more grating than hearing someone refer to children in a settlement conference with both parents present as "my kids": "I don't want *my* kids around his girlfriend."

STAY OFF SOCIAL MEDIA

Part of behaving well in a divorce case is going dark on social media. This is true whether you are embroiled in custody litigation or not. Don't post. Posts can be used in evidence against you, especially that post of you at the nightclub having drinks at 1:00 a.m. when it was your night to be with the kids. Or worse, a post demonstrating you were drinking only a short time before you were to drive the kids somewhere. Posts of the new boyfriend freak out your kids, upset your soon-to-be ex, and do nothing but cause trouble. Keep quiet. (As an aside, it is unethical for a lawyer to recommend deleting older social media posts. This is because it may be illegal in your state to delete old social media posts once you are in litigation—this can be considered "spoliation" of evidence and can be the basis of a civil suit with money damages.)

DON'T FORCE KIDS (ESPECIALLY TEENS) TO SPEND TIME WITH YOU

This comes from the story I mentioned earlier about my son's girlfriend. At the time, she and my son were sixteen years old. Her parents were divorced, and her dad forced her to travel with him to Michigan on the weekends in the summer to a house with his girlfriend, where there was . . . nothing . . . to . . . do. The house was in a remote location, there were no other kids around, and she hated going there. She hated it so much that she swore once she was eighteen, she would not see her father again.

Teenagers have their own lives. A strict parenting schedule is unworkable with most teens, especially older ones. Forcing them to adhere to it only builds resentment, and once they are eighteen, you might not see them again. Remember that they aren't eight years old. It is totally unrealistic to expect that they will love sitting with you watching HGTV or the news after dinner. They have their activities, their friends, and stuff they want to do. Heed those requests, be flexible, and you will be a happier person with a better relationship with your children.

Have cool stuff for your kids to do. I am fortunate enough to have access to a place on a lake and a boat. One of the real saving graces for my relationship with my sons when I moved out and got divorced was that I was still able to take them to the lake and spend the weekends with them. (I give my ex-wife credit for being understanding and helpful in encouraging them to come with me.) This was critical to our relationship in the early months and has continued through today—they still come to the lake, even though they are in their twenties. It is a fun place for them to be, and they can bring their friends. You might not have a lake house, but you can create an environment where your kids will feel welcome, and the chances that they will come will multiply. Maybe it's a nice bedroom, a video game system, and snacks they like in the house, as just a few examples. You can do this in many ways on a smaller scale. Invite your kids and their friends to a sports game. Host a nice birthday party. Take your child and a few friends to a movie or a museum they want to see. Do. Things. With. Them. After they turn eighteen, you won't be able to make them come—and they will only come if they want to.

DEALING WITH BAD-MOUTHING

Frequently, you have situations where your ex bad-mouths you to the kids. You are rightly concerned that they will get a bad impression and think poorly of you. You work hard not to do the same for your kids, which is, of course, best. What to do? Play the long game. Be nice to the kids; don't engage in denigrating or undermining your ex since this only blows back negatively on you. Wait. Over time, the kids see that you are nice to them, that you are nice to their other parent, and that your actions don't match the horrible things your ex says about you. Pretty soon, as time passes, they usually begin to see you as the better person, things come around, and they wonder why their other parent is so nasty.

This is usually a far better strategy than trying to get a court to do something. The court is poorly equipped to address these kinds of behaviors. First, you have proof problems—your ex will deny saying bad stuff about you. That leaves the kids to tell a guardian or the judge about the bad stuff, and they are not likely to tell on your ex. Also, you have then put them in the middle, making you the bad guy and fulfilling your ex's claims that you are a bully and a bad person by dragging your ex (and kids) into court. Don't fall for it. Hang in there, and play the long game.

PARENTING PROVISIONS FROM AN ACTUAL AGREEMENT

The parenting rules reprinted below are from a standard-form parenting agreement. They are rules you see in typical custody judgments and are good guidelines to live by even during your divorce case, before any court order is in effect.

ARTICLE IV
General Parenting Provisions

A.   **SPECIAL CONSIDERATIONS.** It is important for MOM and DAD to foster and encourage affection and respect for both parents. Thus, neither parent will intentionally do anything that would estrange their Children from the other parent. In fostering the Children's love and affection, the Parties shall:

1. Both parents shall prepare the Children, both physically and emotionally, for the Children's return to the other parent. The Minor Children shall be available at the times mutually agreed upon between the parties for everyone's mutual convenience.

2. Both parents shall advise each other as soon as possible if they are unable to have their assigned time of physical access with the Minor Children.

3. Neither parent shall unreasonably question the Children regarding the activities of the other parent, nor shall they use the Children to carry messages between them.

4. Neither parent shall drink to excess or use illegal drugs in the presence of the Children or shortly before being in the presence of the Children, nor allow the Children to witness drinking to excess or the use of illegal drugs.

5. Each parent shall attempt to facilitate the completion of homework assignments during his and her parenting times with the Minor Children.

6. The parties agree that they shall not use physical discipline or extreme foul language of any nature with the Children, nor shall they allow any other third party to use the same.

7. Both parties shall be responsible for maintaining adequate amounts of clothing and articles of personal use for the Minor Children at his and her respective residences but will also allow the Children to take clothing and personal possessions back and forth between his and her residences if the Children wish to do so.

8. In the event of remarriage of either MOM or DAD to a new spouse, the parties agree that they will make known to his or her new spouse the conditions as set forth above and that they will encourage his or her new spouse to act in accordance with the expectations set forth in this agreement.

9. The parties hereto further mutually covenant and agree that they will use his and her best efforts to foster the respect, love, and affection of the Children toward the other party and will cooperate fully in implementing a relationship giving the Children the maximum feeling of security.

10. The Children shall not be used to pass messages between the parties; rather, the parties shall communicate directly with one another. Specifically, the parties shall not communicate with each other through the Children with regard to changes in the parenting schedule. Further, any problems that arise between the parties shall not be discussed with the Children or in the Children's presence.

11. Neither parent shall make disparaging remarks about the other parent, stepparent, significant other (i.e. boyfriend, girlfriend) or other family member to the Children. Neither parent shall, in the presence of the Minor Children, insult, curse, or make disparaging comments to or about the other parent.

12. Neither parent shall undermine the other parent's decisions or authority. The parties agree to discuss and attempt to establish consistent methods of discipline, bedtimes, and curfews.

13. Neither parent shall require the Children to address anyone other than the parties as "DAD" or "MOM" or any name indicating a parental relationship.

14. Parents agree that they shall let each other know they intend to introduce a significant other and shall have the opportunity to meet said significant other prior to the children doing so.

15. Neither parent shall allow his or her spouse, parent(s), brother(s), sister(s), significant others (i.e. boyfriend, girlfriend) or any friend or family member to violate the provisions of this Agreement.

16. Each party shall not show this Agreement or any legal documents regarding the parties' allocation of parental responsibilities and support proceeding to the Children, and each party shall refrain from discussing the legal aspects of this case with the Children.

17. MOM and DAD agree that they shall set aside any issues and feelings of mutual antipathy and discord toward each other for the sake of cooperating in the rearing of the Children.

18. Neither parent shall threaten to withhold parenting time from the other parent. Neither parent shall threaten to prevent or delay the return of the Minor Children to the other parent after a period of parenting time.

BILL'S STORY, CONTINUED

I called Bill the next day.

"I have an out-of-the-box idea, but I think it will work well."

"What is it?"

"I want you to give her sole custody."

"*What?*"

"Yes. Take the steam out of the whole thing. Tsunami wants a custody fight. He is manufacturing one. He knows most guys will get upset and want to fight, and this will make him a ton of money. He figures he can't lose—either he might get sole custody, or if he doesn't, he can just blame it on the judge and the GAL."

"But it doesn't seem right. I am a good dad."

"I know you are. But if we can get you the time with the kids you want, wouldn't that be fine? You said she was a good mom, right?"

"Yes, but . . ."

"And you told me you trusted her with the decisions about the kids . . ."

"Yeah . . ."

"Well, I wouldn't worry about it, then. If you say she's a good mom, and the most likely situation is she just keeps doing what she was doing, it's unlikely there will be any problems. You weren't involved in the medical and school stuff anyway, right?"

"No, I travel a lot, like I told you."

"Yeah, well, what is going to be different now?"

"OK, I get it. But what if she goes crazy and wants the kids to see a quack or something?"

"If she goes off the deep end, you will always be able to bring a motion before the court. Sole custody does not mean that you can't intervene if something harmful is going to happen."

Bill thought about it for a couple of days. He talked with me and agreed to allow his wife Lorelei to have sole custody, but he still had all the parenting time he wanted. We added in a couple of escape hatches, specifically for medical treatment. She had to obtain consent before elective medical procedures and give notice and secure consent prior to any major medical procedure, except in case of emergency. He was satisfied and avoided a two- or three-year custody war. Bill took the biggest issue in the case off the table—his fight for joint custody—and got it done so he could move on with his career and his life. We got it done in months rather than years.

From Bill's perspective, "sole custody" was no different in practice from "joint custody"—Lorelei was a good mom, and he trusted her.

CHAPTER 14

SELF-CARE DURING DIVORCE

O ur receptionist handed me the file (back when we had paper files). "Louise is in room one. It's a little odd—she is wearing one of those foam collars."

"You mean a cervical collar?"

"Yeah. She looks like she's in pain."

"OK." I went through the waiting room toward the main conference room. I was an auto accident lawyer in a past life, so I was familiar with orthopedic injuries, the treatment required for them, et cetera. I knew that soft cervical collars had largely gone out of fashion in the medical community and that more mobility was the recommendation for soft-tissue neck injuries, not less.

Louise was sitting at the table with some papers in front of her and a cup of coffee. She was looking down at the table, shoulders slumped, tears streaming down her cheeks. She was in her early forties, overweight, and wearing the aforementioned cervical collar.

I sat down. "Were you in a car accident?" I asked.

"No, I have a lot of neck pain, so I got this to help with it." That was weird. Seemed like she was moving around just fine and turning her head to talk with me.

"How can I help you today?"

"My husband served me with divorce papers."

She proceeded to tell me how awful her marriage was and how unhappy she was. She was a stay-at-home mom, and their one daughter had just started college. She was totally lost. She described her husband in such a way that I was surprised she wanted to stay married at all. But she was despondent. I got the feeling she was unhappy about a lot more than the divorce.

"Before we talk about the nuts and bolts of your divorce, I want to talk with you about your life."

She looked up at me, brows furrowed. "But I'm here to talk about the divorce . . ."

DIVORCE IS A MARATHON, NOT A SPRINT

People lock down in divorce, stop taking care of themselves, and stop moving. Don't do this. Divorce will take time and energy, and your life continues as well.

We've seen horrible things happen to people in divorce cases. One husband of a client committed suicide. A wife of a client died of a drug overdose. Some succumb to alcohol or drugs and lose custody of their children.

If you look at divorce as the end of things, your negative attitude will spill over into everything you do. You will see life through that lens. If you take a positive approach and see it as an opportunity for a new life, this might be a more rewarding chapter about to unfold. One thing I ask people who do not want the divorce is, "Why would you want to be married to someone who doesn't love you and doesn't treat you the way you deserve?" This helps them shift their attitude from one of loss to one of realizing they deserve better in life and have the right to seek it out.

Self-care is critical to protect yourself and be the best you can be during this process. Here is my best advice, culled from decades of advising clients in divorce.

THINGS YOU CAN DO FOR GOOD SELF-CARE DURING DIVORCE

Get a counselor. If you don't have one, find one. I'd recommend someone your age or older. Young, inexperienced counselors won't have the perspective that life experience brings. In my case, I was referred to John Duffy (his real name), a dynamic, engaging psychologist around my age who had children and had been married a long time. I hoped he would at least understand where I was coming from and also challenge me in a healthy way—and he did. Be sure not to hire a cheerleader. You want a person to bounce ideas off, to ask you the hard questions. Your friends won't likely challenge you. You need someone to give you their unfettered professional opinion. Sticky issues will arise, and you want to be able to tell the counselor everything, things you would not (and should not) tell friends or family. If you have had a counselor for a long time, staying with them might be fine, but I recommend getting a second opinion for a fresh approach—one that is more focused on the present, the future, and the divorce.

Go dark on social media. Many people make the mistake of posting every thought they have online. This is especially true in divorce. Airing your dirty laundry online will drive people away from you, and if you reconcile, how do you explain this to your friends? Also, anything you post on social media can be used in court against you. Avoid photos online showing you partying with your friends. You're a parent and an adult. You can have fun, but do not broadcast it online. Especially avoid photos of you with new significant others. This does nothing but make your children uncomfortable and make you look like a jerk, and it will upset your soon-to-be ex and mess up the meta case.

It will possibly derail settlement negotiations. With that said, photos of the kids doing things with you are fine: your daughter getting ready for prom, birthdays, et cetera. Pictures of the vacation you take with your girlfriend—bad idea.

Maintain your health. Simple things like getting enough sleep, eating well, drinking plenty of water, and getting regular exercise are more important than ever to deal with the stress of divorce. Also, don't miss your medical checkups and dental appointments. You'll avoid compounding a rough situation with brand new health problems even if you were the one asking for it. The stress of the divorce alone may cause you some health issues. My blood pressure shot up high for several months during my divorce.

Be careful about overeating and emotional buying. Stress can make us overeat, drink to excess, gamble, or buy things we don't need to fill the emotional pit in our hearts. Watch for this, recognize it, and address it. Keeping yourself busy with positive things will help you avoid these common pitfalls.

Keep a routine. We thrive best on routines; they make our life orderly and reduce stress. It is easy to get disrupted by new parenting schedules, adjustments to a new home, and more. Try harder than ever to have consistency in your schedule. Go to bed at the same time, do the same things in the morning during the week, et cetera. Reducing uncertainty will go a long way toward making you feel better.

Spend time with your children. They will bring you joy and energy. They need you, and you need them during this time. Do more than the minimum. Drive them home from school even when it is not "your day." Help your soon-to-be ex out when they need a break.

Finish your education. If you don't yet have a college degree, for example, don't be dependent on spousal support and child support. People (especially spouses of high earners) fool themselves that spousal support and child support will be enough. If your ex dies or, more likely, gets terminated or loses income, you and your children will suffer. Build independence by completing your education, which leads to the next point . . .

Get a job. Or take on more at work, but keep balance in mind. Working provides financial security (at least an added measure of it) so you are not entirely dependent on spousal support. Moreover, you can get health insurance, which is expensive to purchase on the private market. Once you are divorced, your ex no longer is required to provide coverage. A job also gives you a useful distraction against thinking about the divorce all the time, as well as purpose and independence. In many cases, our clients were at the point in their lives (kids going away to college, etc.) when a transition back to work for stay-at-home parents was in the offing anyway. Use this as your impetus to go back to work.

Work, but don't overwork. Work can be a salve for heartache. Keeping up at work, and doing your best will reduce stress and give you some regularity in your life when you need it most. If you find yourself having a hard time focusing at work, seek help and let your colleagues know you are getting divorced. They will understand and should give you some space. As with your friends, though, do not burden coworkers with all your woes and the dirty laundry about the divorce. Keep the whys and wherefores to yourself. This is what a counselor is for. People may be curious, but it is none of their business, and you just crank up the gossip machine to no good end at the office.

See your friends and make new ones. One big mistake people make is sitting inside and not doing anything. You may struggle with some friends you had as a couple. People may be reluctant to see you during the divorce (especially if you are talking about it all the time; see my tip about avoiding this below). Get involved in activities where you can meet people. Be social. Get out into the world; don't live on social media. But beware of the next thing, which is . . .

Don't overburden friends and family with your woes. Be careful not to abuse your relationships with other people. It may be nice to complain or cry to a friend, but that can wear on your relationship, and this also breaks the rule about not bad-mouthing a spouse. Be careful who you talk to and what you talk about.

Take a vacation. Take time off. Take your vacation days. Take a half day on Friday. Rest. I like three- to five-day weekends—you can relax because you haven't gone too long, so you don't have a giant pile of work to do in order to prepare, and you don't have five thousand emails in your inbox when you return.

Get a hobby. Not looking at your phone doomscrolling—an actual hobby. Painting, writing, learning the guitar, model building. You may have more time on your hands now that your soon-to-be ex has the kids half the time. You should find productive, creative things to do with your time.

Spend time on your faith. Whether this is church, synagogue, mosque, meditation, whatever. Take time for this. Find peace with yourself.

Be future focused. Fear is based on the unknown. Clients come to us the most fearful in the beginning. It is easy to get mired in the present, to contemplate your navel and be sad about everything. One of the best pieces of advice we can give our clients is to begin answering the questions they have. "Where will I live?" "Can I afford a nice place?" "What am I going to do with my free time?" Focus on what you can control. This is your life. Make the best of it.

Your lawyer will help you answer the basic questions: how much income you will have from support, what asset split you can expect, and so on, but doing some soul-searching and some homework is important, especially if your life is near a transition point anyway. We see this frequently with people who have college-age children. The kids are out of the home, or almost, so there is no longer a need for a big house. (We will discuss the house next.) They may have moved away, even out of state. Downsizing, getting back to work, maybe relocating were already in the cards, but the couple hadn't yet dealt with those issues until the divorce came along.

What this means is find a real estate agent and think about where you might live. Find out what it will cost. Think about where your children are, where your friends and family are, and what you want to do with the next chapter of your life. Figuring out at least short-term answers to these questions brings tremendous peace of mind.

Don't keep the house. This is a big one. In some cases, people keep the house. But it might be a bad idea. People often think they want the house because they want to minimize disruption for the kids and for themselves. This is understandable. There are several things you can do:

1. **One party keeps the house.** One of you keeps the home, and buys the other person out of their equity interest. You will have to agree on a value (an appraiser is handy for this purpose) and use other assets to buy out your spouse's interest. Then, you'll be required to refinance the home if there's a mortgage against it, in order to release your ex from liability for the mortgage. (Typically, you have several months to a year or more to do this.) Disadvantage (to one party or the other): since you are using an appraised value, which is only a snapshot in time of value, the value might be higher or lower when the home is sold. Advantage for the person "selling" to the other: the price is figured at the full appraised value, with no closing costs figured in. This is typical in Illinois because any costs of sale are speculative. (We don't know when the house will sell, and we have no idea what the commission will be, or so goes the logic.) Also, for the "seller": no hassles, no showings, you just get your credit on the balance sheet and walk away.

2. **The parties keep the house jointly but sell it at a predetermined time.** This way, a valuation is not needed. One person stays in the home, typically the kids live there primarily (or at least half the time). The person in the home pays a disproportionate share of the mortgage, insurance, and real estate taxes. (We usually use 60 percent to two-thirds as a guide.) This is essentially "rent" for using the home. The person inside also covers the utilities and the majority of the upkeep costs, outside of major repairs, while the other person pays the remainder. After a set time, usually based on the children moving out into college, the parties place the home on the market, sell, and split the profit (or loss). This can be a useful solution for people who are close to that point and don't want to disrupt the kids for whom a buyout is not optimal. Plus:

you know the exact price, no one is guessing, and you share the proceeds or liability and closing costs (real estate agent commission, attorney fees, etc.).

3. **You put the house on the market right away and sell it.** Of course, you need to know where both of you are going to live, but many times, one person has already moved out. If the kids are already out of the house, this can be an easy choice. The benefit in Illinois is you both share the proceeds (or loss) in whatever percentage you divide your assets, and you both share in the costs of sale.

Rent, don't buy right away. I've seen many people make two mistakes with real estate. First, they jump in and buy something right away, before the dust settles. People have no idea what their lives are going to be like. The best move if you find yourself without a house is to wait: rent something, and let the smoke clear before purchasing. You may find that your kids move to another state, you want to move to a place near your friends, or whatever. You can follow your kids to wherever they're going. Secondly, they sink a ton of cash into real estate rather than taking out a loan. Obviously, being able to manage the loan payments is important, but I would advise against locking up substantial equity in real estate at what undoubtedly is a transitional time for people getting divorced.

Be involved, but not overinvolved, with the kids, and disengage from your spouse. Stop worrying about what your soon-to-be ex is doing. You're getting divorced. Focus on your children, but don't get too enmeshed in their lives. Set time for yourself.

LOUISE'S STORY, CONTINUED

At the conclusion of the case, Louise was smart. She agreed with her husband to sell the house and split the proceeds. She started thinking about what she wanted to do, rather than focusing on what her ex was doing. She rented an apartment so she could clear her head. She worked out, ate better, and got more sleep.

She started seeing friends she had not seen in years. She got a part-time job at a retail store, then was promoted to a full-time job as the assistant manager at the store.

When I saw her the day of the divorce prove-up hearing, she was a changed person. She looked great: no limp, no cervical collar, well dressed. And she had lost a lot of weight. The weight of the divorce was literally lifted from her shoulders. Louise was happy. Even though she had lost a husband, she took control of her life and gained peace of mind.

I JUST WANT THIS DONE

CHAPTER 15

CRISIS CASES

(AND HOW NOT TO BE

ONE OF THEM)

"They're going to put me in jail!"

Jerry panicked. He paced in my conference room, fiddling with his car keys. He kept glancing back at the pile of printed emails he'd laid down on the table.

"What happened?"

"My wife. I just caught her. She's cheating on me. Some doctor. I found out from her email. I figured out where he lives. Some divorced guy renting a house. It's not far from where we live."

"And . . . ?"

"Last night, she went out. She always says she goes out with girl-friends. Bulls——. I just *knew* she was lying to me. She was going to run over to the guy's place to screw around. So I went over there in my car."

"With your son?"

"Yes."

'How old is he?"

"Ten."

"OK. So what happened?"

"I drove over with him in the car so he could see the truth about his mom."

"When was this?"

"About ten o'clock. I pulled up and sent my son up to the front door to knock on it and ask for her."

"OK . . . probably not the best move."

"I know, I know. So they opened the door, and I got out of the car and screamed at her. I told her what a b— and a slut she was."

"She screamed back at me. 'Go away! Why would you do this?' Then she and her little boy toy ran back inside."

"What happened next?"

"My son came back to the car crying. I was so angry. I opened up the trunk of my car and grabbed a golf club."

"You did what?"

"Yeah. I just couldn't help myself. I went over to the guy's BMW and bashed the hell out of it."

"Jeez, Jerry . . . did the guy come out?"

"He heard me yelling, came back out, and shouted at me to get off his property. He went back inside, and I guess he called the cops."

"What did you do?"

"I took off before they came. I got my son home, but my wife never showed. Not even this morning. She must have stayed over . . ."

What Jerry didn't realize was the real trouble he'd gotten himself into. It wasn't the police, although smashing someone's car is a misdemeanor, if prosecuted—"criminal damage to property." In one night, Jerry had given his wife enough ammunition to fight World War III. Jerry's wife was no longer the only "guilty" party. To the court, an affair isn't the end of the world. Dragging your child into a violent situation is. If there was any chance to avoid a huge divorce battle and possible criminal penalties, we had to act fast.

"OK. Let's talk about how to get you out of this."

Crisis cases are a dream for some lawyers because they stand to generate a lot of fees. I want to reiterate something we discussed earlier. The lawyers aren't the problem overall—every lawyer is directed by a client who is in charge. The client embroiled in a crisis case presents an endless cycle of work for the attorney who is either not trained to break the crisis cycle or, worse, is OK with it.

There are many examples of crisis cases in divorce. This is where the personal battle between spouses gets heated to the point where the drama becomes so great that it prevents rational progress toward a solution of the divorce case. Examples include a physical altercation, a cheating issue that boils over, anger over spending, and more.

Divorce lies at the intersection of all we hold dear: love, sex/intimacy, money, and children. We all have those needs. When one of those is not met, we get upset. When several of them are screwed up all at the same time, some people lose it. Thus, the crisis case. Good people in a bad (very bad situation can behave badly. Especially when those people were comfortable with their former situation and perception of control. Suddenly, the steady, comfortable life they lived and felt they had control over is turned upside down.

Fear is based on the unknown. When the unknowns multiply, as they do at the outset of divorce, people's fears also multiply. Some people get sad. Others get angry and feel out of control; they lash out in an attempt to regain it. This leads to a downward spiral into a crisis case.

You see people behaving in ways they never have in their entire lives. For example, the couple who have never had a physical altercation before, ever. One spouse gets angry, drinks too much or whatever, and in a fit of anger, grabs the other spouse or breaks something. This is in a family that has never seen anything like this before. Or someone destroys the property of the other person, blasts out a damaging social media post, or the like. Someone hits one of the kids—and they never did that before. They post embarrassing photos online, or spill gory details to friends and family.

This kicks off a "cycle of violence" between the couple and is damaging to the family as a whole. Sadly, many people get themselves stuck in a downward spiral of accusation, attack, counterattack—on and on until the divorce case itself is totally lost in the shuffle, and the couple is just fighting over everything. It gets expensive when this spills over into the divorce case, resulting in runaway litigation and causing fees to spiral out of control.

Some lawyers sadly feed into this and just do what the client says without critique. We aren't robots. We are allowed to use our professional judgment, and we can and should refuse to take actions that ultimately aren't in the client's best interest. (And, in fact, we have a duty to do so and to avoid harming the children, if any are involved.)

The hardest thing for a lawyer to do is to say no to a client. But many times, taking no action is the best action—it deescalates the situation and avoids making things worse. Taking action where the action does not advance the case just racks up costs and makes everyone upset, usually inciting the other side to ramp up their reactions and deepen the spiral.

As divorce lawyers, we must refuse to be part of this cycle of violence. Attorneys should never be "hit men" for an angry spouse who wants revenge through the court system. They should not bring a custody case when there is no basis to do so. They should avoid needless discovery just to punish someone and rack up expenses.

These cases were a driving force behind this book.

HOW TO AVOID BECOMING A CRISIS CASE

Don't get into a crisis in the first place. Here are some key tips to avoid this.

Allow cooler heads to prevail. The attacks, reprisals, and so on will never net out to any sort of gain in the real-world context of a divorce case. They just raise costs and delay the completion of the case, when things can begin to heal.

Think before you act. As mentioned earlier, the best question to ask yourself when doing anything is "Will this get me *more* divorced?" In other words, will the action you wish to take or are taking advance the ball in the case, getting you closer to being done? Or are you doing it just to aggravate your spouse and poke them in the eye?

Get a counselor. We've talked about the importance of this before. If you have an outlet for your emotions, chances are you won't blow up and vent at your spouse, preventing you from sliding into crisis or helping you dig out from that position.

Take care of yourself. Again, a little recap. If you are feeling good, you will be less likely to enter into a crisis mode with your spouse and better able to pull out of one if you get into it.

Don't bring family and friends into your drama. This isn't *Romeo and Juliet.* Just as we discussed earlier with seeking advice and avoiding bad-mouthing your spouse to your family, bringing them into your drama and getting them involved in the battle with your soon-to-be ex will not end well. This ratchets up the tension, causes embarrassment and upset, and puts your kids in a bad position. Having them tell your spouse off, coming over to the house to yell at them, keeping the kids away from them, et cetera are guaranteed ways to go into a spiral and blow up your case.

Avoid obsessing over the new significant other. It's over. Worrying about what they are doing with the new significant other is a giant waste of time and energy and can get you into real trouble as Jerry found out (the hard way). Let it go. Tracking devices, monitoring phones, watching email, cameras . . . many of these things are not just wrong but illegal in many states. What new information are you going to discover? When your spouse finds out you were monitoring them, it will only serve to make a reasonable settlement more difficult, and evidence of spying/tracking may reach the judge and affect the custody decision, as well as your credibility at trial. You will damage your meta case standing with the court and other professionals.

Don't be Moe. This is my term for soon-to-be exes engaging in generalized back-and-forth, straight out of *The Three Stooges.* Remember when Moe would poke Larry and Curly in the eyes? This is the tit-for-tat exchange of bad behavior we see in cases that causes a spiral. "He went out and bought a flat-screen TV, so I went and bought new living room furniture." This shows up in the form of spending, going out late

I JUST WANT THIS DONE

at night, and more. Just because your spouse does something wrong, that's not a license for you to misbehave. Set the example and take the high road. If you take the bait and engage in similar bad behavior, you just enable them to do more and make things worse. Don't feed this type of negative cycle.

Don't tell their boss. It may seem like a great way to get back at your soon-to-be ex—report them to the HR department at work, saying they were sleeping with a coworker or subordinate. "I'm going to report them to HR because they are cheating, and I want them fired." Not a good idea. You tip the case into something entirely different when you directly attack the way people feed themselves. Moreover, if you expect to receive support (or want your spouse's income to reduce your support payment), why on earth would you jeopardize their income? "Before you embark on a journey of revenge, dig two graves."

Keep moving. Some people freeze in place when they find out they are getting divorced. We talked about the importance of self-care in an earlier chapter. This dovetails with that concept, but the mindset is the focus here. The worst thing is to freeze, take no action, and "drown." You need to adopt a mindset of learning and accomplishment. That is, seek help, and follow professional advice. Think about options for living, work, friends, and family. People who freeze bring a crisis mentality onto themselves and then cannot think clearly about their situation. They frequently then "dig in" in the divorce case, consciously or subconsciously avoiding things in the case to the point where expenses needlessly increase as one lawyer begins to try to push the case forward to trial simply because one spouse has dug in to avoid the inevitable.

Use orders of protection and restraining orders sparingly. They are the nuclear bomb of family litigation. The classic circumstance is when a spouse starts the case by seeking an order of protection. (This is what it is called in Illinois; every state has some version of an anti-domestic violence restraining order.) These orders can be useful tools in cases of genuine domestic violence. However, they are also often abused.

People can obtain emergency orders of this type without notice to the other person by filling out some forms and testifying briefly. If they can convince the judge that they are scared of the other person, and the allegations seem serious enough, the judge will issue a short-term restraining order and set the case for a full hearing on the allegations.

The typical domestic violence restraining order is severe. It is a total block in terms of communication and requires the other person to leave the home and typically not have contact with the children. In our state, it can also cause the police to seize all firearms that person has.

When it is overkill, it can kick off a negative cycle of litigation. The other party feels so offended and screwed up by the emergency order that they want revenge. This is a rough way to kick off a divorce case. Many people get these orders without the knowledge or advice of a divorce lawyer. Then the lawyers have to try to determine whether the order is necessary in the first place and try to deescalate the situation.

Avoid trying to punish with litigation. Taking a spouse to court is not the "punishment" it seems. First, you are spending marital assets on lawyers (more importantly, so is your spouse). So you are punching yourself in the face when you litigate to "teach a lesson" to your soon-to-be ex.

Take these precautions to avoid a crisis case. But you may have learned all this too late. What if you're like Jerry, and the case has devolved into disaster? I'll tell you what I told Jerry.

HOW TO PULL YOURSELF OUT OF A CRISIS CASE

Recognize You're in One

Look for the signs. What are you fighting about right now with your spouse? If you aren't looking at the nuts and bolts of the divorce, chances are you are wasting your time. Realize you are not being productive, and shift your mindset.

Stabilize the Patient

Crisis divorces are like emergency room patients. The crisis client comes into the office much like an injured person comes into the emergency room. There is a lot of drama; they are hurt; they don't know where to start. We have to calm the patient (client) down, stabilize them, and assess their condition (the real legal issues we can address). Any good medical team stabilizes the patient, assesses the actual conditions, and then performs surgery. Similarly, we need to settle down the situation between the parties to give clear space to assess the facts and key issues. Only then can we do the "surgery" of settlement or trial.

Stabilization may include setting up a temporary parenting schedule and getting access to money, a car, clothes, other personal property, and a place to live. Any number of things might be immediate issues that need to be resolved before the parties can start resolving their divorce.

Pull Out of the "Dive"

Stop reprisals. Communicate with your spouse. Stop the negative behaviors. Don't post negative stuff on social media. It would be a good idea to be the bigger person and apologize. This might be hard—your spouse might continue the bad behavior. But if you keep acting badly, who will start to break the cycle? Lead by example to get out of the mess.

You know that old saying about how to get yourself out of the hole you've been digging? "Step one, stop digging." These three tips will help you put down the shovel.

Evaluate the situation. Figure out the facts and the issues. Assess the credibility of witnesses. Determine what is going on and what each party's goals and concerns are. Be honest with yourself about your chances of success and the relevant costs.

Negotiate, if at all possible. Pick up the phone, meet on Zoom, send emails. Whatever it takes to get in communication and stay in communication. Until you get the divorce done, you are stuck with your soon-to-be ex and their lawyer. Start talking and keep talking. Avoid needless motion practice and discovery. Make reasonable offers and consider the responses. Be a good listener. Show basic respect and professional courtesy, and you will be able to demand the same in return.

Litigate, if you must. Use court as the last resort, but concentrate on the issues that matter. If you can settle the parenting part of the case, do that, and only have a trial on the financial portion. Use court as a tool to drive resolution, not as a weapon to cause damage. In the vast majority of cases, you will reach a settlement with your spouse, although it might be on the proverbial courthouse steps.

Fortunately, Jerry didn't have to go that far.

JERRY'S STORY, CONTINUED

After I briefed Jerry on the three steps of case resolution he could expect, I brought us back to the present moment. We needed to bring everyone out of the spiral.

"We can get a divorce case filed, yes," I said. "But you need to call the other guy and apologize."

"What? He's *screwing . . . my . . . wife!*"

"Yeah, I know . . . and there's nothing you can do about it that will benefit you at this point. What you can do is make amends. Look, you wrecked his car. If you're lucky, he won't bring charges against you for criminal property damage."

"I've never even been arrested before—I don't want any trouble with the police."

"Yes, and in your position, you can't afford it."

"OK, OK. Just tell me what I should do."

I did. And Jerry followed my advice to a T. He called his wife to apologize and promised never again to involve their son in the divorce. She accepted, graciously, probably because she felt guilty. Jerry then texted the doctor, apologized, and offered to pay for all the damage.

Jerry also contacted a counselor I recommended to work through his anger and hurt over the affair.

Luckily, the doctor decided not to press charges against Jerry. Everything calmed down as much as we could have hoped. From that point on, the divorce proceeded normally, and the case settled in a reasonable time. Jerry following my advice and taking corrective action defused the situation—and saved the rest of his life from disaster.

CHAPTER 16

THE EVIL
SPOUSE HANDBOOK
(AND HOW NOT TO BE
THAT PERSON)

"The cops just kicked me out of my own house!" Ethan's voice cracked on the phone.

"Are you OK? What happened?"

"I am so *not* OK. I'm outside my own damn house getting into my car with a bag full of my clothes!"

"What . . . why?"

"I caught my wife cheating on me last night. I saw text messages on her phone, and she confessed. We had a big fight last night."

"No one hit anyone, right? You mean you argued?"

"Yeah, I didn't hit her. I've never raised a hand to her in my life."

"So what happened?"

"My wife ran to court today without telling me and got a restraining order. Some BS about me being a danger to her and the kids. The police just came over, handed me the order, and told me I have to leave."

"What does the order say?"

"It says I can't be at the house. I have to stay a thousand feet away, and I can't even talk to my kids. This is insane!"

"Yeah, I know. Those orders are harsh."

"It's crazy! So I called a lawyer friend of mine, and he told me to reach out to your firm first. Can you help me?"

The gears turned as we spoke. I had to stabilize the situation, and fast. Ethan's wife had stirred up trouble for no legitimate reason. Couples fight, even those who are happily married. From what Ethan had told me, he was obviously not a danger to his family or himself.

Playing the restraining order card is rare, but it does happen. In high-conflict cases, some people take advantage of the justice system to just make the person they're mad at go away for a while. All Ethan's wife had to do was fill out a form online and spend thirty minutes at the courthouse in front of a judge. No lawyer was necessary, nor any physical evidence. Judges err on the side of caution; they assume the other party will be able to argue their side in court within a few weeks. Sometimes the situation warrants an order of protection to prevent domestic violence. However, these orders can be abused with ill intent to put a spouse on the defensive from the start of the case.

In situations that don't merit protection from a violent or otherwise dangerous spouse, getting a restraining order is a dirty power play. It doesn't kick the spouse out of the house permanently, and the case devolves into litigation.

A frivolous restraining order is one of many jerk moves I could write an entire book about. If I did, I'd call it *The Evil Spouse Handbook*. The reason I call my hypothetical book a "handbook" is that, time and again, some new guy or gal thinks they've come up with a smart new scheme to get the upper hand on their spouse. The truth is that it's all been done before. When clients tell me they have this great new idea to get back at their spouse, I like to say, "Well, then, you've just invented cold fusion."

TO WIN THE META CASE, DON'T BE A JERK

Remember the meta case? And the cost-benefit analysis? The cost of portraying the Evil Husband or the Evil Wife is far higher than any potential short-term gain or warm, fuzzy feeling you experience getting "even."

Here are a few common examples of the jerky (or downright evil) plays people make in an effort to gain an upper hand or punish the other spouse:

1. **Physical violence** to family, friends, or pets. That this is to be avoided should go without saying.

2. **False allegations of abuse** (worse, sexual abuse) made to authorities, family, or friends. This can be super devastating to a family and set off a chain reaction of unforeseen and unintended consequences, especially in today's highly sensitized culture. Loss of friends, family, and employment can result. And, to top it off, if your state's family services get involved, they might pin the person alleging abuse for allowing the neglect and abuse to take place in their presence—potentially resulting in children being removed from *both* parents. Getting the state involved in any parenting matter can have many undesirable consequences.

3. **Destroy or damage personal property** of the other person (heirlooms, prized photos, collectibles). This is a road to nowhere. You don't want to mimic the characters in the movie *The War of the Roses*.

4. **Cut off access to money, cancel credit cards, close joint bank accounts.**[6]
5. **Sell valuable assets without telling.** The eBay sale of the Star Wars collectibles. Dumping the baseball card collection. Unloading the jet skis for cash.
6. **Concealing or transferring assets.** This takes many forms. Siphoning off money in cash withdrawals and depositing it into a separate account or, better yet, a safe deposit box. We once busted a person who claimed to have nothing in the box by obtaining the bank security camera recordings along with the sign in sheets for the box area. The person went to the bank right before the divorce started on the ledger, pulled the video for that day, and lo and behold—she walked in with an empty bag and left with a full bag. This can also include transferring an asset like a home into a parent's or sibling's name, moving cash around, having a friend hold a substantial sum of money, and so on. Many times, with today's electronic records, the "leaks" of these funds can be found, if not the ultimate destination of the money. Finding the outward movement of cash can oftentimes be enough to gain negotiating leverage.
7. **Get an unwarranted restraining order** without notice. As described above, the order blocks all contact between you and your spouse and your spouse and the kids. They are not permitted to have *any* contact with you or the kids for a period of time, and violating the order is a crime. In many cases, such as Ethan's, this is a far more severe remedy than is necessary.

---

6   A caveat re: financial moves. Restricting your spouse's access to money might be advisable, given the facts of your case. If your spouse has their own income, and bills are being paid, your attorney might advise you to cancel joint cards, place your income in an individual account, and move money as needed into the joint account to pay bills. This can protect a large sum of money from being spent by the other party without your knowledge.

8. **Blasting embarrassing stuff onto social media.** Bad-mouthing, embarrassing photos, and nasty comments on social media aren't worth it and ultimately make *you* look bad. Furthermore, photos of your spouse containing nudity, posted without their permission, may well be illegal (i.e., revenge porn).

9. **GPS tracking** of spouse, spouse's significant other, or vehicles (may be illegal).

10. **Hacking** into the spouse's phone, computer, et cetera. to track emails and texts (likely illegal).

11. **Hidden microphones/cameras** (likely illegal, depending on what is recorded in many states).

12. **Bad-mouthing or demonizing** the other parent to the children.

13. **Cutting off or blocking parenting time** whether at the outset ("We don't have a court order yet, so you can't see the kids") or later on.

14. **Cutting off communication with the kids.** "Johnny is in bed now and can't talk" at 7:00 p.m.

15. **Leaving your soon-to-be-ex in the dark** about events for the children (school, sports, etc.).

16. **Taking the children to the doctor, dentist, et cetera without notice** for any reason other than routine appointments.

17. **Not allowing the children to move toys and clothes** between homes. Why put them in the middle?

18. **Moving out suddenly, without warning, and taking the kids.** (Be advised, moving far away or across state lines—known as "removal" or "relocation"—can subject you to a court order forcing return of the children, could result in fines (and having to pay your soon-to-be ex's attorney's fees), may result in you being permanently barred from moving the children out of state, and could result in a custody award to the other spouse.

19. **"Adultizing" the children**, or trying to make them your pals. Showering money on them to curry favor. Telling them gory details about the divorce.

20. **Sex, drugs, and rock 'n' roll.** (Well, rock 'n' roll is fine.) But the other two, while maybe making you feel like you are getting back at your spouse, don't end well. This includes showing off the sexy significant other on social media, parading them in front of the family, and partying hard to show your spouse how much fun you are having without them. Cavorting around can be used against you in a custody case, unnecessarily aggravate the ex, and lose you respect in your children's eyes.

Whatever perceived short-term gain you think you might get from any of these jerky tactics is far outweighed by the negative (and potentially serious) impact. Follow *The Evil Spouse Handbook*, and one or more of these may happen:

1. **You may have committed a crime or a tort (a wrongful act that can be punishable in a separate civil case).** Eavesdropping, hacking into email, false statements made to an employer that result in termination, defaming someone online, and revenge porn all can result in serious consequences.

2. **You lose the meta case.** The judge, the GAL, and the other professionals in the divorce case will learn how you cut off cash, took all the keys to the cars so she couldn't take a car anywhere, and had her followed by a private investigator and filmed with her boyfriend (in a state where adultery is not relevant). Now, your credibility is shot, and you are wearing the black hat—even if your spouse "started it" and was a jerk to you first.

3. **Your spouse is more determined than ever to fight you.** Good luck trying for a reasonable settlement in a reasonable amount of time. You will end up in the swamp, and you

just gave your soon-to-be ex a great reason to hire the number-one swamp creature to fight WWIII for them against you.

4. **You handed your spouse ammo** so they can tell everyone else, "See, he is a jerk like I told you. He did X, Y, and Z!" And then anything bad that your soon-to-be ex did is buried by the more recent and worse stuff you've just done. They will tell your kids, your friends, your family, and their family what a jerk you are. "This is why I am leaving your father. See how nasty he is?"

Remember that when you have children, you're still a family after the divorce.

You won't feel good at the end of all this, believe me. You don't want to crush each other. You want both parties feeling like they were reasonable to each other and behaved well. If you fail to do that, your children and other relationships will be the casualties. At eighteen, your kids will vote with their feet.

ETHAN'S STORY, CONTINUED

I looked up Ethan's restraining order online and discovered that his wife hired a lawyer and filed a divorce case after the restraining order. That was not necessarily a bad thing because I can talk to a lawyer and, most times, have a reasonable discussion.

I was able to speak with the lawyer about the restraining order, as I'd hoped. After some back-and-forth between and among Ethan, me, Ethan's wife, and her attorney, we worked out a plan that dropped the restraining order, set up temporary parenting rules, and barred each spouse from harassing the other. Within days, we de-escalated the situation. That meant Ethan got to see the kids again.

They'd missed their Daddy.

I JUST WANT THIS DONE

CHAPTER 17

DEALING WITH THE NARCISSISTIC SPOUSE (OR HOW TO STOP BEING ONE)

E mily nervously slid her empty coffee cup in circles on the conference room table.

"You'll love Cal. Everyone does. That's the problem."

"What do you mean?" I asked.

"He does all the bad stuff when no one else is around. He's great in public, seems nice to everyone he meets, but then when we're at home, he can be . . . horrible. To me. I don't think I can take it anymore."

"How is he at work?"

"Oh, his business is doing great. He reminds me all the time. I don't know, but money has never been a problem, and the company just keeps growing."

Emily paused. "He'll come home from work, and something—anything—will set him off. And he'll yell at me, call me a stupid b—, tell me I'm worthless . . . stuff like that. Then he tells me he loves me, that he's sorry, and pretends nothing ever happened. If I say anything at all negative or ask him to do something, he tells me I'm crazy, that no one will believe me, and everyone else thinks I'm nuts."

"Who handles the money in the family?"

"Oh, of course, *Cal* does. He won't let me have access to any of the accounts. I'm given an allowance of four hundred dollars a month. He doles out cash to me, but I have to tell him what it's for and give him receipts."

I shot her a look across the table. "Really?"

"Yeah, I know. It's crazy, right? He demands the receipts or throws a fit. I gave up fighting a long time ago. I just want out now." She started into her empty cup. "I take care of the kids. I make dinner. I even make some good money on the side counseling from my home office. It's never enough for him."

"Have you talked about counseling?"

"He agreed to go to a counselor, but *he* picked the counselor. After a few sessions, when the counselor said he might have to make some changes, he quit counseling and said, 'The guy's full of it.'"

"Did you talk with Cal about divorce?"

"Oh yeah, a few years ago. He basically said, 'If you leave me, people will think you're crazy, including your family. The judge will agree with me, not you. I'll get the kids, and you won't get any money. I'll see to it that you get nothing from the business and no support because I will just stop taking on clients, and business will go to zero. You can't win." Emily looked like she had believed him. Not anymore. "So I did nothing. But things never got better. He started talking this way to the kids. And I just can't stand it anymore."

I've seen this movie before, I thought to myself.

Divorcing a genuine narcissist like Cal is difficult. Many successful, type-A people have narcissistic personality disorder (NPD) and bipolar disorder (BPD). They are otherwise social and popular people.

The Mayo Clinic defines NPD as follows:

> Narcissistic personality disorder—one of several types of personality disorders—is a mental condition in which people have an inflated sense of their own importance, a deep need for excessive attention and admiration, troubled relationships, and a lack of empathy for others.[7]

Many people label their spouses "narcissists" as an insult. It's not true in all cases. Some divorcing partners exhibit classic NPD behaviors like egomania, selfishness, and vindictiveness but are not diagnosable narcissists. Not every controlling jerk is a narcissist. When divorce lawyers hear a spouse call their soon-to-be-ex a narcissist, we listen, but we take the label with a grain of salt.

If you have NPD—and it can be a little secret just between us—you would do well to rein it in to get divorced smarter and sooner. I'm not a psychiatrist or psychologist. I'm not equipped to diagnose or treat NPD, and I will not attempt to do that here. A single chapter in this book cannot serve to deal with all the issues attendant to NPD in divorce. In fact, excellent books exist on the subject. I recommend *Splitting* by Bill Eddy and Randi Kreger if you're divorcing a narcissist. However, it's worth addressing NPD in this book because so many cases we deal with involve self-assured, high-income type-A business owners, entrepreneurs, and professionals. Get a counselor or see a psychiatrist for your own benefit.

If you recognize narcissistic traits in your spouse, be prepared. Divorce is normally not easy. If experience is a teacher, you may be in for a rough ride. If you recognize NPD in yourself, admit it and address the behaviors.

Research on NPD indicates it is not "curable" but treatable. The Mayo Clinic states that NPD can be treated by psychotherapy (talk therapy) to address the behaviors and help the narcissistic person improve

---

7   "Narcissistic Personality Disorder," The Mayo Clinic, www.mayoclinic. org/diseases-conditions/narcissistic-personality-disorder/symptoms-causes/syc-20366662#:~:text=Narcissistic%20personality%20disorder%20%E2%80%94%20one%20of,lack%20of%20empathy%20for%20others.

personal relationships. Medication might help if NPD is present with other psychiatric issues, such as depression or anxiety.

It's common for someone married to a narcissist to wonder, "Why do they treat me so badly if they have a girlfriend, and we're getting divorced?" Because. Just because. No other real reason. They want the emotional energy from you. You've failed them. People don't leave a narcissist; the narcissist leaves *them.*

Understand that narcissists have a hard time dealing with their behavior, never mind acknowledging it. Many will believe nothing is amiss and deny any problems at all. So you need to be prepared to deal with this harsh reality if your soon-to-be-ex is a narcissist. Here are a few tips to help.

1. **Get a counselor or see a psychiatrist.** Professionals can help you understand what's going on inside the narcissist's mind to weaken their attacks. It may not end the negativity, but knowledge is power—in this case, that's the power to blunt the attacks and deal with them.

2. **Don't feed the monster.** Narcissists feed on the emotional energy provided by others—especially those close to them. Your attention, positive or negative, is a narcissist's "food." Cut it off, and the narcissist ramps up attention-seeking behavior just to get a meal. They keep "pushing your buttons" that worked in the past to get you to notice them. When that stops working, they mash your buttons harder.

3. **Hang in there.** Remember, divorce is a marathon, not a sprint. A narcissist will try to wear you down. Ignoring the negativity is essential. They're trying to get your goat, to make you make mistakes or react in a way that makes you look bad.

4. **Remember that words are just words.** Most divorce issues are proved by documents. You may be concerned that everyone will believe the narcissist because they often seem convincing. Documents count more in most divorce cases than oral testimony does. Admittedly, in parenting cases,

oral testimony is significant, but even then, documents can make a big difference. For example, a calendar on which you track the dates and times you were with the children and the time your soon-to-be-ex spent with the kids can be persuasive evidence that their claim they were with the kids "all the time" is a wild exaggeration.

5. **Call the police.** Most people with NPD don't want actual trouble with police. If a narcissist is abusive in any way, an appropriate response may be calling the police and requesting a wellness check. "My husband is verbally abusing me and the kids. Can you send someone out here for a wellness check, please?" They can, and they likely will. No one will get arrested, but this one phone call signals to the narcissist that you're serious and refuse to be pushed around. If there is physical abuse at all, call 911. Have zero tolerance for domestic violence. A restraining order may be warranted as well.

6. **They won't all think you're crazy.** You're being told that to get your compliance. Your friends and family are not likely to believe everything your spouse tells them, especially in a divorce. The more your soon-to-be ex bad-mouths you, the more they suspect it is not true—especially when it does not match their observations of you.

7. **They won't get the kids.** This is a classic threat made by the narcissist. The court ultimately decides who has custody and who has visitation. The court, as a general rule, wants children to have parenting from both parents. Visitation is only prevented in extreme abuse situations. As I've told many clients, "Even child abusers get to see their kids." Obviously under controlled conditions, but the point is the same. Why in the world would Mr. or Mrs. Normal be forbidden to see their children?

8. **They won't get "all the money."** Here's another typical narcissist threat. As related elsewhere in this book, the court will award you an equitable share of the marital estate. This could be an equal division, but several factors we covered

earlier can alter that. The bottom line is that if the facts support it, you may receive support and an equitable share of the marital assets.

9. **Ninety percent of what bothers you, we can't address with the court.** Most of what the narcissist does drives you nuts but won't impact the endgame of the case. I recommend *BIFF* by Bill Eddy, a book with effective techniques for getting through to narcissists.

EMILY'S STORY, CONTINUED

I shared all this advice with Emily. I also handed her copies of *Splitting* and *BIFF* and told her to read both books as soon as she could. The information would help her tremendously over the next twelve months as we navigated a challenging court case.

Emily worked to stop "feeding" her husband's narcissism. He ramped up his negative behavior, but after he discovered he no longer got a rise out of Emily, he stopped. Things improved over time after they initially got worse.

We had to complete discovery and, unfortunately, prepare for trial—we had to go the distance and pursue litigation in court. When Cal's back was against the proverbial courtroom wall, he agreed to settle. The result was a reasonable deal for both parties.

At the end of the case, Emily told me, "You were right. Hanging in there and not fighting back was the hardest thing. But it was the best thing in the end. I stopped listening to the crazy talk and trusted myself. I stopped listening to the negativity and was finally able to see things clearly for myself and get a fair result. Thank you."

CHAPTER 18

HOW TO NOT BE A JERK BEFORE, DURING, AND AFTER DIVORCE

When I worked as a guardian *ad litem*, I investigated child custody cases for judges in DuPage County, Illinois, my home court. My job was to learn the facts of parenting situations and report back to the judge. This involved interviewing the children, which judges don't like to do. They're aware of the courthouse intimidation factor. Getting ushered past uniformed bailiffs into a judge's chambers is upsetting and can cause children to shut down and lie.

I hated the job. Kids got caught between angry parents. Parents cursed each other and fought in front of the children. Sometimes worse.

I had to interview each parent, normally at our office, then schedule a visit to both homes. We'd interview the kids, usually at one of the parents' homes. I vividly remember sitting on the floor of a little girl's room while she and I played with a LEGO set. Her name was Amanda. She was eight years old.

After playing for a while, I asked a few simple questions about the girl's life. Who were her friends, what were her favorite things to do, what did she like about school? I started with her grass-stained soccer uniform.

"I like LEGOs . . . those horses." Amanda glanced at the open toybox in the corner. "And video games. I play soccer."

After a few quiet moments, unprompted, she opened up about her parents.

"I live with my mom. Well, usually."

I knew her parents' divorce was acrimonious. Amanda's dad, Brad, and mother, Kirsten, did not get along. At all. Brad had complained to me that any time he called Amanda, Kirsten would answer and give an excuse as to why Amanda could not talk. Or she would just cut off the phone call. Brad also told me that Kirsten would never encourage Amanda to call him, so he always had to call . . . which he did—every night.

When Kirsten left Brad, she had claimed he was verbally abusive and controlling. Brad, a big, muscular guy who worked for the Park District, said that Kirsten met a guy at a new job. He made a lot more money, and they had an affair. The marriage collapsed. To say Brad was bitter would be an understatement.

Kirsten moved about fifteen minutes away into a rental. The move made it harder for Brad to see Amanda. It also took Amanda away from her friends and Brad's extended family, who all had been nearby.

"My mom says Daddy is mean," Amanda said. "She says we had to leave because Daddy was mean to her."

Kirsten claimed that she never blocked Amanda from phone calls. When I got around to asking Amanda about how much she talked to her dad, she was vague.

"Daddy calls me . . . sometimes . . ." Amanda said.

Brad had also complained that Kirsten never offered extra parenting time. Brad only got every other weekend and a couple of evenings a week for dinner.

Despite my effort to get Kirsten to open up communication with Brad about Amanda, things got worse. And Brad was his own worst enemy, leaving Kirsten nasty voice mails, emailing her, calling her a b——, showing up unannounced demanding to see Amanda, and more. I understood why. He felt out of control yet justified in his anger. But he was losing the meta case, and it was his own fault.

Brad informed me that Kirsten was dumping their dirty laundry all over the place. Her family avoided him at Amanda's school events. The couple's friends would not talk to him anymore. Kirsten monopolized communications with Amanda's teachers and school counselor.

Unfortunately, Brad's reaction was to pump Amanda for information. And punish her. He would alternately yell at her when he had parenting time and beg her to talk to him. He also blamed Amanda for not talking to him and not wanting to be with him.

Brad then bad-mouthed Kirsten to his family. He posted photos and personal info about Kirsten's new boyfriend on social media, calling him a "homewrecker" and worse.

The case reached the point that the judge, against my recommendation, drastically limited Brad's access to Amanda. I thought that more time for Brad with Amanda would help normalize the situation. The judge, exasperated at Brad's reactions and treatment of Amanda, devastated Brad with a reduction in visitation time.

A few years went by. I forgot about the case. But acrimonious cases like Brad's taught me many useful lessons about what to do and not do in order to improve a client's chances of success in a divorce.

How you treat other parties before, during, and after the divorce affects the meta case and the actual case itself. In fact, I've noticed more than twenty different ways that acting like a jerk (or not) changes the outcome of the case.

1. **There is no substitute for professional counseling help.** Get a counselor, psychologist, or psychiatrist to assist you on this journey. Even if you don't think you need a "shrink," even if you have never had counseling before—now is a good time to start. They will help you understand and anticipate your feelings and better communicate with your soon-to-be ex, family, friends, and coworkers.

2. **Avoid bad-mouthing your spouse to your family and friends.** If you decide to reconcile, and you have told your family a lot of bad stuff about your spouse (like cheating, verbal abuse, etc.), they will not be able to deal with it; the reconciliation will make your family and friends question *you*. Don't expect your family and friends to welcome the person back into the family. The saying "You can't unring a bell" is truer than ever in this instance. Even if you don't reconcile, how will you convince your family and friends to even tolerate the presence of your ex at sports events, scouts, graduations, and so on?

3. **Don't confide in the children.** They aren't your friends; they are your children. This is adult information, and they should not be exposed to it.

4. **Don't take it out on the kids.** It's your divorce, not theirs. They have enough to deal with now that their parents are breaking up. Being hard on the children is only going to make it worse and hurt your chances with regard to custody and visitation to boot.

5. **Don't do anything when you're angry.** Sleep on it. It is always better in the morning. You will do dumb things when you are mad, things you may regret later in a divorce trial— or something that might convince your soon-to-be ex that they should not agree to settle the case with you.

6. **Don't use the kids as pawns.** Threatening to withhold parenting time, bringing them home late, showing up early, or grabbing them from school when you know your spouse was supposed to pick them up puts the kids in the middle and makes you the jerk.

7. **Don't send nasty text messages, emails, or voice mails.** They can all be used in evidence against you later. Again, a major loss of the meta case and potentially the actual case as well. You are manufacturing evidence showing your bad character and handing it to your spouse.

8. **Don't threaten your soon-to-be-ex.** Threats of violence, property damage, and the like can result in temporary restraining orders, you being kicked out of your home, restriction of visitation, and more. A bad move to be avoided at all costs.

9. **Don't abuse drugs or alcohol.** This should go without saying, but understand that you are under a spotlight during the divorce. Coming home drunk on Saturday night may have happened before the divorce, but now is not the time to be drunk or high. Again, you are creating ammunition against your parenting claims and handing your soon-to-be ex free bullets to use against you. Also, evidence of alcohol or drug abuse will jeopardize your custody case.

10. **Don't show anger in front of the judge, the GAL, your soon-to-be-ex, or the kids.** This is a bad look and will bias the court against you. The judge will think, *If he's being rude here, I can only imagine how he was with her.* The GAL will think you're a hothead and not to be trusted with the children.

11. **Send a unified message to the world about the divorce**— to the public, to friends, to family, to children. Don't feed the gossip monster. Best if you can coordinate this with your soon-to-be ex. If you and they are telling different stories to the world, this will only increase conflict and lead to more questions—from everyone.

12. **Take the high road.** "We grew apart" is all you need to say. To the world, this says, "Nothing to see here; move along." These three simple words are universally understood. They shut down the conversation. Even if you feel like telling the truth about the facts, in the long run, it is much better and easier to be vague. Famous people like Jeff Bezos, Bill Gates, and Gwyneth Paltrow have famously said little about their divorces, preferring to keep things private. The "We've agreed to part ways" message is the best way to handle a divorce announcement.

13. **Keep the "dirt" private.** Telling people about the affair, abuse, drug use, et cetera is bad for you in the long run, even if it feels good to vent right now. This becomes a circular firing squad. At first, you might have people on your side. But at some point, this blows back on you if you 1) don't acknowledge your part in the breakdown of the marriage and 2) keep talking about it when people expect you to move on within a reasonable period of time. If they hear enough about how bad your soon-to-be ex is, they will then wonder why on earth you would marry that person in the first place. Again, keep this stuff between you and your counselor.

14. **Don't reject the entire marriage.** Don't armchair quarterback your life. No one gets married hoping to get divorced. Kicking the whole thing to the proverbial curb and blaming your soon-to-be ex for ruining your life is false and cowardly because you try to shift all blame for the divorce onto your spouse. This is sour grapes and makes you look bad, not the other person. Your marriage was good until it wasn't good. Don't go around saying, "So-and-so wasted twenty good years of my life." "I never should have married that person." You were free to leave. You chose to stay. Never surrender agency. You're free to get divorced. You could have left each other five years ago or ten years ago. It takes two people to marry and two to get divorced.

15. **Use mature language.** You had children with that person; they're not a b-word or c-word. This is no way to speak about the children's other parent in front of them, even if your ex deserves it. Again, take the high road. Set a good example for your kids, family, and friends. You are on stage with your kids all the time, and they take cues from you. If you bad-mouth the other parent in front of them, it does two things: it shades their opinion of them (maybe you intended that), and it may backfire. When the kids figure out eventually that Mom or Dad is not the terrible person you repeatedly said

they were, they will see you as the liar and decide you aren't to be trusted.

16. **Don't leave divorce papers and financial materials out where they can be found.** The kids should not see your divorce documents. It is none of their business and will only hurt their feelings.

17. **Avoid referring to the children as "my" kids.** They are collectively your children as a couple. Saying this in the presence of the other parent is demeaning, hurtful, and unproductive.

18. **Be consistent and responsive** with your soon-to-be ex and your children. Show up on time; do what you say you will do; follow through. Now more than ever is the time to step up your parenting.

19. **It's not "your" money; it's "ours."** The law considers the assets gained during the marriage as marital or community property in general. The law in the United States thinks of marriage as an equal partnership. Again, you were OK with the marriage until you weren't. Avoid revisionist history.

20. **Have hard conversations directly rather than by text or email.** Emotion and intention are missed in writing. Stick to in person or on the phone for sensitive topics. But when notice is important or you make an agreement, put it in writing. Remember, some agreements (like any change of support) should be approved by the court in a court order.

21. **If it is in writing, write it as if the whole world (and the judge) will read it.** Because they will. This goes for everything from the shortest text to your ex to email threads to family and friends. Assume everything you say will be public and in court and act accordingly. That confidant you think is your friend may be forwarding everything to your spouse. It's happened before. It can happen to you.

AMANDA'S STORY, CONTINUED

Six years after Brad and Kirsten's divorce, I received an email notice that I was being reappointed to Amanda's case. Unfortunately, Brad and Kirsten were fighting over Amanda, now a teenager. I learned she was doing well in school and sports.

Kirsten came into the office and talked with me. She blamed Brad for the problems with Amanda again. Brad was seeking more time with Amanda, saying that Amanda wanted to live with him.

Since Amanda was older, I met with her in my office. She related her story. She told me that over time, she came to learn that her mother had been constantly working to keep Amanda away from Brad. That she loved her dad and found her mother to be incredibly controlling and domineering. And that Kirsten treated Amanda like her friend and not her daughter. Amanda told me her mom would not let her have her cell phone except for limited times. She monitored all her communication and limited her contact with friends as well as her own dad.

Brad had lightened up since the divorce and tried to make the best of his visitations with Amanda. Amanda's positive experiences with her father did not line up with her mother's vitriol. Eventually, Amanda came to realize that Kirsten had been driving a wedge between them all along.

Due to all of the negativity and bad-mouthing from Kirsten, Amanda strongly urged me to recommend that she move in with her father. After further investigation, I agreed with her.

The custody case went to trial, and the court ordered that she move in primarily with her dad. Amanda's constant bad-mouthing of Brad, coupled with other negative behaviors, led the court to believe that living with Brad was in Amanda's best interest. The meta case drastically affected and merged with the actual case, turning the court in Brad's favor.

CHAPTER 19

REBUILDING YOUR LIFE WHEN THE MARRIAGE IS OVER

"We have a problem."

I was finishing lunch when I got a call from Terri, the collaborative lawyer representing my client's wife. She and I had worked together for fourteen years and never felt like we were "opposing attorneys." Every divorce we've done settled successfully out of court to everyone's satisfaction. Was that about to change?

"What happened?" I asked.

"You haven't heard?"

"Heard what?"

"Oh boy. . . . Well, Erin apparently didn't tell Peter about the prom picture event for parents, which was last Saturday. So Peter didn't know about it, and Erin showed up there to take pictures of their son and his date with . . . her boyfriend."

My eyes rolled up to the ceiling. "You've got to be kidding me."

Long story short: Erin had had an affair. Peter found incriminating emails on the computer. And that was the end of a twenty-year, two-child marriage. The divorce case was young, and Peter was still angry. A crucial meeting about alimony was supposed to take place in twenty minutes back at the office.

"I just wanted you to know as soon as I heard so we can deal with it," Terri said.

"I appreciate it. I'll call him right away."

I hung up and called Peter.

"Pete, I just heard about the prom photo thing."

"Can you believe it?" he boomed. "And right after we just started dealing with her running around with that a——, and she not only intentionally keeps me away from the photo thing, but she has the balls to bring 'Bill' with her? Tommy is just starting to wrap his head around the divorce to begin with!"

"I know, I know . . ."

"Erin begged me to do this collaboratively. And I did. Against my better judgment. I wanted to drag her ass to court . . . cost her everything . . . make her *hurt*."

"Right . . ."

"But you told me to stick with collaborative, to not get into a spiral with this."

"I know; you're trying to hang in there," I said.

"And here I am, like a total loser, and she's literally rubbing my nose in it."

"Yeah."

"It doesn't make me f—— happy! She's not 'winning friends and influencing people' here."

"I know. I—"

"I mean, I don't want to be anywhere near her right now, much less meet with her."

"Right, I get it. But settling this case still is the best option, and you should stick with it."

"OK. What should I do?"

"You and Erin need to meet with your divorce coaches first. We'll push the alimony meeting back an hour so you four can talk it out. Deal with it. Work through it. Me and Terri will stay out until you're ready."

"OK . . . OK . . ." Peter finally sounded calm. "I'll do it. But if this doesn't work out, we're going to court. Deal?"

"Deal."

• • • •

People like Erin sabotage their own cases with dumb, easily avoided mistakes during divorce and afterward. Under normal circumstances, Erin was probably not the type of person to pull a stunt like that. But the end of a long marriage is no normal circumstance. Emotion runs high and logic low. The animal brain takes over, and it's you against yourself.

A little advice for the Erins of the world and their new significant others: if you had an affair, put that relationship on ice until the divorce is done (or you reconcile) so you have a clearer head and heart. If you continue with the affair during counseling or divorce, you're giving yourself conflicting signals. And you certainly cannot reconcile with your spouse if you continue to see your paramour. If you're going through with the divorce, continuing the relationship upsets your soon-to-be ex (this should go without saying) and your family and friends. You also have the risk of another voice, another person with strong influence on you affecting your judgment at a critical time when you need to think rationally about the future.

What if you don't want to follow my advice? What if you're "in love" and "want the whole world to know"? At the absolute least, keep them away from the kids—and your spouse. As Erin proved, reminding your spouse about the affair is a bad idea. The scorned spouse feels taken advantage of. They're in shock and grieving both the betrayal and the end of their marriage.

If you're in Peter's role, you may not be able to imagine dating another person again. Sooner or later, you'll emerge from the fog of divorce. You'll reenter the dating market ready to rebound harder than you thought. This extreme change results in complications with your ex-spouse and your kids.

HOW TO HANDLE YOUR "FREEDOM" DURING AND AFTER DIVORCE

Whether you wanted the marriage to end or not, you'll inevitably realize you are now free to try new things, meet new people, and fall in love again. With this freedom comes responsibility. Here's how to wield it the smart and successful way.

1. **Wait before jumping into a new relationship.** You are emotionally fragile. You need time to focus on the divorce, your career, and your children. A new relationship takes energy, and you are in a state of mind where you are likely not at your best.

2. **Resist partying and acting like a child.** It is tempting to go out and have fun, and some of that in moderation is a good thing. Getting drunk, getting a DUI, and causing yourself or others injuries or financial harm is a bad thing.

3. **Keep your spending under control.** It is tempting to go crazy, buy new clothes, go out to dinner, and travel. You open yourself up to a dissipation claim (waste of marital assets), and every dollar you spend is theoretically shared between you and your spouse. This can also lead to a "spending arms race," in which your soon-to-be ex cranks up spending to match (or best) yours, afraid of being left behind. Divorce is expensive enough, and increasing your cash burn rate won't make things better.

4. **Don't obsess over your new significant other.** Resist the urge to brag that you have moved on. The kids don't want to know about your girlfriend. Your family does not want to know about her. And for sure, your soon-to-be ex does not want to hear about her. Too soon! A corollary: keep your fun new situation off social media. This is not the time to rub your spouse's nose in your great life or to show off your

fun vacation with your shiny new SO. This can cause major blowback in your divorce case, derail a settlement, and push your spouse into taking you to trial.

5. **Don't bring the kids around the new SO.** Wait until the divorce is done for this. Too soon!

6. **Don't spend big money on the new SO.** Spending marital assets on a purpose outside the marriage is considered dissipation (waste) of marital assets. You will have to reimburse the marriage (pay your soon-to-be ex) for their share of any spending for a purpose outside the marriage. You also stir the pot, and large-scale spending can tip the meta case against you.

7. **Keep your SO out of court**, and don't get them involved in your divorce case. It is a big mistake to allow the GF/BF to come to court in a sexy outfit or to bend your ear, telling you what to do. I have had problems with clients when the BF or GF intervenes in the case and inserts themselves into decisions the client has to make about their divorce. This is not the time to be influenced by a third party you might not know well, who possibly has a vested interest in the situation.

8. **Don't get pregnant, and don't get anyone pregnant.** This should go without saying, but you'd be surprised how some people compound their problems by getting someone pregnant or getting pregnant. This is 100 percent avoidable. This makes a hard situation even worse, and yes, we've seen the couple getting divorced get pregnant, and now you add a late-breaking baby to a tough situation. Bad move. Plus, you may delay a divorce case as the court will now want to determine the paternity of the child to assess whether additional child support and custody issues need to be determined.

9. **Don't stalk your soon-to-be ex or their significant other.** This goes for in-person creeping or cyberstalking. First, focusing on the past is not healthy for you—learn what you can from the past relationship, work with a counselor, but don't obsess over your spouse. Avoiding constant focus on

them will help you move on and be future focused. Stalking may bring potential criminal liability, and it's a bad look if you are caught.

10. **Avoid recording devices or monitoring, whether remote, GPS, or cameras in the home.** You will likely violate criminal eavesdropping laws, potentially get into trouble with revenge porn statutes, and worse. You'll look like a creep and damage your meta case. You don't need to track your soon-to-be ex (except in limited circumstances; see a local lawyer for your specific case), and you shouldn't. Remember, in many states, affairs are not relevant except for money spent on a significant other. Even where they are relevant, the impact they have on divorce cases is waning. Put your energy into the key components of the case and, again, be future focused.

HOW TO MANAGE FAMILY AND CHILD RELATIONSHIPS

Just as there are dos and don'ts (mostly don'ts) with your lover, I can offer practical guidance for maintaining your relationship with your kids as Mom and Dad head their separate ways.

1. **Remember, the kids don't want to hear about your new love.** You are excited to have a new relationship. That is totally understandable. But the kids aren't and probably won't ever be excited about your newfound love. The vast majority of kids want nothing more than their parents being together. Your girlfriend or boyfriend just makes them relive the divorce all over again.

2. **Comply with the divorce decree to the letter.** This means turn over assets, disclose financial information, and follow the parenting agreement. Don't create more problems (and legal fees) for yourself by failing to comply with the divorce

judgment. If you aren't sure what you need to do, consult with a local divorce attorney and have them review your divorce decree.

3. **Tactfully introduce your new significant other to the kids when the time is right.** Please wait until the relationship is serious. Absolutely avoid the "boyfriend of the week club"— this is hard on the kids as they have to get introduced, they might get used to a person, and then you break up.

4. **If at all possible, wait to move in with your new SO until it's serious.** Sometimes moving in together sooner is unavoidable because of post-divorce financial circumstances. By all means, try to avoid this situation until you're in a long-term, committed relationship. You're setting an example for the children. If the person moves in, and you break up, you ratchet up your own stress and that of your kids. They'll be hurt all over again and relive the divorce process. This is not healthy.

5. **Let kids accept the significant other at their own pace.** Don't force it.

6. **Be generous with your ex.** If they need help, consider that doing a little more for them than is in the divorce decree would be a nice thing. Keeping your ex happy will make things easier for you and the children. If they were supposed to pay for something for the kids, but they need help, cover it yourself. If they are in a jam at work and need you to pick up the kids from school, do it, even if it is not your day to have the kids in your parenting plan. A little goodwill goes a long way. Do you want to be cheap with the kids' mom?

7. **Don't be surprised when your ex disappoints you.** You got divorced for a reason, right? (Probably several.) Why would you expect your spouse to behave well now? You got divorced. Clients will complain from time to time that their ex is behaving badly. Many times, their ex acts just the same way they did during the marriage, maybe worse, and clients

act surprised. Why would you expect your ex to be better now, when they don't care what you think anymore?

8. **Don't take your SO (and especially their kids) on vacations with your kids.** That can come later when the kids are familiar and more comfortable with your SO. Focus time immediately after the divorce on your family. There will be time later to introduce your new relationship to the children.

9. **Don't force the kids to spend time with the new SO.** Earlier in the book, I told a story about my son's former girlfriend. Her father made her go on trips to a vacation home with his girlfriend, where there was nothing to do. Her resentment built up to the point where she did not want to spend any time with her father and vowed to not see him again once she turned eighteen. If you are getting married or entering into a committed relationship, obviously, this changes—what I'm addressing is when people needlessly force the situation before the kids are ready. Best to work with a counselor on this and all the issues in this chapter to get direct, specific advice.

10. **Keep your SO out of your children's extracurricular activities.** This is a judgment call, naturally. These types of activities should be family time for you, your kids, and your ex. Even though you are divorced, you still are a family. If possible, it is best if you can sit with your ex for these events. Your children will appreciate it. A few visits at games or events are fine, but keep it to a minimum, especially early on in a new relationship.

11. **Never make the kids call your significant other "Mom" or "Dad"** or anything similar. Also, don't force them to get gifts, cards, et cetera for the SO. This is usually barred in parenting judgments, but it's good to keep in mind regardless. There is a desire to create a new family with an SO that is understandable, but remember that the kids aren't as excited about your new life as you are. Go slowly. Keep their feelings in mind.

12. **Be flexible with parenting time.** Let the kids' lives control the schedule rather than artificial scheduling imposed by the parenting document. The best parenting judgment is the one you never have to look at again. Keep the kids' needs in mind, and be willing to bend. You will need flexibility from your ex at times. You need to give a break to get a break.

13. **Put everything in writing.** When you are giving notice about a vacation, asking for something, or complying with a term in your decree—put it in an email and save it. You may need evidence later that you made the request at a certain time or that you complied with a requirement of your divorce judgment.

PETER'S STORY, CONTINUED

Erin's prom photo antics brought Peter a lot of heartache, much more than was necessary. He cycled forward and backward through the stages of grief, mostly between and among denial, anger, and acceptance. As a result, the case took longer than it otherwise could have.

In the end, the divorce coaches' counsel, Terri's urging Erin to get her act together, and my guidance to Peter to use his better judgment kept the case on track. We kept the case out of court, settled amicably only two months after the blowup, and sent everyone on their way.

I JUST WANT THIS DONE

CONCLUSION: THE LAST WORD

Thank you for reading my book. I sincerely hope you've found valuable advice here. My goal was to convey all my years of hard-won advice in an entertaining, informative way. If I help even one person save time and money and prevent pain, it will have been worth it. And if I help other divorce lawyers with their clients, particularly through alternative dispute resolution, so much the better.

If nothing else, remember this: use your head, not your heart. Consider facts, not feelings, when deciding what to do in your divorce. Because that's what a judge will do. Keep the cost-benefit analysis always at the forefront, whether you're going to trial after all or are considering a settlement offer. Always consult a skilled divorce lawyer in your jurisdiction who has experience with the local court.

Finally, I cannot overemphasize the benefits of alternative dispute resolution. If you think it may work for you, I urge you to consider it over costly, painful litigation. Remember: evaluate, negotiate, litigate—only as a last resort.

Good luck. Things *will* get better.

HOW TO STAY IN TOUCH

Want to continue our conversation? Find me via my website www. IJustWantThisDone.com, on Twitter @raifordpalmer, on TikTok @raifordpalmer, or on YouTube @raifordpalmer.

Also, please email me at Raif@IJustWantThisDone.com. I look forward to hearing from you!

ACKNOWLEDGMENTS

This book would not have been possible without the help of many. First, I want to thank the world's best editor, Joshua Lisec, for his guidance and assistance through the entire process of developing the ideas for the book and for getting them down on (digital) paper. Second, I must thank my wife and law partner, Juli Gumina, JD, AAML, as well as my friend and colleague collaborative attorney James Lenahan, JD, of Wheaton, Illinois, for taking the time to review the book and provide valuable input. My good friend and the dean of Illinois divorce law scholars, attorney Gunnar J. Gitlin, JD, AAML, provided invaluable advice and was kind enough to write the foreword. Next, thank you to business valuation expert Tony Garvy, ASA, CPA/ABV/CFF at Corporate Valuation Services, who took the time to read and provide valuable input on the chapter discussing business assets in divorce.

Thank you to Mike Black and Kirsten McKinney at Told Media, for all the help with our social media outreach and general encouragement. Alison Beckwith has been invaluable with her firm's support in getting the word out about the book to the media.

Next, I want to thank the entire team at my law firm, STG Divorce Law, for backing me with this project. They keep the law firm humming and our clients delighted so I can accomplish my mission of spreading the word about a better way to get divorced to the world.

I have special appreciation for my mother, Patricia Palmer, and my dad, Doug Palmer, who are still married. (As of the time I am writing this book, fifty-three years!) They have supported and guided me my entire life. My dad, with his commonsense advice to people, has been an inspiration to me. My mom, with her caring and high emotional intelligence, has been invaluable in helping me understand other people and my own feelings throughout my life.

I must mention my maternal grandfather, Edward James Flickinger, my "Papa," who wanted me to go to law school and for whom my publishing company is named. He would have been thrilled to see this book.

I've had my own "tribe of mentors" along the way. From my scout leaders to favorite teachers (Ward F. Chick, Walter Lacyk) and college professors like Ira Carmen at the University of Illinois, who showed me how interesting and human the law could be; Shuseki Shihan Miyuki Miura at USA Karate Dojo, for hammering home the values of discipline and hard training. Within the practice of law: Professor Jamie Carey at Loyola University-Chicago School of Law, who taught me trial practice and evidence. Judge Theodore M. Swain, who taught me not to make leaps of faith and to have patience at my first five-dollar-per-hour clerking job before law school. The late William J. Sneckenberg, a highly talented, natural trial lawyer, gave me encouragement and my first Christmas bonus in the law business as a young law clerk. The Honorable James F. McCluskey, my first boss as a young associate attorney, taught me so much about lawyering and client service and has been a good friend ever since. My former law partner, Michael J. Angelina, for believing in me when he had plenty of business, and all I had was hustle and bright ideas. Attorney Joseph F. Emmerth, who suggested that my law firm, STG Divorce Law, consider hiring me to help manage the firm, and STG partner Juli Gumina and founder Maureen Sullivan Taylor for taking that advice and taking a chance on me. (Maureen, I know you didn't expect the marriage—thanks for trusting us.) Pam Kuzniar, AAML, and Jeffrey Brend, AAML, for encouraging me and mentoring me as I worked to join the American Academy of Matrimonial Lawyers, the most elite group of family law attorneys in the world. Attorneys Danya Grunyk and Margaret Bennett, for encouraging me to try collaborative practice. Collaborative practice guru Theresa Kulat, for encouraging my work in collaborative practice and for trusting me to work on cases. Thanks to my friend and adviser on complex Illinois divorce law issues Gunnar Gitlin for the amazing Foreword and his support with the AAML. I must also mention colleague Nancy Chausow Shafer, for getting me involved in speaking opportunities with the AAML and the Illinois State Bar.

To my counselor, Dr. John Duffy: thank you for your extremely valuable advice during my own divorce. You helped me think clearly at the time I needed it most. I've often recalled your advice when helping our own clients.

To our divorce clients, past, present, and future: thank you for your trust in us, and we hope we can help you to A Better View in your lives and those of your children.

ABOUT THE AUTHOR

Raiford Dalton Palmer, JD, AAML, is an experienced Illinois attorney concentrating in family law with a focus on complex divorce cases, especially those involving business owners and high-income earners. His work includes divorce, collaborative divorce, mediation, child custody, post-divorce matters, and premarital/postmarital agreements. Achievements include multiple successful jury and bench trials, numerous successful arbitrations and mediations, and many successfully resolved divorce and family law matters. Raiford has also argued an appeal before the Illinois Appellate Court. Raiford is the managing shareholder of STG Divorce Law, a premier divorce law firm located in the Chicagoland area. A multi-year winner of client service awards from Avvo.com as well as multi-year awardee of the SuperLawyer and LeadingLawyer designation for family law in Illinois, he is a frequent lecturer on Illinois divorce law and law firm management topics. Raiford is also a fellow in the American Academy of Matrimonial Lawyers and the Collaborative Law Institute of Illinois.

Raiford is also the author of *I Just Want This Done: How Smart, Successful People Get Divorced without Losing their Kids, Money, and Minds*. Learn more about the book at www.IJustWantThisDone.com.

Made in the USA
Las Vegas, NV
08 July 2024

92057610R00184